SPEAKING FREELY

SPEAKING FREELY

The Case Against Speech Codes

Edited and with an Introduction by Henry Mark Holzer

Second Thoughts Books is an imprint of the Center for the Study of Popular Culture, 12400 Ventura Blvd., Suite 304, Studio City, CA 91604.

ISBN 1-886442-00-2

Printed in the United States of America
1 2 3 4 5 6 7 8 9 10

President: David Horowitz
Vice President: Peter Collier
Publications Director: Elizabeth Larson
Cover and Interior Design: Jean-Paul Duberg

DEDICATION

This book is dedicated to Jacob Abrams, Joseph Beauharnais, Walter Chaplinsky, F. J. Chrestensen, Eugene V. Debs, Ralph Ginzburg, Benjamin Gitlow, Charles T. Schenck, Charlotte Anita Whitney, and the too many others who offended merely by speaking words the authorities did not wish to hear. It matters not that some of those words may have been odious. Because the speakers were in America, they had a right to speak.

ACKNOWLEDGEMENTS

No book project that I have been involved in has come to fruition without the help of a considerable number of other people. So, too, with *Speaking Freely*. Erika Holzer's encouragement, as always, was unbridled. The library staff at Brooklyn Law School, especially Carmen McPhail, enabled me to assemble the necessary materials in record time, and the school's 1994 Summer Writing Stipend Program provided financial support. At the Center for the Study of Popular Culture's Individual Rights Foundation, David Horowitz's enthusiasm for this project and Maura Whalen's and Elizabeth Larson's assistance greatly contributed to its realization. And, perhaps most important, there were the thousands of students I taught in twenty-two years at Brooklyn Law School, against whose beliefs many of my own ideas on free speech were tested.

TABLE OF CONTENTS

INTRODUCTION

HENRY MARK HOLZER*

The Vice Chancellor of a state university decides that a T-shirt printed by a fraternity is "politically incorrect," and the fraternity is banned from the campus. A candidate for student office is disqualified from running because his views are "offensive" to the incumbent majority. A college conservative newspaper is deemed "unsuitable" for distribution because of its viewpoint. A University of Michigan student is forced to write and publish a "confession" of political error for merely raising the morality of homosexuality in a classroom discussion. A Sarah Lawrence student is charged with "inappropriate laughter" for guffawing at someone else's joke about gays.[1]

These examples could be multiplied many times over, revealing a systematic attack on the First Amendment of unprecedented magnitude. It is shocking that this assault on free speech had its genesis with those whom one would expect to be most solicitous of the First Amendment: law school professors. Indeed, the seminal law review article that gave birth to the "Hate Speech Movement" was written by Richard Delgado, the Charles Inglis Thomson Professor of Law at the University of Colorado. In this article Professor Delgado informed the academic, legal and judicial communities what speech would be acceptable and what unacceptable:

> [A]n epithet such as "You damn nigger" would almost always be found actionable, as it is highly insulting and highly racial. However, an insult such as "You incompetent fool," directed at a black person by a white, even in a context which makes it highly insulting, would not be actionable because it lacks a racial component. "Boy," directed

---

*Henry Mark Holzer is Professor of Law at Brooklyn Law School. He is author of *Sweet Land of Liberty?: The Supreme Court and Individual Rights* and editor of *Government's Money Monopoly* and *The Gold Clause*. Professor Holzer serves as a director of, and Special Counsel, to the Individual Rights Foundation.

> at a young black male, might be actionable, depending on the speaker's intent, the hearer's understanding, and whether a reasonable person would consider it a racial insult in the particular context. "Hey, nigger," spoken affectionately between black persons and used as a greeting, would not be actionable. An insult such as "You dumb honkey," directed at a white person, could be actionable. . . .but only in the unusual situations where the plaintiff would suffer harm from such an insult.[2]

It is, of course, true that even if the First Amendment were intended to be absolute—the proscription is that "Congress shall make *no* law"—the Supreme Court has never *held* it to be without exceptions: "Speech is not an absolute, above and beyond control by the Legislature when its judgment. . .is that certain kinds of speech are so *undesirable* as to warrant criminal sanction";[3] any attempt to restrict freedom of speech "must be justified by *clear public interest.*"[4] Thus, it is in the name of the "public interest" that various kinds of speech have been suppressed in the past, among them: commercial speech, pornography, sedition, defamation.

Whether one identifies the root of the "public interest" standard superficially as "the claims of the state versus the individual," or of society vs. the individual, or more philosophically as the utilitarian greatest good of the greatest number, or ethically as altruism,[5] it is the same old collectivist claim over individual rights that is invoked today by the Hate Speech Movement. In the name of some public interest, they seek to silence "words that wound" on subjects that embrace race, religion, gender, sexuality, ethnicity, multiculturalism, and more.

It was bad enough when obeisance to the god of "public interest" was invoked to silence discrete, perhaps even marginal, groups such as anarchists and Communists, pornographers, and pacifists. It is much more dangerous when a movement seeks to silence not some definable and limited category of speakers, *but everyone who dares make an "unacceptable" statement concerning any class which the movement deigns to certify as "victim."*

Professor Delgado's presumptuous parsing of who will be allowed to say what to whom, and with what intent, is a potentially limitless assault on thought and word. There can be no doubt that he and his colleagues mean business. They are frank in stating their intention to censor expressed ideas which they, in their self-appointed role of moral guardians, deem "unacceptably" insensitive to some select groups of individuals.

Regrettably, it is too late to stop the Hate Speech Movement in its tracks; it has a decade's head start on those of us who still believe that "Congress shall make no law." More importantly, with the help of radical law professors it has rationalized the establishment of speech codes at hundreds of American universities and colleges. And, until now, there has been far too little rigorous intellectual opposition to the Movement's anti-individual rights, anti-free speech, program.

Of the approximately three hundred law review articles written on the subject of hate speech—most of which support, or fail to squarely and consistently oppose, the *au courant* attempt to violate free speech—the eight law review articles and one Supreme Court decision that appear in this book have been selected to make the case *against* "words that wound" and *for* unfettered, uninhibited, unself-conscious, uncensored free speech.

Professor Linzer's context-setting article identifies and explains the alleged racism that serves as the Hate Speech Movement's rationale. He provides a thorough survey of the solutions proposed by the Movement's leading thinkers, by affected universities, and by the American Civil Liberties Union.

Mr. Alexander's article compliments Professor Linzer's in its analysis of the various rationales for justifying regulation of hate speech; to wit: outsider jurisprudence, the "equality principle," "politically correct" speech, and hate speech as non-speech.

With the context of the problem and its proffered solutions in place, Professor Massey's important contrasting contribution consists of a comprehensive explication of the basic principles of free speech and the traditional rationales that have been advanced to justify them.

Messrs. McGowan and Tangri identify and elaborate on a point crucial to the Hate Speech debate but rarely considered as thoroughly as it deserves to be: the university as a "special environment" for the nurturing of free speech.

Building upon the idea of a university as a special environment, Professor Sedler's article squarely addresses the constitutionality of campus bans on racist speech, resting his conclusion in part on the 1992 U.S. Supreme Court decision in the *R.A.V.* case—the first time the Court has addressed the constitutionality of hate speech.

The text of Justice Scalia's majority opinion for the Supreme Court in *R.A.V.* is set forth in its entirety, an opinion which, to some extent, rests on theoretical aspects of the free speech guarantee of the First Amendment.

Professor Wolfson's article rounds out the discussion of hate speech by addressing free speech theory, against which the prohibition of hate speech cannot stand.

In *Wisconsin v. Mitchell,*[6] however, the U.S. Supreme Court reached an entirely different conclusion concerning a legal phenomenon closely related to hate speech: the enhancement of criminal penalties based on "hateful motivation." In a devastating critique of *Mitchell,* Professor Fleisher makes a convincing case for why the Court erred in upholding the constitutionality of penalty enhancement statutes.

And in a riveting report on the proceedings of a University Academic Council—hard at work on an "offensive conduct rule"—Professor Van Alstyne dramatizes where the road of politically correct speech inexorably leads: Tiananmen Square.

In sum, then, the materials collected in this book cumulatively make two important and timely points.

First, that people offended—justifiably or not—by mere words, should not be allowed to prohibit their utterance. Permitting them to wield that inevitable tool of dictators—censorship—is at once dangerously unworkable, flagrantly unconstitutional, and profoundly un-American.

Second, that the "public interest" standard, which has infected the First Amendment's unambiguous free speech guarantee from the Founding to the present, forms the core of the

Hate Speech Movement's broadbased assault on "words that wound."

Unless the infection is fought vigorously and without apology or compromise, the cornerstone of this Republic—the First Amendment—may not survive. This book is intended to provide some strong medicine.

Endnotes

1. *The Defender*, Vol 1, No. 1, March 1994, page 1.

2. Delgado, *Words that Wound: A Tort Action for Racial Insults, Epithets, and Name-Calling*, 17 HARV. C.R.-C.L.L. REV. 133, 179-80 (1982).

3. Dennis v. United States, 341 U.S. 494 (1950); emphasis added.

4. Thomas v. Collins, 323 U.S. 516 (1945); emphasis added.

5. See, for example, Ayn Rand, "Man's Rights" and "Racism," *The Virtue of Selfishness* (The New American Library, 1965), pp123, 127, 175; Ayn Rand "The Objectivist Ethics," *The Virtue of Selfishness* (The New American Library, 1965), pp32-33.

6. _____U.S._____, 113 S.Ct. 2194 (1993).

CHAPTER 1

THE NATURE OF THE PROBLEM, AND PROPOSED SOLUTIONS

"White Liberal Looks at Racist Speech"*

*Peter Linzer***

* * *

I am what in Texas is called a "Yellow Dog Democrat": I'd sooner vote for an old yellow dog than for a Republican. Not only am I a card-carrying member of the American Civil Liberties Union ("ACLU"), but I'm also on the chapter and state affiliate boards, and I wrote the National ACLU's amicus brief to the United States Supreme Court in *Texas v. Johnson*,[3] the first flag-burning case. I am about as close to being an absolutist about the first amendment as a rational lawyer can be, but the problem of racist speech has me troubled. And Matsuda's article[3A] and others by articulate writers of "outsider jurisprudence" almost have me convinced. Almost.

I. The Problem

Until recently I was convinced that America had a serious race problem, but that the problem was primarily economic,

---

*The complete article from which the following is excerpted appears at *65 St. John's Law Review* 187 (1991). Footnotes have been changed to endnotes and are numbered as in the original. Reprinted with permission.

**Professor of Law, University of Houston Law Center. A.B. 1960, Cornell University; J.D. 1963, Columbia University School of Law. I am grateful to friends and colleagues of widely different outlooks who generously read and criticized the manuscript of this essay or discussed the topic with me at length. They include David Crump, Sashe Dimitroff, David Dow, Marc Franklin, David Gregory, Steven Huber, Bill Kaplin, Mari Matsuda, Micheal Olivas, Laura Oren, Irene Rosenberg, Rhea Stevens and Patricia Tidwell. m. elisabeth bergeron, Executive Articles Editor of the *St. John's Law Review*, was invaluable.

and no longer the result of raw prejudice. This was not to say that there was no prejudice left, but that it was relatively discrete; lower-income whites and old, rural southerners were still fond of words like "nigger" and "wetback," and there were still places where the civil rights acts were not enforced, but the bulk of the population was at least fairly tolerant of the notion that a person deserves a fair shake regardless of color.[4] But I have seen enough evidence now to reject my conclusions about the eradication of traditional prejudice. An excellent student Note recently published gave examples of the happenings in contemporary university settings:

> The reports of racist incidents on college campuses recur continually in the popular press. The National Institute Against Prejudice and Violence collected reports of seventy-eight incidents of racial violence or allegations of prejudice that occurred in the spring semester of 1988 alone, and that did not purport to be a comprehensive survey. The recurrence of old-fashioned intentional racism on campuses is the most obvious form of hostility, and a sampling demonstrates the ferocity of some such incidents, which have variously involved: graffiti containing swastikas and antiblack epithets; cross-burning; the protesting of an all-white fraternity's "White History Week" party; the shouting of racial slurs; the distribution of openly hostile leaflets; racial brawls; and black student class boycotts and protests. The comprehensive list of such incidents is much longer, and that list does not include unreported incidents, which may well be the majority.[5]

Furthermore, many violent incidents occurring outside the college setting have made headlines: for example, Vincent Chin's death by baseball bat in Detroit[6] and the Howard Beach and Bensonhurst killings in New York City.[7] The problem is real. The evidence has been put forth by many writers, citing both systematic studies and journalistic accounts.[8]

II. The Solutions Proposed

A number of proposals have been put forth to deal with "hate speech" through some form of legal sanction. They range from criminal statutes to tort remedies to a variety of university regulations. Even the ACLU has gotten into the act. The criminal statutes may make an existing crime, such as assault and battery, more serious if motivated by racial harassment,[9] or make the uttering of offensive words a crime in itself, either as a form of harassment[10] or as criminal group libel.[11] Tort remedies have been suggested for many years, dating back to the seminal writing of sociologist and lawyer David Riesman during World War II.[12] Most significantly, universities all over the country have been debating and adopting conduct codes forbidding racist and other forms of "hate speech" according to various formulas.

A. The Writers

Modern scholarship on the subject usually dates from Richard Delgado's *Words That Wound: A Tort Action for Racial Insults, Epithets, and Name-Calling.*[13] Professor Delgado showed at some length that racial insults cause injuries of the type traditionally compensated by tort law.[14] He reviewed ways in which traditional torts such as defamation and intentional infliction of emotional distress and statutory torts involving discrimination have been used in racial insult situations.[15] He concluded, however, that none of the existing remedies work well and proposed the establishment of an "action for racial insult." Under the proposal, a plaintiff could recover by proving that

> [l]anguage was addressed to him or her by the defendant that was intended to demean through reference to race; that the plaintiff understood as intended to demean through reference to race; and that a reasonable person would recognize as a racial insult.[16]

Professor Delgado's proposal was quite modest and relatively limited. Whether racially demeaning language would be actionable would depend on the context of its utterence.

> [A]n epithet such as "You damn nigger" would almost always be found actionable, as it is highly insulting and highly racial. However, an insult such as "You incompetent fool," directed at a black person by a white, even in a context which made it highly insulting, would not be actionable because it lacks a racial component. "Boy," directed at a young black male, might be actionable, depending on the speaker's intent, the hearer's understanding, and whether a reasonable person would consider it a racial insult in the particular context. "Hey, nigger," spoken affectionately between black persons and used as a greeting, would not be actionable. An insult such as "You dumb honkey," directed at a white person, could be actionable under this formulation of the cause of action, but only in the unusual situations where the plaintiff would suffer harm from such an insult.[17]

Mari Matsuda, in what has become the leading article on the topic, proposed that we consider "racist hate messages" as unprotected by the first amendment if three characteristics are present: "1. The message is of racial inferiority; 2. [t]he message is directed against a historically oppressed group; and 3. [t]he message is persecutorial, hateful, and degrading."[18]

Professor Matsuda gave very little detail on the specific remedies that she would make available to victims of an unprotected racist hate message. She said only that "a range of legal interventions, including the use of tort law and criminal law principles, is appropriate to combat racist hate propaganda."[19] She elaborated in a footnote:

> In addition to judicial modification of first amendment analysis, the forms of remedy could include creation of a new crime of racist speech, enhanced sentencing for existing crimes where racial motivation is found, administrative mechanisms for fines and injunc-

> tive relief, civil actions for damages, or a combination of the above.[20]

Matsuda devoted her article to a description of the impact of racist speech on the victims, an analysis of first amendment law and an argument that by taking the victim's perspective into account and narrowly defining prohibited speech with the three criteria set out above,[21] one could, consistent with the values of freedom of speech, read the first amendment to exclude racist speech from its protection.[22] She also considered several "gray area" case scenarios, and indicated where she thought line-drawing appropriate.[23] For example, rather than stretching present exceptions to the first amendment like "fighting words" or obscenity, and rather than trying to conceal anti-racist laws in a neutral mask, "[i]t is more honest, and less cynically manipulative of legal doctrine, to legislate openly against the worst forms of racist speech, allowing ourselves to know what we know."[24]

In the past few months there has been a flood of writing on the issue.[25] One of the most notable and eagerly awaited articles was Charles Lawrence's *If He Hollers Let Him Go*,[26] an expansion of Professor Lawrence's debate with Nadine Strossen at the Biennial Conference of the ACLU.[27] Lawrence argued that *Brown v. Board of Education*[28] was itself a regulation of racist speech:

> *Brown* held that segregated schools were unconstitutional primarily because of the *message* segregation conveys—the message that black children are an untouchable caste, unfit to be educated with white children. Segregation serves its purpose by conveying an idea. . . .Therefore, *Brown* may be read as regulating the content of racist speech.[29]

Lawrence also argued that distinctions between speech and conduct are inapposite ("[r]acism is both 100% speech and 100% conduct"),[30] and that the distinction between public and private conduct is overdrawn in the area of racism:

> When a person responds to the argument that *Brown* mandates the abolition of racist speech by reciting the state action doctrine,

> she fails to consider that the alternative to regulating racist speech is infringement of the claims of blacks to liberty and equal protection. The best way to constitutionally protect these competing interests is to balance them directly. To invoke the state action doctrine is to circumvent our value judgment as to how these competing interests should be balanced.[31]

In this Symposium, Mary Ellen Gale, a noted civil libertarian, has challenged what she calls "the heroic ideal of the first amendment."[32] Professor Gale concludes:

> We can expand our vision of the first amendment beyond the libertarian paradigm—to acknowledge a more complicated world. We can regulate speech to combat the harms done when speakers themselves perpetuate prejudice and repression: silencing the voices of targeted victims, undermining equality, and decreasing both individual liberty and democratic dialogue. A more complex theory of free speech, informed by social context and lived experience, can take the harms of racist speech seriously and allow us to weave a remedy into our continuing constitutional story of individual rights.[33]

B. The Universities

The issue's major battleground has become the universities. Some of the reasons are clear. As the number of non-white students has increased, particularly ugly forms of racism have become endemic on campuses that had prided themselves on their sophistication and tolerance of difference.[34] Universities traditionally adopt regulations concerning student conduct, and their administrations are at least somewhat more susceptible to pressure from minorities than the government in general.

I have been told that more than one hundred universities have adopted some degree of regulation of racist speech. I will limit myself to the regulations of three state universities, Michigan, Texas, Wisconsin,[35] and one private university, Stanford, each of which take a somewhat different approach.

A federal district court struck down as unconstitutional the University of Michigan's Policy on Discrimination and Discriminatory Harassment of Students in the University Environment (the "Policy"),[36] and the university has since replaced it. As this decision is the only judicial opinion on this topic thus far, it warrants a detailed examination. The Policy subjected to university discipline

> 1. Any behavior, verbal or physical, that stigmatizes or victimizes an individual on the basis of race, ethnicity, religion, sex, sexual orientation, creed, national origin, ancestry, age, marital status, handicap or Vietnam-era veteran status, and that
> a. Involves an express or implied threat to an individual's academic efforts, employment, participation in University sponsored extra-curricular activities or personal safety; or
> b. Has the purpose or reasonably foreseeable effect of interfering with an individual's academic efforts, employment, participation in University sponsored extra-curricular activities or personal safety; or
> c. Creates an intimidating, hostile, or demeaning environment for educational pursuits, employment or participation in University sponsored extra-curricular activities.[37]

Section 1(c) was withdrawn less than three months after the Policy took effect (but after the federal lawsuit had been filed), on the ground that "a need exists for further explanation and clarification" of the provision.[38]

Together with the Policy, the university issued an official "Interpretive Guide" ("Guide") that contained a number of poorly thought out illustrations of what constituted violations of the Policy. The Guide was a major reason that the court invalidated the Policy, primarily because, together with the university's actual enforcement, it revealed the Policy's overbreadth and demonstrated its potential for misapplication by well-meaning but overzealous administrators.[39]

Some parts of the Policy, dealing with physical behavior

and express threats, are not particularly controversial and do not require examination here. For our purposes, we may concentrate on the fact that the Michigan approach focused on "verbal behavior"[40] that "stigmatizes or victimizes" an individual on the basis of any of a rather long list of factors.[41] In addition, the complainant had to show either a threat, express or implied, or an intention or reasonably foreseeable effect of interfering with the individual's academic efforts, employment, extracurricular participation or personal safety. While the "stigmatizes or victimizes" language is vague, the additional requirement did have a narrowing effect. Section 1(c), had it not been withdrawn, would have been very troublesome, since what "[c]reates an intimidating, hostile or demeaning environment" is more difficult to define than threats and purposes. Even without section 1(c), a complainant had a case, on the text of the Policy, if she could prove that the speech "victimized or stigmatized" her on one of the forbidden grounds, and had the reasonably foreseeable effect of interfering with the complainant's academic efforts.

The University of Wisconsin's rules permit discipline of a student

> [f]or racist or discriminatory comments, epithets or other expressive behavior directed at an individual or on separate occasions at different individuals, or for physical conduct, if such comments, epithets, other expressive behavior or physical conduct intentionally:
>
> 1. Demean the race, sex, religion, color, creed, disability, sexual orientation, national origin, ancestry or age of the individual or individuals; and
>
> 2. Create an intimidating, hostile or demeaning environment for education, university related work, or other university-authorized activity.[42]

Intent is to "be determined by consideration of all relevant circumstances."[43] The Wisconsin Administrative Code contains, along with its rules, three illustrations of violative conduct.

> In order to illustrate the types of conduct which this subsection is designed to cover, the following examples are set forth. These examples are not meant to illustrate the only situations or types of conduct intended to be covered.
>
> 1. A student would be in violation if:
>
> a. He or she intentionally made demeaning remarks to an individual based on that person's ethnicity, such as name calling, racial slurs, or "jokes"; and
>
> b. His or her purpose in uttering the remarks was to make the educational environment hostile for the person to whom the demeaning remark was addressed.
>
> 2. A student would be in violation if:
>
> a. He or she intentionally placed visual or written material demeaning the race or sex of an individual in that person's university living quarters or work area; and
>
> b. His or her purpose was to make the educational environment hostile for the person in whose quarters or work area the material was placed.[44]

A fourth and last illustration gives an example of what is not considered a violation:

> A student would not be in violation if, during a class discussion, he or she expressed a derogatory opinion concerning a racial or ethnic group. There is no violation, since the student's remark was addressed to the class as a whole, not to a specific individual. Moreover, on the facts as stated, there seems no evidence that the student's purpose was to create a hostile environment.[45]

The University of Texas proposal[46] rejects the stigmatization or victimization approach of the University of Michigan which had been declared unconstitutional before the Texas report appeared.[47] Instead, it takes a double approach. Somewhat like the Wisconsin rules, it provides that physical misconduct can be treated as an aggregated offense for university disciplinary purposes if it has a discriminatory purpose.[48] This is not terribly controversial.[49] With respect to speech alone, the

Texas plan focuses on the intentional infliction of emotional harm. It prohibits "racial harassment," and, building on section 46 of the *Restatement (Second) of Torts*,[50] it defines "racial harassment" as "extreme or outrageous acts or communications that are intended to harass, intimidate, or humiliate a student or students on account of race, color, or national origin and that reasonably cause them to suffer severe emotional distress."[51] The commentary on the proposal conceded that its formulation substitutes "acts or communications" where the Restatement uses "conduct," but insisted that this was "in the nature of a clarification and not a substantive revision."[52] Violation could lead to punishment ranging from an admonition to expulsion.[53]

Stanford University is a private institution that, under current views of state action, is not subject to the first amendment. Nonetheless, the proposal to add a racist speech "Interpretation" to Stanford's "Fundamental Standard" led to a constitutional debate involving the cream of Stanford Law School's faculty.[54] Stanford's Fundamental Standard, written in 1896, states: "Students at Stanford are expected to show both within and without the University such respect for order, morality, personal honor and the rights of others as is demanded of good citizens. Failure to do this will be sufficient cause for removal from the University."[55]

The "Interpretation," created by Stanford's Student Conduct Legislative Council, begins with a strong statement of commitment to the principles of free inquiry and free expression, including toleration "even of opinions which [students] find abhorrent."[56] It continues, that "Stanford is also committed to principles of equal opportunity and non-discrimination" because of race and other factors. Thus, "[h]arassment of students on the basis of any of these characteristics contributes to a hostile environment that makes access to education for those subjected to it less than equal. Such discriminatory harassment is therefore considered to be a violation of the Fundamental Standard."[57]

The two remaining paragraphs of the Interpretation

contain the operative provisions:

> 3. This interpretation of the Fundamental Standard is intended to clarify the point at which protected free expression ends and prohibited discriminatory harassment begins. Prohibited harassment includes discriminatory intimidation by threats of violence, and also includes personal vilification of students on the basis of their sex, race, color, handicap, religion, sexual orientation, or national and ethnic origin.
> 4. Speech or other expression constitutes harassment by personal vilification if it:
> a) is intended to insult or stigmatize an individual or a small number of individuals on the basis of their sex, race, color, handicap, religion, sexual orientation, or national and ethnic origin; and
> b) is addressed directly to the individual or individuals whom it insults or stigmatizes; and
> c) makes use of insulting or "fighting" words or non-verbal symbols. In the context of discriminatory harassment by personal vilification, insulting or "fighting" words or non-verbal symbols are those "which by their very utterance inflict injury or tend to incite to an immediate breach of the peace," and which are commonly understood to convey direct and visceral hatred or contempt for human beings on the basis of their sex, race, color, handicap, religion, sexual orientation, or national and ethnic origin.[58]

Appended to the Interpretation is a very thoughtful series of comments in the form of questions and answers. It limits the application of disciplinary action to face-to-face or similar insults intentionally directed at a single person or a small group of individuals.[59] Moreover, only those words and symbols that are "understood across society as a whole" as insulting or offensive to members of the groups covered in the Interpretation would be sanctioned.

> The kinds of expression covered are words (listed, not exhaustively, and with apologies for the affront involved even in listing

> them) such as "nigger," "kike," "faggot," and "cunt"; symbols such as KKK regalia directed at African-American students, or Nazi swastikas directed at Jewish students. By contrast, a symbol like the Confederate flag, though experienced by many African-Americans as a racist endorsement of slavery and segregation, is still widely enough accepted as an appropriate symbol of regional identity and pride that it would not in our view fall within the "commonly understood" restriction. The direction of profanities or obscenities as such at members of groups subject to discrimination is also not covered by the interpretation, nor is expression of dislike, hatred, or contempt for these groups, in the absence of the gutter epithets or their pictorial equivalents.[60]

The sincerity of the attempt to keep the Interpretation within narrow bounds is apparent. However, the distinction between the Confederate flag and the swastika, while tenable, points up the subjectivity involved in defining what words or symbols are "commonly understood" to be insulting to the groups covered by the Interpretation.[61]

The Interpretation also makes clear that it concerns only words and symbols and not ideas, however racist or hurtful:

> Making the prohibition so narrow leaves some very hurtful forms of discriminatory verbal abuse unprohibited. Substantively, this restriction is meant to ensure that no *idea* as such is proscribed. There is no view, however racist, sexist, homophobic, or blasphemous it may be in content, which cannot be expressed, so long as those who hold such views do not use the gutter epithets or their equivalent. Procedurally, the point of the restriction is to give clear notice of what the offense is, and to avoid politically charged contests over the meaning of debatable words and symbols in the context of disciplinary proceedings.[62]

C. The American Civil Liberties Union

The National ACLU recently adopted a policy statement

deploring racism and other biases on campus and calling for aggressive educational methods to deter them.[63] The preamble to the policy statement says that "some" have set up a dichotomy of either restrictions on speech or acceptance of bias as unremediable, but that "[t]he ACLU rejects both these alternatives and reaffirms its traditional and unequivocal commitment both to free speech and to equal opportunity."[64] The policy itself provides in part:

> 1. Freedom of thought and expression are indispensable to the pursuit of knowledge and the dialogue and dispute that characterize meaningful education. All members of the academic community have the right to hold and to express views that others may find repugnant, offensive, or emotionally distressing. The ACLU opposes all campus regulations which interfere with the freedom of professors, students and administrators to teach, learn, discuss and debate or to express ideas, opinions or feelings in classroom, public or private discourse.
> 2. The ACLU has opposed and will continue to oppose and challenge disciplinary codes that reach beyond permissible boundaries into the realm of protected speech, even when those codes are directed at the problem of bias on campus.
> 3. This policy does not prohibit colleges and universities from enacting disciplinary codes aimed at restricting acts of harassment, intimidation and invasion of privacy. The fact that words may be used in connection with otherwise actionable conduct does not immunize such conduct from appropriate regulation. . . .[65]

The ACLU policy states that the constitutionality of disciplinary codes has to be considered on an individual basis, but it does not address the hard question of whether the first amendment permits any sanctions against speech.[66]

The California affiliates of the ACLU, however, have adopted a somewhat more explicit policy about harassment on college campuses.[67] The California ACLU Policy begins with a preamble reiterating the ACLU's commitment to "protecting freedom of speech to guarantee the free exchange of ideas," including abhorrent ones expressed offensively. It also sets forth a commitment to full participation in the education process on a non-discriminatory basis, and claims that harassment of minority students based upon their minority status could functionally exclude them from such full participation.

> In light of the First Amendment considerations outlined above, however, any attempt to punish such harassment must be carefully drawn so as to address the severe or pervasive nature of the conduct as directly as possible, and to avoid infringement on the First Amendment protected expression of even repugnant ideas. In particular, campus policy should not bar the ability of professors to teach their philosophies or students to express their views no matter how offensive, but must instead focus on speech or expression used as a weapon to harass specific victims on the basis of their protected status.[68]

The California ACLU Policy itself provides that campus administrators "are obligated to take all steps necessary within constitutional bounds to minimize and eliminate a hostile educational environment which impairs access of protected minorities to equal educational opportunities."[69] The policy refers to administrators speaking out vigorously against hate speech, promoting equality, mutual accommodation, and understanding among the minority groups and the rest of the college community, by assuring diversity among faculty, staff, students and administration, and eliminating discrimination on campus.

Thus far, the California Policy does not differ much from the National Policy. However, the California Policy, without explicitly advocating the enforcement of restrictions on speech, implicitly approves narrow limitations:

> Campus administrators may not, however, enact campus codes of conduct prohibiting

> discriminatory harassment of students, faculty, administrators and staff on the basis of speech or expression unless at a minimum all of the following conditions are met:
>
> 1. The code of conduct reaches only speech or expression that:
>
> a) is specifically intended to and does harass an individual or specific individuals on the basis of their race, sex, religion, sexual orientation, national alienage; or ethnic origin, and
>
> b) is addressed directly to the individual or individuals whom it harasses; and
>
> c) creates a hostile and intimidating environment which the speaker knows or reasonably should know will seriously and directly impede the educational opportunities of the individual or individuals to whom it is directly addressed. . . .[70]

Professor Mary Ellen Gale of Whittier College School of Law, a participant in this Symposium, was a principal drafter of the California ACLU Policy. In a letter to the New York Times she defended it, noting that, as of the date of her letter, it was narrower than any university's "speech code." "Offensive speech—in classroom debates, public discourse or private conversation—is something students must endure or challenge with speech of their own; harassment that threatens personal safety and educational opportunity is not."[71]

Thus, a number of approaches attempt to remedy this admittedly serious problem. However, there is no agreement on how a particular policy squares with the first amendment.

* * *

ENDNOTES

3. 109 S. Ct. 2533 (1989).

[3A. Matsuda, *Public Response to Racist Speech: Considering the Victim's Story*, 87 MICH. L. REV. 2320 (1989).]

4. Affirmative action was another matter. Many (perhaps most) whites oppose affirmative action, and while I disagree, I am unwilling to call their opposition racist. How to break the connection between poverty and race is a serious problem, but to my mind disagreement about means is not prejudice pure and simple. One of the

points of this essay is that "prejudice pure and simple" is itself simplistic. For a thoughtful analysis along these lines, see Pettigrew, *New Patterns of Racism: The Different Worlds of 1984 and 1964*, 37 RUTGERS L. REV. 673, 682-86 (1985).

5. Note, *Racism and Race Relations in the University*, 76 VA. L. REV. 295, 315-16 (1990) [hereinafter *Virginia Note*] (citations omitted). Like Pettigrew, *supra* note 4, the *Virginia Note* goes beyond traditional racism in its discussion. Doe v. University of Michigan, 721 F. Supp. 852, 854 (E.D. Mich. 1989) (describing lack of attention given to racial incidents that prompted university to adopt its policy on discrimination). For other examples of the recurrence of traditional racism, in several settings, see Delgado, *Words That Wound: A Tort Action for Racial Insults, Epithets, and Name-Calling*, 17 HARV. C.R.-C.L. L. REV. 133, 135 n.12 (1982) (citing various authorities who describe recent incidents of verbal racism); Matsuda, *supra* note [3A] , at 2320-21, 2326-38, 2370-73 (specific instances and effects of racism, especially on college campuses); *Soltis, Sensitivity Training 101*, 76 A.B.A. J. 47, 47 (July 1990) (discussing specific instances of racial harassment on college campuses); Williams, *The Obliging Shell: An Informal Essay on Formal Equal Opportunity*, 87 MICH. L. REV. 2128, 2132-37 (1989) (describing "Ujamaa House incidents" at Stanford).

6. *See* Matsuda, *supra* note [3A] , at 2330 n.55.

7. *See* Williams, *Spirit-Murdering the Messenger: The Discourse of Fingerpointing as the Law's Response to Racism*, 42 U. MIAMI L. REV. 127, 136 (1987).

8. *See* France, *Hate Goes to College*, 76 A.B.A. J. 44 *passim* (July 1990). For a perceptive view by an American-born Israeli, see Chafets, *The Tragedy of Detroit*, N.Y. Times, July 29, 1990, § 6 (Magazine) at 22, *reprinted in* Z. CHAFETS, *Devil's Night and Other True Tales of Detroit* (1990).

9. *See, e.g.*, ILL. ANN. STAT. ch. 38, para. 12-7.1(a), (b) (Smith-Hurd Supp. 1990) ("[a] person commits ethnic intimidation when, by reason of . . . race, . . . he commits assault. . . . [A]ny person who commits ethnic intimidation as a participant in a mob action . . . which results in the violent infliction of injury . . . shall be guilty of a Class 3 felony"); MASS. GEN. LAWS ANN. ch. 265, § 39 (West 1990) ("Whoever commits an assault or a battery upon a person . . . for the purpose of intimidation because of . . . [the] person's race, . . . shall be punished by a fine . . . or by imprisonment . . . or both"); MINN. STAT. ANN. § 609.2231(4)(a) (West 1991) ("Whoever assaults another because of the victim's or another's actual or perceived race . . . may be sentenced to imprisonment for not more than one year or to payment of a fine of not more than $3,000, or both").

10. *See, e.g.*, N.Y. CIV. RIGHTS LAW § 40-c (2) (Consol. Supp. 1990) ("No person shall, because of race . . . be subjected to any discrimination in his civil rights, or to any harassment . . . in the exercise thereof, by any other persons . . . or by the state. . . . "); WASH. REV. CODE § 9A.36.080(1)(a)- (b), (3) (1990) ("A person is guilty of malicious harassment if he maliciously and with the intent to intimidate or harass another person because of . . . that person's race . . . [c]auses physical injury to another person; or [b]y words or conduct places another person in reasonable fear of harm to his person . . . . Such words or conduct include . . . words [that] historically or traditionally connotate hatred or threats toward the victim, or written or oral communications designed to intimidate or harass because of . . . that person's race. . . . Malicious harassment is a class C felony").

11. *See, e.g.*, MASS. GEN. LAWS ANN. ch. 272, § 98C (West 1990) (prohibiting publication of "any false written or printed material with intent to maliciously promote hatred of any group of persons . . . because of race"); Note, *A Communitarian Defense of Group Libel Laws*, 101 HARV. L. REV. 682, 695-96 (1988) (group libel laws satisfy demands of first amendment).

12. *See* Riesman, *Democracy and Defamation: Control of Group Libel*, 42 COLUM. L. REV. 727, 775-80 (1942).

13. *See* Delgado, *supra* note 5.

14. *Id.* at 135-49.

15. *Id.* at 150-65.

16. *Id.* at 179.

17. Id. at 179-80 (footnotes omitted). In a footnote accompanying the last sentence of the quoted passage, Delgado stated that the cause of action was designed primarily to protect members of racial minority groups traditionally victimized, but that there were some circumstances where a racial insult might cause harm when directed to members of the majority. *Id.* at 180 n.275. He gave the example of a white child being called a "dumb honkey" by a black teacher in a predominately black school. *Id.* In this respect, Delgado offered somewhat more protection to whites than does Mari Matsuda, who requires that the message be "directed against a historically oppressed group." Matsuda, *supra* note [3A] , at 2357. Professor Matsuda agreed that some whites would fit within the concept of a "historically oppressed group," but focused more on group status than on the vulnerability of the person insulted in the particular incident. *Id.* at 2361- 63. Although both Professors Delgado and Matsuda argued that members of the majority have greater support and "safe havens" from racial insults, and thus need less protection, they recognize that some majority members are nonetheless vulnerable and should be protected. *Id.* at 2358; Delgado, *supra* note 5, at 180; *see also* Wright, *Racist Speech and the First Amendment*, 9 MISS. COLL. L. REV. 1, 14 (1988) ("[i]t is, at least, hardly self-evident that anti-black and anti- white speech must rationally be regarded as symmetrical harms in nature and degree").

18. Matsuda, *supra* note [3A] , at 2357.

19. *Id.* at 2360 (footnote omitted).

20. *Id.* at 2360 n.207.

21. *See supra* note 18 and accompanying text.

22. Matsuda, *supra* note [3A] , at 2356-61.

23. *Id.* at 2361-73.

24. *Id.* at 2374.

25. *See, e.g.*, Bartlett and O'Barr, *The Chilly Climate on College Campuses: An Expansion of the "Hate Speech" Debate*, 1990 DUKE L.J. 574; Dubick, *Freedom To Hate: Do the Criminal Code Proscriptions Against Hate Propaganda Infringe the Charter?*, 54 SASKATCHEWAN L. REV. 149 (1990); Gale, *Reimagining the First Amendment: Racist Speech and Equal Liberty*, 65 ST. JOHN'S L. REV. 119 (1991); Hodulik, *Prohibiting Discriminatory Harassment By Regulating Student Speech: A Balancing of First-Amendment and University Interests*, 16 J. COLL. & UNIV. L. 573 (1990); Lawrence, *If He Hollers Let Him Go: Regulating Racist Speech On Campus*, 1990 DUKE L.J. 431; Love, *Discriminatory Speech and the Tort of Intentional Infliction of Emotional Distress*, 47 WASH. & LEE L. REV. 123 (1990); Post, *Racist Speech, Democracy, and the First Amendment*, 32 WM. & M. L. REV. 291 (1990); Smolla, *Rethinking First Amendment Assumptions About Racist and Sexist Speech*, 47 WASH. & LEE L. REV. 171 (1990); Strossen, *Regulating Racist Speech On Campus: A Modest Proposal?*, 1990 DUKE L.J. 484; Note, *Closing the Campus Gates to Free Expression: The Regulation of Offensive Speech At Colleges and Universities*, 39 EMORY L.J. 1351 (1990) [hereinafter Emory Note]; Note, *Racist Speech on Campus: A Title VII Solution to a First Amendment Problem*, 64 S. CALIF. L. REV. 105 (1990). Still others are listed in Post, *supra*, at 291 n.5.

26. 1990 DUKE L.J. 431.

27. *See infra* notes 66 and 90-91, and accompanying text.

28 347 U.S. 483 (1954).

29. Lawrence, *supra* note 25, at 439-40.

30. *Id.* at 444.

31. *Id.* at 446-47 (footnotes omitted). Professor Lawrence's article is up to his usual high standard, but I think he is well answered by Nadine Strossen in an article printed together with his in the Duke Law Journal. *See* Strossen, *supra* note 25, at 541-49.

32. Gale, *supra* note 25, at 136-41.

33. *Id.* at 184. Given time and space constraints, I cannot discuss Professor Gale's article in any depth. I do not think that she and I are really that far apart, just as I do not think that she and Nadine Strossen are that far apart. In fact, I find Gale's conclusions about what she would restrict much milder than her rhetoric. Similarly, I frequently noticed that after making fairly outrageous (and in my lights irritating) remarks in text, Gale felt obliged to modify them in her supporting footnotes. For instance, though she states in text that: "[h]eterosexual white males . . . often exalt the heroic ideal of the first amendment while seldom, if ever, suffering its consequences," she immediately follows this with a footnote conceding that "I realize that the statement in the text is easy to undermine," and appends a list of eleven people who are either heterosexual white males who do not exalt "the heroic ideal" or are white women or people of color who do. *Id.* at 138 n.58 and accompanying text. I conclude that Professor Gale would like to be more radical than her considerable legal and academic ability allows her to be.

34. See *supra* note 5 and accompanying text.

35. Each of the three state universities is actually a system with several campuses. The Michigan and Texas regulations applied only to their main campuses, at Ann Arbor and Austin respectively. The Wisconsin regulations seem to apply to the entire university system.

36. *See* Doe v. University of Michigan, 721 F. Supp. 852, 866-67 (E.D. Mich. 1989); *see also* Emory Note, *supra* note 25, at 1357-78 (extensive discussion of both University of Michigan policy and Doe decision); Comment, *First Amendment—Racist and Sexist Expression on Campus—Court Strikes Down University Limits on Hate Speech*—Doe v. University of Michigan, 103 HARV. L. REV. 1397 (1990) (further analysis of the court's opinion); *infra* notes 108- 14 and accompanying text (in-depth discussion of *Doe* court's analysis).

37. *Doe*, 721 F. Supp. at 856.

38. *Id.* at 856. The Policy had a second section dealing with "[s]exual advances, requests for sexual favors, and verbal or physical conduct that stigmatizes or victimizes an individual on the basis of sex or sexual orientation," which had provisions paralleling sections 1(a)-(c). *Id.* Section 2(c) was not withdrawn. *Id.*

39. *See id.* at 861-67. The Interpretive Guide helped give the plaintiff standing, as discussed *infra* notes 109-11 and accompanying text. On the standing question, the court stated, "[I]f the plain language of the policy were all the Court had before it, it would probably conclude that Doe had failed to demonstrate a reasonable probability that the Policy would be construed to cover his anticipated speech. . . . The slate was not so clean, however." *Doe*, 721 F. Supp. at 859.

40. This kind of double-talk is just a rhetorical way to avoid the word "speech."

41. Some of these factors approach the trivial ("[y]ou old, married, Vietnam-era Vet" would seem to violate the Policy three times).

42. WIS. ADMIN. CODE § UWS 17.06(2)(a) (1989).

43. *Id.* § UWS 17.06(2)(b).

44. *Id.* § UWS 17.06(2)(c)(1)-(2). A third illustration makes the destruction of property with a discriminatory motive a violation. *Id.* § UWS 17.06(2)(c)(3).

45. *Id.* § UWS 17.06(2)(c)(4). *Compare id. with infra* notes 111-12 and accompanying text (addressing University of Michigan's Interpretive Guide which described similar conduct as sanctionable). On the Wisconsin rules, see generally Hodulik, *supra* note 25 (discussion by University's senior system legal counsel).

46. *See* REPORT OF PRESIDENT'S AD HOC COMMITTEE ON RACIAL HARASSMENT (Nov. 27, 1989) [hereinafter TEXAS REPORT]. The Committee was comprised of three students, three faculty members, and three administration members, and was chaired by Mark G. Yudof, Dean of the University of Texas Law School, and a prominent civil libertarian.

47. *Id.* at 16-17.

48. *Id.* at 7-8, 10-11.

49. This approach is used in the federal civil rights acts and in many local criminal statutes that already make the underlying act a crime regardless of motivation. *See, e.g.*, CAL. PENAL CODE §1170.75 (Deering 1990) (racial motivation is factor in felony sentencing).

50. *See* TEXAS REPORT, *supra* note 46, at 13-15.

51. *Id.* at 4-5.

52. *Id.* at 12. The full passage reads:

The primary difference is that the recommended policy refers to "acts or communications," whereas [section] 46 generically refers to "conduct." Since the tort of intentional infliction of emotional distress always has included harms brought about by "verbal conduct," the change in wording is in the nature of a clarification and not a substantive revision.

Id.

53. *Id.* at 6-7.

54. Paul Brest, Bill Cohen, Tom Grey, Robert Rabin, Charles Lawrence and Gerald Gunther all took part, and the opposing positions of Lawrence and Gunther were reprinted in the *Stanford Lawyer*. *See Good Speech, Bad Speech— Should Universities Restrict Expression That Is Racist Or Otherwise Denigrating? Two Views . . .* , STANFORD LAW. 4, 7 (Spring 1990) [hereinafter *Good Speech, Bad Speech*].

55. STANFORD UNIVERSITY, FUNDAMENTAL STANDARD INTERPRETATION: FREE EXPRESSION AND DISCRIMINATORY HARASSMENT (June 1990) [hereinafter STANFORD INTERPRETATION].

56. *Id.* para. 1.

57. *Id.* at para. 2.

58. *Id.* at paras. 3-4 (quoting Chaplinsky v. New Hampshire, 315 U.S. 568, 572 (1942)); *see infra* notes 157-68 and accompanying text (discussion of *Chaplinsky's* "fighting words" doctrine). The University of Texas Ad Hoc Committee expressly disclaimed reliance on the fighting words approach. TEXAS REPORT, *supra* note 46, at 17-20.

59. STANFORD INTERPRETATION, *supra* note 55, at 2-3.

60. *Id.* at 4.

61. The Interpretive Guide issued by the University of Michigan to flesh out its Policy reached the opposite conclusion and declared that it was harassment if "[y]ou display a confederate flag on the door of your room in the residence hall." Doe v. University of Michigan, 721 F. Supp. 852, 858 (E.D. Mich. 1989); *see infra* text accompanying note 113.

62. STANFORD INTERPRETATION, *supra* note 55, at 4 (emphasis in original).

63. American Civil Liberties Union, *Policy Statement on Free Speech and Bias on College Campuses* (October 13, 1990) [hereinafter ACLU Policy Statement].

64. *Id.* at 1.

65. *Id.* at 1-2 (footnotes omitted). The policy continued by warning against overbreadth and noting that the ACLU had opposed several codes that it deemed overbroad. It also called for universities to take affirmative steps to reduce the problem by education, communication, increases in minorities on campus, course offerings, orientation, and counseling and "such other steps as are consistent with the goal of ensuring that all students have an equal opportunity to do their best work and to participate fully in campus life." *Id.* at 3.

66. The ACLU also devoted a plenary session at its biennial national meeting in June of 1989 to a debate over the issue between Professor Charles Lawrence of Stanford and Nadine Strossen, one of the ACLU's General Counsel, and now its President. *See* AMERICAN CIVIL LIBERTIES UNION, BIENNIAL CONFERENCE REPORT 1989, at 9-19 [hereinafter ACLU CONF. REP.]; *see also* Lawrence, *supra* note 25, at 438-39 (arguing that Constitution requires some regulation of racist speech); Strossen, *supra* note 25 *passim* (responding to Professor Lawrence's article).

67. There are three ACLU affiliates in California, the ACLU of Northern California, Southern California, and San Diego. Each has adopted the same policy, with

minor conforming changes. I have quoted from the Southern California version.

68. ACLU of California, *Policy Concerning Harassment on College Campuses* (1990) [hereinafter California ACLU Policy] (copy on file with the *St. John's Law Review*).

69. *Id.*

70. *Id.* at para. 1. Paragraph 2 of the California Policy calls for due process in enforcement of any code of conduct and promulgation of illustrations showing when the policy does and does not apply.

71. N.Y. Times, July 28, 1990, at 20, col. 5. Professor Gale's letter was dated July 5, though it was not published by the *Times* for another three weeks. Although the *Stanford Interpretation, supra* note 55, is dated June, 1990, it was not available until somewhat later, and it is not clear whether Professor Gale was including the Stanford approach in her statement. The *Stanford Interpretation* seems very close to paragraphs 1(a) and 1(b) of the California ACLU Policy, but it uses a "fighting words" standard where the ACLU requires in paragraph 1(c) that the forbidden speech "create a hostile and intimidating environment."

CHAPTER 2

THE RATIONALES FOR REGULATION

"Regulating Speech on Campus: A Plea for Tolerance"*

William Shaun Alexander

* * *

II. Rationales for Regulation

A. Critical Legal Studies Approaches

This part of the comment will discuss four major rationales for supporting the imposition of anti-hate speech codes. They are: (1) Outsider jurisprudence, (2) the "equality" principle, (3) "politically correct" speech, and (4) hate speech as non-speech.

1. Outsider jurisprudence

The most serious challenge to the tolerance requirements of the first amendment has come from critical legal scholars, who charge that tolerance is merely a pseudonym for continued oppression of minority groups traditionally excluded from the marketplace of ideas.

Professor Mari Matsuda, a noted feminist legal scholar, wrote, "Racism is more than race-hatred or prejudice. It is the structural subordination of a group based on an idea of racial inferiority. [It] is particularly harmful because it is a mechanism of subordination, reinforcing a historical vertical relationship [between oppressed and majority groups.]"[119] Indeed, the latter idea

---

*The complete article from which the following is excerpted appears at 26 *Wake Forest Law Review* 1349 (1991). Footnotes have been changed to endnotes and are numbered as in the original.
Reprinted with permission.

of the dialectic between the oppressors and oppressed is the battle cry of "outsider jurisprudence," the school of legal thought which values principles of an extreme social equality and deference extended to groups who have been historically deprived of economic and social advantage. It is a philosophy which rejects "Eurocentric" legal thought and its emphasis upon the concepts of legal reasoning and content-neutrality because these concepts were conceptualized by members of the Anglo oppressor class to the detriment of minority groups.[120] Therefore, it is also a rejection of first amendment jurisprudence in favor of a more aggressive state posture in speech regulation.

Professor Matsuda would welcome the imposition of radically conceptualized and executed anti-hate speech codes provided that they are not applied, as the Michigan code was, against minority groups. She cries that "subordination exists by looking at social indicators: wealth, mobility, comfort, health, and survival [which] tend to mark the rise to the top and the fall to the depths."[121] According to her thesis, this "victim's privilege" should be the new standard of review, since it would theoretically cure the defects in the disjointed and racist application of the *Doe* code,[122] for example, by removing the oppressed person from beneath it and applying the codes only against members of oppressor groups. Matsuda argues that because the fault of the oppression lies at the feet of the very people who have controlled and continue to control the evolution of the legal system, namely whites and the wealthy, a minority person cannot be sanctioned under an anti-hate speech code because his "racist" statements are the angry, passionate, and poetic responses to the power monopoly of his oppressors.[123] According to Matsuda, forbidding the oppressor from sanctioning a minority group member under such a code would help equalize prior injuries done to minority groups,[124] breaking the monopoly in favor of a new egalitarian ideal.

Professor Matsuda also asserts that her subjective "victim's story" should be the relevant standard of review, measuring the speech and its effects against the mores and sensitivities of the subrogate group attacked. For example, Matsuda insists that a Jewish Anti-Defamation League could collect Nazi memorabilia for a Holocaust display, because of their "sensitivity" about the event, but a hypothetical "Gestapo Collector's Club" could be legally prevented from doing so because of its noninvolvement in "careful debate" about the devastation of the Nazi experience and its peculiar attraction to the Nazi epoch, which could be offensive to Jewish people.[125] The same standard would apply to a reading of Mark Twain's works which, based on contemporary standards, are peppered with racially insulting language, unless an African- American were teaching the novel.[126]

Matsuda also insists that universities in particular have the duty to identify and punish racist and sexist expression, because perpetrators will infer from the institution's silence that their behavior is ethically acceptable.[127] She theorizes that victims of campus hate speech will learn a fundamental mistrust of educational institutions which will further impair their world view and discourage their pursuit of educational goals.[128] The problem is exacerbated by the fact that the college student is in a very sensitive transitional and developmental phase. Therefore, the young adult is still amenable to pedagological control as to acceptable social mannerisms. Likewise, the student is likely to suffer a "psychic wound" if he is the hate speech victim or perpetrator because of this psychological presumption.[129]

The "victim's privilege" theory and its assertion that hate speech causes grave psychological injuries are bolstered by the work of Professors Charles Lawrence and Richard Delgado. These commentators rely on social sciences to illustrate that hate speech in any form is unendurable to its victims and should be culled out of the language through legal sanctions. Delgado, for example, argues that if racist speech is delivered directly or indirectly against the same victim over a long period of time, it has a cumulative effect upon the listener's physical and mental well-being which should override any first amendment concerns about regulating speech on the basis of content.[130] He asserts that racist speech is in this sense racist *conduct* which causes palpable injuries, like a blow to the head or a kick in the stomach.[131] Delgado claims that racist speech could be an aggravating factor in psychic deterioration and stress-related physical ailments predominant among African-Americans, such as hypertension and susceptibility to stroke.[132]

To Delgado, racial identity is a focal point in assessing self-worth,[133] and therefore, a race-based assault is more than a mere comment; it is almost a physical violation of the person. Because of the ingrained racism in American society, Delgado presumes that the "oppressed" group member has an "eggshell skull" on the psychological level, which adds injury beyond the temporary hurt feelings when one is the brunt of a racist or sexist attack.[134] He writes, "[T]he maker of a racial slur necessarily calls upon the entire history of slavery and social discrimination. . .in order to injure the victim."[135] His legal conclusion is that the slur, which causes real damage, should not be protected expression, following the principle that the first amendment does not sanction the use of physical violence or abuse as a speech form.[136]

In accord with Delgado and Matsuda, Charles Lawrence argues that tolerance of racist and other hate speech has desensitized American society to racist behavior to the point where most people have become covert racists.[137] This means that while the polite member of a majority group might not think of physically harming a minority group member, neither would he invite the person to his dinner party, nor hire the more qualified minority applicant because the less-qualified majority applicant was somehow "better" on an unidentifiable, subconscious basis. The oppression, whether overt, covert, or sublimated into the subconscious, is a stigmatizing force, "the process by which the dominant group in society differentiates itself from others by setting them apart, treating them as less than fully human, denying them acceptance."[138] Therefore, as an overt manifestation of racist ideology, hate speech necessarily leads to the perpetuation of negative stereotypes about minorities, which in turn leads to the sublimated desire to oppress them. Lawrence therefore agrees with Matsuda that the counter hate speech of minority against majority is an acceptable self-affirmation device in the face of oppression.[139]

Upon these theses, the school of outsider jurisprudence

finds a compelling societal interest in avoiding harms sufficient to breach the wall between speech and conduct because of hate speech's noncommunicative impact. Under this theory, that would bring hate speech into the areas of permissible regulation, much like obscenity,[140] where the harm it causes is greater than the need to allow it free dissemination.

2. The "equality" principle

Allied to the school of outsider jurisprudence are scholars who see, within the free speech clause, the requirement of equality before words. Proponents of this philosophy believe that fourteenth amendment equality is more important than first amendment free speech.[141] The central premise of the argument for equality in the marketplace of ideas is that racist speech, by its very nature, carries an overt denial of the fourteenth amendment's promise and social agenda.[142] Such stigmatic effect is not only conceptualized as a debilitating psychic injury; but a legally redressable one following *Brown v. Board of Education of Topeka*[143] and its empathetic response to the damaging effects of segregation upon African-American children.[144] The argument goes that, just as the *Brown* decision enabled the federal government to eradicate damaging stigmatic effect by compelling desegregation under the fourteenth amendment, so should the fourteenth amendment compel the government to enter the linguistic battle as a Platonic guardian instead of merely binding the government against using racist speech or endorsing racist ideologies.[145]

Owen Fiss argues that the so-called marketplace of ideas is ruled by those with the most wares to sell, with the added idea that government acts as a silent partner in terms of content regulation.[146] "The duty of the state is to preserve the integrity of public debate—in much the same way as a great teacher. . .to safeguard the conditions for true and free self-determination."[147] The right of free speech, therefore, should not be an individualistic phenomenon, but a "democratic" phenomenon—the "Aristotelian" principle as opposed to the "Kantian" principle.[148] And, "[b]ecause equality is a centerpiece of a. . .participatory democracy, speech that promotes inequality based on race does not contribute to an understanding of our society any more than the argument that the world is flat."[149]

Like the outsiders, the "equality" school insists that the law, acting as a teacher, can act in such a way that it molds behavior. "Speech that promotes the good life and affirms values of community, justice, and the rule of law will be fostered by the state; speech destructive of these ends will be condemned."[150] To therefore tolerate an equal speaking to another equal in a way that denies the dignity and truth of equality is an implicit betrayal of the whole body politic, hampering positive social evolution. There is a ruthless emphasis upon the old revolutionary ideal, "Liberty, Equality, Fraternity." To be achieved, of course, through the rule of egalitarian law and enforced through the coercive functioning of the state legal machine. Racist speech, by denying the validity of egalitarian philosophy, is an automatic degradation of an equal and tantamount to a societal suicide pact.

Therefore, those cases which hold that false ideas are sacrosanct, impliedly elevating the sanctity of the individual mind over the concerns of the corporate state, are anathematic rejections of the concept that the state should stand at the apex of human affairs, intervening with a choosy regulatory hand whenever it senses that the balance of total equality is threatened. By guarding even the outrageous opinion,[151] the government covers the racist and his cause with the patina of legitimacy and even appears to be an accomplice to the racist and his mission.[152] Also, the egalitarian school argues that assent through silence is a subversion of the government's moral claims that it rules a free and equal society and that there is such a thing as an American "community" which safeguards the interests of all of its participants.[153]

3. "Politically correct" speech

Other commentators have proposed expanding the hate speech debate into further censorship of "exclusionary" speech—speech that implies that those who are not heterosexual, caucasian, and male with "Eurocentric" thought patterns are somehow "less" than those who possess these attributes. The expressed intention of those who use such language is to compel others to adopt their viewpoint and thereby enhance awareness of cultures other than the predominant European one and bring all groups into a full equality. It is a sublime contradiction, to say the least.

It has been discussed at length in the popular media that just as episodes of hate crime and hate speech have increased, so has official intolerance for not only hate filled expression, but what could be called "conservative" views on sensitive issues.[154] The premium, according to the "politically correct" model, is upon division of the human race into majority and minority groups. For example, the word "heterosexist" is the politically correct way of saying "homophobia." "Homophobia" is merely a bland psychological term which describes an irrational fear or dislike of homosexual people. On the other hand, "heterosexism" slices people into two groups, homosexual and heterosexual. Inclusion of the negative word "sexist" imputes this vile attribute to the "hetero" group. This spat of verbal gymnastics supposedly empowers the oppressed homosexual or lesbian by positing an "enemy" against them, one who disapproves or hates their chosen lifestyle. In turn, this gives the homosexual person a battle to fight against an identifiable yet depersonalized thing in the pursuit of equality and the acceptance denied them because of an adverse historical evolution.

4. Hate speech as non-speech

The final major strand in the justifications for regulation is the theory that racist speech cannot be protected because it is not speech at all. The proposition is that hate speech does not serve any of the underlying purposes of the first amendment, which are "(1) to permit informed choices by citizens in a self-governing democracy, (2) to aid [the individual in his] search for truth, (3) and to permit each person to develop and exercise his or her capacities, thus promoting the sense of individual self-worth."[155] The argument is that hate speech inspires fear, impeding the victim's own search for dignity and self-determination.[156] Hate speech is conceptualized as the "denial of self" of both victim and aggressor.

Hate speech has no claim to being a protected opinion or fact because it has no relationship to the speaker's faculty of reason. Rather, it is designed to cause a reaction and not a two-sided conversation valued by the first amendment.[157] But, as one result of exposure to one-sided and unreasoned assaults on college campuses, "[b]lack students [exposed to hate speech] say they feel. . .like outsiders, isolated and unwelcome."[158] The preconditions for speech as understood and protected under the first amendment, therefore, are the willing speaker and the willing listener engaged in discussion. Otherwise, there is no search for truth or realization of self- autonomy benefitting either.

Commentators who argue that hate speech cannot be speech conceive of a requirement that thoughts must be sifted through the mind's reflective processes before gaining any constitutional legitimacy when expressed.[159] Hate speech, according to them, does not meet this requirement; otherwise, the self-autonomy and self-determination rationales for allowing free discourse become endangered because while self-autonomy may be a cherished precept, tolerance of the hate-speaker's self-autonomy as he attempts to strip that armor off of another is, in fact, acceptance of excessive individualism.[160] The thesis is that society, or the community, cannot tolerate that degree of self-indulgence because if it became a majority practice, the rule of law and the respect for persons promoted by the law would begin to collapse into anarchy.[161]

B. Summary

The collection of the critical legal studies arguments have several recurrent themes. First, proponents of outsider jurisprudence argue that hate speech creates special types of harms to both the individual victims and the speakers in the sense that the "communication" causes injury to the mind and the affirmation of neurotic, discriminatory world-views.[162] Additionally, the targets must endure societal exclusion and suffer cumulative injuries manifested by unhealthy physical and psychological symptoms.[163] Therefore, the social sciences indicate that hate speech is not speech in any sense, but a substitute for an actual physical blow with no claim to any first amendment protection. Further, hate speech reaffirms an ongoing relationship between oppressors and oppressed groups.[164] The touchstone of this world view includes perpetuation of the idea that others, on the basis of some characteristic, belong in a servient position as sub-human, unequal, and undeserving of legal protection.

The "equality" principle supplies the concept that the first amendment, as a matter of principle and fourteenth amendment law, must serve the community and not the individual.[165] Since hate speech degrades the individual, who is an integral part of the community, it rips at the fabric of society itself. By degrading people who are granted full rights to equality under the fourteenth amendment, hate speech is a cut *against* the constitutional guarantee of that equality, which is understood to be more important than the free speech guarantee and its greater solicitude for individual as opposed to collective rights.[166]

The final major theme is the concept that the fourteenth amendment also commands the government to take an active regulatory role in the leveling of language, which, according to the Aristotilean ideas of the law as a teacher and shaper of social attitudes, will result in the slow death of discriminatory thought and ideology.[167] For example, the "politically correct" school of thought maintains that the college should take an aggressive role in eliminating those behaviors and words which perpetuate subordination of oppressed groups, with the community interest in a vapid harmony overriding the individual focus of the first amendment free speech guarantee.

III. Analysis

The varied justifications offered for these codes are not so much grounded in protecting the *individual* student as in protecting a community of people. This means that the college, as an enclave unto itself, can claim the power to use tactics like those in *Doe v. University of Michigan*[168] and *Wu v. University of Connecticut*[169] to evolve some uniform thought standard among its students.

Succinctly, hiding behind speech codes denies people three major fruits of the first amendment. First, the victims of college hate speech could be given a false sense of security unavailable outside of the college environment. Second, codes deny the individuality of the hate-speaker and his right as a participant in public debate. Third, they deprive society, which will hopefully find its most able servants in the educated, the chance to raise the level of public discourse about topics like race, gender, and human sexuality. Whether oppressor, victim, or bystander:

> [E]very individual is entitled to equal opportunity to share in common decisions which affect him. . . .To cut off his search for truth, or his expression of it, is thus to elevate society and the state to a despotic command and to reduce the individual to the arbitrary control of others. [170]

This section will analyze the various justifications for regulating hate speech, concluding that none of these rationales are adequate.

A. Hate Speech as Fighting Words

Given the Court's broad tolerance of speech in general, the definition of "fighting words"[171] in the *Chaplinsky* dicta is not practically definable to the point where it can provide the basis for any kind of state sanction. For example, in *United States v. Eichman*,[172] the Court struck down a federal flag burning statute because it restrained the freedom of political expression. The Court noted: "We are aware that the desecration of the flag is deeply offensive to many. But the same might be said, for example, of virulent ethnic and religious epithets, vulgar repudiations of the draft, and scurrilous caricatures."[173]

Practically, the distinction between the categories of speech listed in *Eichman* and the "fighting words" left undefined in *Chaplinsky* is meaningless because "fighting words" spoken to provoke only a visceral reaction may be different things to different people. What might provoke a violent reaction in one person could bring a grin to another's face. Therefore, "fighting words" has an innate subjectivity that makes it impossible to apply as a uniform standard and measures the value of expression upon the reactions of its listeners. Further, adverse emotional impact, standing alone, is never a sufficient justification for regulating the content of speech. As the Court in *Hustler Magazine v. Falwell*[174] wrote:

> "Outrageousness" in the area of political and social discourse has an inherent subjectiveness about it which would allow a jury to impose liability on the basis of the jurors' tastes or views, or perhaps on the basis of their dislike of a certain expression. An "outrageousness" standard thus runs afoul of our. . .refusal to allow damages to be awarded because the speech in question may have an adverse emotional impact on the audience.[175]

It would thus appear that the Court has backed off from any extended exploration of *Chaplinsky*'s meaning, bleeding it white rather than overruling or formally limiting the effects of its outdated dicta. By analogy, it makes no sense that a student, in violation of his rights of free speech and expression, should be forbidden from advocating hateful ideas which also happen to frustrate or psychologically harm members of his audience. An emotional revulsion, even fear, is not compelling enough to override the constitutional protections speakers enjoy, and it is certainly not enough to squeeze hate speech into *Chaplinsky*'s shadowy proscription of fighting words.

The Court has repeatedly pointed out that individually held beliefs and opinions are beyond the reach of state regulation.[176] An anti-hate speech code would seem to violate this legal norm, because it forces speakers to answer for their advocacy. Mere advocacy, or even an offensive conversation, cannot by itself amount to a substantial interference[177] that rises to the level where there is physical disruption of the university itself. The existing precedents[178] indicate that the mere advocacy of undesirable and anti-social ideas or threats of disruption cannot be constitutionally prohibited.

B. The Justifications for Regulation—Insufficient Bases and Questionable Motives

The question at the heart of the hate speech debate is why

some people must suffer when another person vents his hatred. But the question of moral evil aside, it must be stated unequivocally that the various justifications for anti-hate speech codes fail to overcome the jurisprudence underpinning the first amendment and its requirement that, in the area of free speech, the person and not the state or community is paramount.

1. Outsider jurisprudence and "politically correct" speech

In terms of sources and thought, there is little difference between the politically correct school and that of "outsider jurisprudence," and identical ideological deficiencies plague both. Consider first the social scientific justifications for anti-hate speech codes. Delgado and Lawrence[179] claim that speech can be the functional equivalent of a physical act where hurt feelings over a long period of time alienate the victim from society and irreparably damage the sense of self and well-being, as well as affirm in the hate speaker's mind the twisted justice and "rightness" of his self-destructive cause.[180] However, as much as common wisdom might validate Delgado's and Lawrence's viewpoint, legal thought is highly skeptical of using social sciences as a vehicle for evolving lasting precedents which must be applicable in the future.

For example, in the famous "two-doll test," a child is presented with four dolls, two white and two black, two male and two female. If an African-American child is asked to select the "good" or "correct" doll, high incidence of white doll selection could indicate that the child has internalized the belief that being white is better than being black. Similarly, a high incidence of male doll selection among girls could indicate a belief that being male is "better."[181] However, this test has not yielded a vast change in results from the pre- to post-segregation eras, according to author Richard Posner.[182] Posner, therefore, questions the test's validity as used to demonstrate the injury of stigma in desegregation cases.[183]

In contrast, Professor Lawrence impliedly interprets the failure of test results to "even out" over time as evidence that caucasian aggression into African-American cultural life still proceeds apace, suggesting that social conditions since 1954 may have physically changed, but that mental attitudes remain the same.[184]

Therefore, in the hands of law professors and judges, different results from a single test can suggest two very different things. The use of social scientific data is not in and of itself content-neutral, and its meaning will be different according to the interpreter and his own beliefs and prejudices. The gravity of harms suffered by different hate speech targets cannot be accepted as conclusive, then, but merely indicate that hate speech could substitute for physical conduct relative to the physical injuries it allegedly causes. A further conclusion is that when the social sciences are advanced as legal proofs, they must yield because of their doubtful nature, to alternative theories of "political history, common sense, and ethical insight."[185] So tenuously justified, the argument that hate speech causes palpable injury cannot be enough of a basis to override the protections of the first amendment or serve as the reason to implement a speech code. By censoring the hate-speaker in the public forum, society gains only an illusion of security.[186]

Additionally, the social sciences do not support the conclusion that speech codes will ameliorate the problem of hate, because attitudes about race, gender, and sexual orientation are probably formed at a young age. Commentators do not explain how punishment under a speech code will help the young adult attending college shed his hatred. Such negative reinforcement could have an adverse impact as well, because punishment may convince the young person that he is being dominated by those he despises.

Another justification of the regulations is the concept of balancing the needs of an "out group" with those of an "in group." This call for balancing is the hallmark of Professor Matsuda's outsider jurisprudence and the politically correct movement. This excessive deference is an insult to the fortitude and mental capacities of "out group" members.[187] Moreover, Matsuda and her colleagues fail to draw any lines or define what constitutes hate speech exterior to the subjective reactions of each victim of this form of aggression.[188]

Following these arguments, if minority race, gender, and sexual orientation assume the pre-eminent position in the lives of people who possess these certain immutable characteristics, the struggle against real or imagined villains of history becomes the focal point of living. First, by seeking to punish a racist or sexist under a speech code on the basis of historical errors, an institution asks a person to bear the costs of his ancestor's sins.[189] Matsuda's assertion that the victim's story should become the standard of review[190] slashes against the most fundamental precept of the law—that no one should be punished when he is innocent, or be blamed for past events over which he had no control.[191] But a victim's personal and subjective settling of accounts is not the law of the land. It is the law of the jungle, the art of vendetta bound up in legal phraseology that does not conceal the fact that what politically correct and outsider jurisprudence adherents desire is the blood of a paschal lamb in order to expunge their own latent guilt over being who they are.

Further, arguing that the content of speech must be subject to a regulatory code in order to balance current societal inequalities betrays the ideal of true equal justice. By carving people into groups and labeling them as "oppressor" and "oppressed," Matsuda and her allies are committing the identical sin that they allege the Anglo oppressor committed and justifying their philosophy on the basis of their own minority status. This is not to accuse these schools of thought of anything so facile as reverse discrimination, but:

> [s]ome versions of moral philosophy are particularly greedy, tending to divide human conduct into the two domains of the morally prohibited and the morally required. If courts were to enforce the judgments of those versions of moral philosophy, they would make all [of] society's decisions. But because judges can make moral mistakes too, we might end up with less good in the long run than if we let *people* learn from their mistakes.[192]

The deliberate imposition of intellectual morality is precisely what the doctrine of content neutrality seeks to avoid. Thereby, every person can be assured that he or she will have at least the reasonable opportunity to speak his or her mind in the pursuit of truth within that *individual's* chosen community, doctrine, or cause.[193] However, this is only a license to persuade, not to impose, require, or dictate. The criteria that proponents of political correctness employ are so self-referential and non-self-defining that they can have no continuing relevance to the communities they seek to "protect" as social mores evolve.

The final criticism that can be leveled at those who advocate linguistic equality for the benefit of oppressed groups is the crass insensitivity to group members who perhaps do not care to be classified at all, much less protected. The Bourbon Street Party has been cited as an example of hate *behavior* which should be prohibited under a university regulatory code.[194] According to commentators, this type of behavior should be *abolished*, not discussed,[195] yet they do not stop long enough to ask if the women who attend this sort of function have *chosen* to attend or wear revealing clothing. By assuming an air of righteousness, the authors do not credit the women they are seeking to protect with autonomous mental processes. They do not take into account the individual's desire to go to a certain party or dress in a certain manner. If there is any worth in any of these approaches, it lies in their desire that people learn to treat one another with basic decency. But by preparing a gamut of abolishing, correcting, punishing, and elevating, they go too far. A utopian dream is a noble thing. A utopia supported by fatuous egomania and the assumption that the unenlightened must be driven in a herd into the false light of some amorphous equality is a lie. This is not to say that people should cease talking about the evil people do and continue to do. But, as has been pointed out over and over by people surveying destruction, the end never justifies the means.

2. The community ideal—dream and reality

The recurrent desire to build a sense of collegiate community at the expense of the individual is a related thesis, and one that is also unacceptable under an amendment that supposedly guards the individual's quest for self-determination and self-autonomy as well as his personal right to speak his mind.[196] The perception is that a college is a distinct community without reference to the exterior world,[197] giving some members of the academic community reason to justify the enactment of a speech code, despite the district court's express contrary declaration in *Doe v. University of Michigan.*[198] If the college claims to be the greatest of all marketplaces of debate and discourse, adoption of a speech code is a betrayal of that very boast and an act of moral cowardice.

Realistically, the liberal arts and free speech are inseparable, because it is only through communication, the "multitude of tongues,"[199] that "[induces] skepticism and tolerance, which are a direct result of the perception that human error has existed throughout human history until challenged and exposed."[200] The college is not a hothouse where one cultivates socially correct thinkers like one might cultivate orchids. A campus which draws students from a vast range of regional and ethnic backgrounds cannot reasonably hope to impose a meaningful sense of community in four short years.[201] The best the institution can do is provide exposure to diversity by enrolling students from wide backgrounds and shaping a diverse and challenging curriculum. Whether the student elects to read a book, accept a professor's interpretation of history or literature, or have a discussion with a person different from himself is a decision which will always vest in the student alone, speech code or no speech code. The most distressing aspect about the hate speech controversy is that the image of a college faculty, supposedly a repository of the keenest intellect in the nation, hides behind something so grossly unimaginative as a speech code rather than applying the traditional tools of education—enthusiasm, reason, and persuasion—to evolve critical thought and inculcate a sense of the social responsibility.

As a societal microcosm, the college is destined to reflect the turbulence and cultural tensions ingrained into the national structure. The idea of a directly imposed community philosophy through a speech code is ludicrous, and would be laughable but for the aggression displayed in the pursuit to create an "enclave" contrary to the *Tinker*[202] decision's proscription against just such an experiment. In imposing these codes, colleges are asserting that the student cannot have the protection of the first amendment. The often-decried institutional neutrality which allegedly legitimizes hate speakers is infinitely preferable to state intervention, because it would be a far better thing to learn to distrust the government and its structures than to distrust the Bill of Rights.

3. The equality principle

The argument that the fourteenth amendment demands that the state intervene in the marketplace of ideas is similarly bankrupt, even if the intention is to alleviate the stigma others feel because of status-based abuse. Keeping in mind that minor state actors attempting to expand a right at cost to others is generally disfavored and legally questionable,[203] the university which seeks to impose a linguistic form of the fourteenth amendment upon private persons is wrong. First, the fourteenth amendment is not simply a tool for equalizing every sphere of human endeavor which brushes areas where a perceived inequality exists.[204] It has no reach into a person's private mind, just as it has no reach into a private institution. Further, an equality achieved through imposing equal protection methodology upon linguistics is not equality at all, but the imposition of intellectual vices upon a population which has come to view the freedom of speech clause as a secular godhead,[205] distilled into the popular wisdom of "I have the right to say whatever I want to say whenever I want to say it."

The proponents of hate speech regulations also do not explain how the fourteenth amendment can retain its "colorless" character if used as a club to silence people who advocate discrimination or race hatred. The fourteenth amendment is concerned with regulating race relations in particular, insuring a basic level of equal treatment in the struggle to evolve a longed-for "race-neutral society."[206] This is not to say that the fourteenth amendment has been used well, as current social conditions indicate. However, social conditions are not identical to personal views and predilictions, because speech is a non-physical entity outside the scope of the fourteenth amendment's power.

Speech, as non-physical, is the domain of the first amendment. Any resultant conduct insofar as it creates a palpable social barrier is the province of the fourteenth amendment.[207] In the collegiate context, this is the very essence of substantial interference.[208] Only if the physical results of the speech, like a riot, palpably prevent the student from accomplishing his studies may the university attempt to regulate the speech. Another conclusion necessarily enables the stated mechanism to regulate what people do beyond the physical impact of their actions upon others. And that means invasion of the mind and punishment for the mind's essential workings.

4. Hate speech as non-speech

Finally, the assertion that hate speech is not speech because it is a raw statement of emotional force intended to produce some non-communicative negative impact upon its listener cannot be seriously accepted.[209] The law has not embraced this position, and it would be exceptionally foolish to do so.[210] All speech has an emotive element—to deny that speech may not be dominated by a predominant emotion, like hatred, and still remain speech suggests that love poetry is not speech, that the graphic sexual violence in the Marquis DeSade's books is not speech, or that the rage of the revolutionary or the platitudes of the saint are not speech. If speech is subjected to a qualitative standard, and inquiry moves backward from its utterance to divine the actual motives of the speaker, then the speech is not what is being judged, but the quality of the individual himself. This "scapegoating" could provide the justification for any amount of censorship, and society would be reduced to regulating what it finds offensive according to a changeable political standard.

C. Regulation—A Threat to Personal Autonomy

The terse free speech clause is far removed from its aggressive sister, the fourteenth amendment.[211] Unlike the fourteenth amendment, it posits no goal, nor does it authorize the use of force. Therefore, the clause cannot be understood as a law in the strictest sense of the term because it has no coercive power to forge some pattern of behavior throughout the Republic, like the prohibition against murder.[212] The clause is merely a restraint against the government, compelling the Congress and the states, through the imperative command "shall not," from abridging the freedom of speech.

> [T]he social compact establishes among the citizens such an equality that they all pledge themselves under the same conditions and ought all to enjoy the same rights. . . .[T]he sovereign never has a right to burden one subject more than another, because then the matter becomes particular and his power is no longer competent.[213]

* * *

ENDNOTES

119. Matsuda, *supra* note 1, at 2358.

120. *Id.* at 2324, 2363-68.

121. *Id.* at 2362.

122. For a discussion of the *Doe* code, see *supra* notes 9-17 and accompanying text.

123. Matsuda, *supra* note 1, at 2361-62.

124. *Id.*

125. *Id.* at 2368.

126. *Id.* at 2369.

127. *Id.* at 2371-72.

128. *Id.* at 2371-73.

129. *Id.* at 2370-71. Matsuda's assertion about the mental fragility of college students in relation to racial attitudes is questionable because "there is no persuasive psychological evidence that punishment for name-calling changes deeply held attitudes." Strossen, *supra* note 16, at 554 n. 358. However, as one commentator explains:

> At some point between the ages of seven and eleven, the child [exposed to racism] learns to reject those who are the target of his parents' verbal slurs. In this stage, the child blindly condemns all members of the hated category. [At or during adolescence], the behavior of the prejudiced young person begins to harden into the familiar pattern of adult bigotry.

KU KLUX KLAN, *supra* note 3, at 27.

130. Delgado, *Words That Wound: A Tort Action For Racial Insults, Epithets, and Name-Calling*, 17 HARV.C.R.-C.L.L.REV. 133, 136-39 (1982); *but see* Heins, *Banning Words: A Comment on "Words that Wound,"* 18 HARV.C.R.-C.L.L.REV. 587 (1983).

131. Delgado, *supra* note 130, at 136-39.

132. *Id.*

133. *Id.*

134. *Id.* at 169.

135. *Id.*

136. *See, e.g.*, Samuels v. Mackell, 401 U.S. 66, 75 (1971) (Douglas, J., concurring). ("[U]se of weapons, gunpowder, and gasoline may not. . .masquerade under the

guise of advocacy."); *See also* NAACP v. Claiborne Hardware Co., 458 U.S. 886, 916 (1982) ("The First Amendment does not protect [physical] violence."); Vietnamese Fisherman's Ass'n. v. Knights of the Ku Klux Klan, 518 F.Supp. 993, 1001-02 (S.D.Tex.1981) (group engaged in overt acts of intimidating violence cannot claim first amendment protection).

137. Lawrence, *The Id, the Ego, and Equal Protection: Reckoning with Unconscious Racism*, 39 STAN.L.REV. 317, 324-37 (1987).

138. *Id.* at 350.

139. *Id.* at 341-42.

140. For further discussion of areas of permissible regulation, see *supra* notes 35-36 and accompanying text. However, the argument for oppression as a justification for regulation is not sufficient. For example, in American Booksellers Assoc. v. Hudnut, 771 F.2d 323 (7th Cir.1985), *aff'd* 475 U.S. 1001 (1986), a causal connection between the oppression of women in pornographic materials and the oppression they experience in society was offered as a justification for regulation. The court refused to accept this argument because it constituted viewpoint-based discrimination.

> The difficulty with this proposition, appealing though it may seem, is that the Supreme Court has been strongly resistant to arguments that would justify governmental restrictions on speech as a means of equalizing power in the market-place of ideas. . . .More generally, arguments in favor of suppressing a type of speech on the ground that it has the ultimate effect of devaluing or disempowering others' speech appeal to unverifiable and deeply contested intuitions.

L.TRIBE, *supra* note 19, at 928.

141. Lawrence, *supra* note 1, at 442-44.

142. *Id.*

143. 347 U.S. 483 (1954).

144. Henderson, *Legality and Empathy*, *supra* note 120, at 1593-1609 (1987).

145. *See, e.g.*, Bob Jones Univ. v. United States, 461 U.S. 574 (1983).

146. Fiss, *Free Speech and Social Structure*, 71 IOWA L.REV. 1405 (1986). *See also* M. SHIFFRIN, THE FIRST AMENDMENT, DEMOCRACY, AND ROMANCE 21 (1990) ("[F]rom the perspective of government there is no 'equality of status' in the field of ideas. Government plays an enormous role in the intellectual marketplace. By subsidizing some speech and shunning other speech, it rejects the equal status ideas. . . .").

147. Fiss, *supra* note 146 at 1416.

148. *Id.* at 1410; Smolla, *Rethinking First Amendment Assumptions about Racist and Sexist Speech*, 47 WASH. & LEE L.REV. 171, 173-75 (1990). The "Kantian" argument is that self-autonomy, in itself and without reference to a community goal, is in and of itself a cherished and inalienable condition unique to the individual. *See* Fiss, *supra* note 146, at 1410. The "Aristotelian" principle, on the other hand, is the idea that the state stands at the apex of affairs with the duty to provide its participants with at least the chance of attaining "the good life." *See generally* ARISTOTLE, THE POLITICS, Book I, Ch. I., *reprinted in* G. CHRISTIE, JURISPRUDENCE: TEXT AND READINGS ON THE PHILOSOPHY OF LAW 13, (1973).

149. Note, *supra* note 1, at 740.

150. Smolla, *supra* note 148 at 173.

151. *Id.* at 182.

152. This sense of philosophical violation is common, and knows no ethnic or color barriers. It occurs, according to one author, when four key elements are present: (1) A sense of violation will arise when one cultural group is "invaded" by another, (2) viewed as the perpetuation of a master-slave relationship, (3) that when tolerated by society as government in an atmosphere of apprehension makes the "invader" and the "government" synonymous, (4) evolving a counter-productive "us" against "them" mind set. D. DOWNS, NAZIS IN SKOKIE: FREEDOM, COMMUNITY, AND THE FIRST AMENDMENT 88-90

(1990).

This attitude development is not rare. It was observable in the South during desegregation, for example, and provided the psychological impetus, presumably, behind most revolutionary philosophies and actual revolutions. On the most generic level, it explains, perhaps, why people of different educational backgrounds, class backgrounds, or any other diametric relationship possess such an antipathy for one another. Race, regrettably, has often been seen as just such a diametric relationship, as if people, Black and White, had been erected on a chessboard. The moral claims of a government, therefore, will only exacerbate the problem if the government is populated by persons believed to be invaders or oppressors.

153. It is very unclear if American society, much less a state college, can claim "community" status, given its mass heterogeneity. The United States, for example, is a "state," or a parcel of land with artificial walls thrown up around it, as a college is on the tiny level. A "nation" or "community," on the other hand, is a cultural product denoted by some shared characteristic, from language to cuisine. The problem for the "hate-speech" debate, particularly on the issue of the college as "community," is that,

> [U]ndue love of one's own can lead to hatred or contempt of others. Family pride can degenerate into snobbery, love of one's university into an elitist contempt for the unscholarly, honorable national sentiment into the. . .evil of Nazism, firm religious commitment into harsh sectarianism.

M. MacCormick, Legal Right and Social Democracy, 247-52 (1982).

154. Karst, *Equality as a Central Principle in the First Amendment*, 43 U.Chi.L.Rev. 20, 23 (1975).

155. Karst, *supra* note 154, at 23.

156. Whitney v. California, 274 U.S. 357, 375 (1927) (Brandeis, J., concurring), *overruled by* Brandenburg v. Ohio, 395 U.S. 444 (1969) (speech enables people to shed fear).

157. *See generally* Richardson, *Racism: A Tort of Outrage*, 61 Or.L.Rev. 267, 270-71 (1982) (allegory of two African-American's reactions to racial mistreatment); *see also* D. Downs, *supra* note 152, at 85-86.

158. Graham, Baker & Wapner, *Prior Interracial Experience and Black Student's Transition into Predominately White Colleges*, 42 J. Personality & Soc. Psychology 1146, 1147 (1985). This study concluded that the pattern of racism perpetuated in American society as a whole has contributed to the demoralization of the black college student, who is thrust into a world of cultural unknowns when he attends a university primarily populated by whites. *Id.* However, the study draws no explicit correlation between hate speech occurring upon college campuses and feelings of isolation, which could be the product of other discriminatory phenomena like continuing segregated living patterns. *Id.* The relationship between segregation and hate speech has not been demonstrated with any clarity in terms of direct causal connections. *Id.*

159. Smolla, *supra* note 148, at 182-86.

160. M. Shiffrin, *supra* note 142, at 90-95.

161. *Id.*

162. For a discussion of this type of effect, see *supra* notes 130-36 and accompanying text.

163. For further discussion of Delgado's arguments, see *id.*

164. For further discussion of oppression in this context, see *supra* notes 137-39 and accompanying text.

165. For a discussion of the interaction between the first and fourteenth amendments, see *supra* notes 141-51 and accompanying text.

166. For further discussion, see *id.*

167. For a further discussion of the Aristotilean Principle, see *supra* notes 148-53 and accompanying text.

168. 721 F.Supp. 852 (E.D.Mich.1989).

169. No. Civ. H89-649 PCD (D.Conn.1989); for further discussion of the Wu

case, see *supra* note 7.

170. Emerson, *Toward a General Theory of the First Amendment*, 72 YALE L.J. 877, 880 (1962).

171. For this definition, see *supra* note 42.

172. 110 S.Ct. 2404 (1990) (citations omitted).

173. *Id.* at 2409.

174. 485 U.S. 46 (1988).

175. *Id.* at 55.

176. *See, e.g.*, Gertz v. Robert Welch, Inc., 418 U.S. 323, 339-40 (1974). There the Court said, "Under the First Amendment there is no such thing as a false idea. However pernicious an opinion may seem, we depend for its correction not on the conscience of judges and juries but on the competition of other ideas."

177. For a discussion of "substantial interference," see *supra* notes 51-96 and accompanying text.

178. *Id.*

179. Delgado, *supra* note 130; Lawrence, *supra* note 133.

180. *Id.*

181. R. POSNER, THE PROBLEMS OF JUISPRUDENCE 309 (1990).

182. *Id.*

183. *Id.*

184. Lawrence, *supra* note 133, at 360 n. 4.

185. R. POSNER, *supra* note 179.

186. R. WRIGHT, THE FUTURE OF FREE SPEECH LAW 79 (1990). Regarding affirmative action, Wright argues:

> [I]t is predictable that. . .minorities and the cause of equality would suffer from the disease of any legally enforced secular orthodoxy, in which any vividly held principles, tempered in the fire of intellectual combat, gradually approach the. . .extreme of lifeless platitudes and cliches which lose their power to inspire.

Id. See also GREENAWALT, SPEECH CRIME, AND THE USES OF LANGUAGE 300-01 (1990):

> What will be the benefits to [minority] groups if [hate mongers] are prosecuted and given the public forum of a trial to present. . .all the damaging facts they can find about the group they hate? . . .The trials over truth could easily do much more harm than the original communications.

187. Alan Keyes, former Assistant Secretary of State, said of Stanford University's hate speech regulation:

> The basic problem with all these regimes to protect various people is that the protection incapacitates. . . .To think that I [as an African-American] will. . .be told that [Whites] have the moral character to shrug off insults, and I do not. . . .That is the most insidious, the most insulting, the most racist statement of all!

Stanford News, Press Release (Mar. 19, 1990), *quoted in* Strossen, *supra* note 16, at 486.

188. *See, e.g.*, Doe v. University of Mich., 721 F.Supp. 852, 859 (E.D.Mich.1989) ("stigma" and "victimization" are terms of art, undefinable with any precision).

189. "[T]here is a measure of inequity in forcing innocent persons . . .to bear the burdens of redressing grievances not of their making." Regents of the Univ. of Cal. v. Bakke, 438 U.S. 265, 298 (1978) (Powell, J., concurring).

190. *Id.*

191. For a discussion of Matsuda's theory, see *supra* notes 119-29 and accompanying text.

192. M. TUSHNET, RED, WHITE, AND BLUE: A CRITICAL ANALYSIS OF CONSTITUTIONAL LAW 110 (1988) (emphasis added).

193. "If the Constitution forces government to allow people to march, speak, and write in favor of peace, brotherhood, and justice, then it must also require government to allow them to advocate hatred, racism, and even genocide." L. TRIBE, *supra* note 19, § 12-8, at 838 n. 17.

194. The "Bourbon Street Party" is an asinine but popular fraternity function where women dress as whores and men wear "john" outfits. Of course, the unstated objective is for these people to have sex at some point in the evening.

195. Bartlett & O'Barr, *supra* note 1, at 578.

196. *See* D. RICHARDS, TOLERATION AND THE CONSTITUTION 169 (1986). "[A person's] ethical independence [becomes endangered by] state judgements about the worth of communications that usurp a person's control over the range of. . .facts and values central to the self-determination of rational and reasonable powers." *See also* Emerson, *Toward a General Theory of the First Amendment*, 72 YALE L.J. 877 (1963).

197. Adler, *supra* note 7, at 52 (quoting President of Mt. Holyoke College who suggested that free speech must bow to the pursuit of college community); *but see* Dorsen, *The Need For a New Enlightenment: Lessons in Liberty From the Eighteenth Century*, in THE CONSTITUTION, THE LAW, AND FREEDOM OF EXPRESSION: 1787-1987 (J.B. Stewart ed. 1987).

> There are many who lust for the simple answers of doctrine and decree. . . .They are the terrorists of the mind. Doctrine closes the mind and kills the spirit whenever it is construed as self-contained and closed, whenever it requires exclusivity of adherence or application or both, and whenever it claims to explain all that has happened or will happen.

Id. at 33 (quoting Giamatti, Freedom of the Mind Comes First, U.S. NEWS AND WORLD REPORT, June 16, 1986, at 64).

198. 715 F.Supp. 852 (E.D.Mich.1989). For a discussion of the University of Michigan's rationale in enacting a speech code, see *supra* note 19 and accompanying text.

199. United States v. Associated Press, 52 F.Supp. 362, 372 (D.N.Y.1943), *aff'd*, 326 U.S. 1 (1945).

200. Dorsen, *supra* note 197, at 23-24.

201. W. MACCORMICK, *supra* note 153, at 247-51. MacCormick defined "community" as a homogenous cultural structure evolved over time, not a heterogenous short-term structure like colleges or departments within them. *Id.*

202. Tinker v. Des Moines School Dist., 393 U.S. 503, 511 (1969).

203. For a discussion of the limitations of power placed on minor state actors, see *supra* notes 102-11 and accompanying text.

204. *See, e.g.*, Hernandez v. Texas, 347 U.S. 475, 478 (1954) ("The Fourteenth Amendment is not directed solely against discrimination due to a 'two-class theory'— that is, based on differences between 'white' and [black]."), *overruled* by Taylor v. Louisiana, 419 U.S. 522 (1975).

205. M. SHIFFRIN, *supra* note 142, at 87. Shiffrin writes: "[The first amendment] affords a positive boost to the dissenters and the rebels. It has helped shape the kind of people we are, and it influences hopes about the kind of people we would like to be." *Id.*

206. City of Richmond v. J.A. Croson, Co., 488 U.S. 469, 507 (1989) (O'Connor, J.).

207. *See, e.g.*, United States v. City of Parma, 494 F.Supp. 1049 (N.D.Ohio 1980), *aff'd*, 661 F.2d 562 (6th Cir.1981), *cert. denied*, 456 U.S. 926 (1982) (racially derogatory epithets made by city council members prior to election led federal court to strike down election results); Gomillion v. Lightfoot, 364 U.S. 339 (1960) (court struck down deliberate alteration of township boundaries based on race).

208. For a discussion of substantial interference, see *supra* notes 51-96 and ac-

companying text.

209. For a discussion of "hate speech" as "non-speech," see *supra* notes 155- 61 and accompanying text.

210. Much "purely emotional" speech has received protection, even if deeply offensive. *See, e.g.*, Gooding v. Wilson, 405 U.S. 518 (1972) ("White Son- of-a-Bitch, I'll kill you."); Cohen v. California, 403 U.S. 15 (1971) ("Fuck the Draft"); Street v. New York, 394 U.S. 576 (1969) (statement of anger and flag burning).

211. U.S. CONST. amend. XIV. The text reads in pertinent part: Section 1:

> No State shall make or enforce any law which shall abridge the privileges and immunities of citizens of the United States; nor shall any State deprive any person of life, liberty, or property, without due process of law; nor deny to any person. . .the equal protection of the laws.

212. Compare the text of the first amendment, *supra* note 3, with the text of the fourteenth amendment, *supra* note 211, which expressly authorizes enforcement.

213. Rousseau, *The Social Contract*, Book II, Ch. IV (Tozer transl. 1902), in F. COKER, READINGS IN POLITICAL PHILOSOPHY 646-47 (rev. ed. 1938).

CHAPTER 3

THE RATIONALES OF FREE SPEECH

"The Influence of the Foundational Paradigms of Individualism, Pluralism, and Cultural Authoritarianism upon Free Expression"*

Calvin R. Massey[**]

* * *

There are no easy answers in the American constitutional law of free speech. Repeated involvement in speech cases by the United States Supreme Court "has produced a complex and conflicting body of constitutional precedent,"[43] a veritable "Sargasso Sea of drifting and entangled values, theories, rules, exceptions, predilections."[44] Scholars and courts are unable to agree on a single purpose for the existence of a guarantee of free expression. Rather, the justifications for securing free speech fall into one of two broad categories: free expression is regarded either as a means to some other desirable end, or free expression is seen as an end in itself. Despite the diversity of rationales for free expression, their application to speech that is a part of public discourse has been borne along on a common current: the primacy of individualism. When speech occurs in a context unrelated to public discourse, however, judicial application

---

*The complete article from which the following is excerpted, entitled "Hate Speech, Cultural Diversity, and the Foundational Paradigms of Free Expression," appears at *40 UCLA Law Review* 103 (1992). Footnotes have been changed to endnotes and are numbered as in the original. Reprinted with permission.

**Professor of Law, University of California, Hastings College of Law.

of the rationales for free expression, while still steeped in individualism, is also apt to reinforce culturally authoritarian patterns of legal thought. This dichotomy may be seen most clearly by contrasting the rationales for free expression with the actual development of free expression law as applied to speech that forms little or no part of public discourse. Sections A and B of this Part briefly describe the rationales for free expression in relation to the pluralist, culturally authoritarian, and individualistic paradigms; section C examines, in relation to the same paradigms, a few representative examples of the law pertaining to speech thought to be outside or on the periphery of public discourse.

A. Free Expression as a Means to an End

Those who view free expression as a means to an end have posited a variety of overlapping ends that the guarantee serves. It has been claimed that free expression is a necessary precondition for self-governance,[45] of invaluable assistance to the search for truth,[46] indispensable to the development of moral virtue,[47] a mechanism to enable the society professing it to cultivate the virtues of tolerance and self-restraint,[48] a safety valve to preserve social stability,[49] and an indispensable check upon the power of government.[50]

1. Self-Governance

Perhaps the foremost instrumental rationale is the notion that free expression is indispensable for the promotion of the free flow of ideas that is necessary for a democratic polity to govern itself. If the people are to govern, they must choose; to do so, they must be informed; and to be informed, governments must be disabled from restricting the dissemination of ideas. In short, free expression is thought to be the precondition for democratic self-governance, for "when [people] govern themselves, it is they—and no one else—who must pass judgment."[51]

This view encounters a theoretical obstacle, posed by those who see democracy as simply another term for unfettered majoritarian rule. If free speech is simply an instrumental means of furthering majoritarian rule, and if the majority decides to muzzle certain speakers or suppress certain thoughts, it is conceptually difficult to invoke ideals of free expression rooted in preservation of democracy to frustrate the will of the majority.[52] One advocate of this position boldly asserts that "[t]here is nothing undemocratic about censorship initiated or ratified by a majority vote."[53] The error of this view is that it fails to recognize the distinction that legal philosophers have drawn between autonomy and heteronomy.[54] Autonomy inheres in the manufacture of laws by the same people to whom they apply. Heteronomy results when laws are produced by people who are not subject to those laws. The distinction is critical to understanding democracy as something other than unvarnished majoritarianism.[55]

The moral claim of democracy is that it is an autonomous institution; it thus embodies not simply majoritarianism but self-determination. This cannot mean that all people are free to do what they wish in every respect for such a condition, writ large, is anarchy rather than democracy. Democracy necessarily implies some social order; the trick is to arrive at that social order in a way that leaves every member of the polity with a sense of his or her own self-determination. The only way in which this can be accomplished is through a social system that permits, if not invites, each person to participate in the creation of the social order. This participation is not just by voting, or through the vicarious speech of one's representatives in the councils of government, but inheres in all the various aspects of public opinion: books, newspapers, speeches, conversations, posters, letters, open-air harangues, buttons and bumper stickers, flags and symbols, and all the other countless ways in which a community carries on the dialogue that is ultimately distilled into the social order.[56] Thus, "democracy serves the principle of self-determination because it subjects the political and social order to public opinion, that is the product of a dialogic communicative exchange open to all."[57]

If coercion is injected into this public debate, either

through compelled speech[58] or by suppression of speech, the central meaning of the process is utterly lost. The reason for public debate is to enable every person within the polity to express his or her view in the hope that it will convince others. Ideally, this public dialogue would produce consensus. If it did, the social order would be truly self-determined and in harmony with the individual views of every constituent member of the polity. Of course, this ideal is impossible. The fact of its impossibility is what makes the prevention of coercion in public discourse such a critical link in the maintenance of democracy in the service of autonomy rather than heteronomy. If majorities can censor the vernacular of public discourse, from the perspective of silenced individuals the process by which the majority rules is as tyrannically heteronomous as that employed by the Khmer Rouge. It is only because democratic legal norms are subject to shaping by an unfettered public discourse that democracy can retain its moral claim that it serves autonomy.

The development of this individualistic rationale in free expression law can be seen most starkly by contrasting a handful of major free speech cases, vastly separated by both time and attitude. *Debs v. United States*[59] upheld the conviction of Socialist leader Eugene Debs for his anti-World War I speech delivered at a Socialist gathering, because the speech had as its "natural tendency and reasonably probable effect"[60] the obstruction of armed services recruiting. The Court ignored the fact that Debs was preaching to the converted, that his speech was essentially "bitter criticism of government and government policy,"[61] and that there was no showing that Debs's exhortations were likely to result in actual obstruction of the armed forces' recruiting efforts. In writing for the Court, Justice Holmes provided "no discussion of the sense in which Debs's speech presented a clear and present danger."[62] Indeed, Holmes did not discuss free speech at all in the course of deciding *Debs*. By implication, the constitutional issue was so simple it did not merit comment. It was permissible to suppress Debs's speech simply because it was deemed to have had a bad tendency on the audience: it might increase the likelihood that his auditors would obstruct military recruitment.

Debs employed a profoundly culturally authoritarian mode of thought. The underlying premise was that, the majority having determined that American military participation in World War I was desirable, any speech deviating from that sentiment could be suppressed so long as it possessed a "natural and intended effect"[63] of even remotely increasing the likelihood of law- breaking. In similar vein are such notorious classics of suppression as *Frohwerk v. United States*,[64] which upheld criminal convictions for speech merely critical of governmental policy; *Gitlow v. New York*,[65] which upheld criminalizing the advocacy of ideas deemed dangerous to the dominant portion of the polity; and *Whitney v. California*,[66] which upheld a criminal conviction for mere membership in an organization advocating such dangerous ideas.

By 1969, the Court's foundational understanding of free speech was radically different. In *Brandenburg v. Ohio*[67] the Court reversed the criminal conviction of a Ku Klux Klan leader for his racist speech suggesting the possibility of violence at some future time. No longer could a mere bad tendency suffice to support governmental suppression; rather, suppression was permissible only if the speech "is directed to inciting or producing imminent lawless action and is likely to incite or produce such action."[68] The bedrock of cultural authoritarianism was plainly fractured. If there was a theoretical foundation for *Brandenburg*, it was individualism. However small the value of Brandenburg's speech, it was necessary to permit its utterance because, at bottom, it was an aspect of the unfettered public discourse required for self-governance to operate legitimately.

A similar phenomenon attends the constitu-tionalization of tort law's "civility rule"[69]—defamation, invasion of privacy, and intentional infliction of emotional distress. *New York Times Co. v. Sullivan*[70] and its family of related cases constellate around the proposition that the central meaning of free speech is the "profound national commitment to the principle that debate on public issues should be uninhibited, robust, and wide-open."[71] *Hustler Magazine, Inc. v. Falwell*[72] found the free speech guarantee applicable to intentional infliction of emotional distress, rejecting the claim that "outrageous" speech was outside the scope of constitutional protection. In these cases, the Court not only aligned itself with the self-governance rationale for unfettered public discourse but also with the individualistic mode of thought as a base for free speech doctrine. *New York Times Co. v. Sullivan* does so by removing most of the inhibitions of tort law placed upon individuals who speak ill of others who occupy a place in the public sphere. *Hustler* echoes that aspect of Sullivan but does even more. By rejecting "outrageous" speech as a category to be placed beyond the First Amendment, the Court implicitly rejected both pluralist and culturally authoritarian values and embraced individualist ones. Within "the commonly accepted norms of a particular community,"[73] speech that is outrageous can be identified, but those norms are apt to differ *between* communities. Thus, the community of fundamentalist Christians is likely to regard 2 Live Crew in quite a different light than the community of young African-Americans. [74] To permit governments to sanction outrageous speech "is unacceptable. . .because it would enable a single community to use the authority of the state to confine speech within its own notions of propriety. . . .[T]he concept of public discourse requires the state to remain neutral in the 'market-place of communities.'"[75]

Hustler can thus be seen to be a repudiation of pluralism as a foundation for free speech, but an even deeper meaning may be derived from the case. If "outrageousness" were to have been recognized as an exception from free speech, the standards of *every* community would prevail, thus regulating public discourse at the level of the most restrictive community. Alternatively, if some "objective" standard of "reasonableness" were to be employed in testing "outrageousness," the standards of the community most "objectively reasonable" would govern. In either case, the prevailing mode of legal thought would have been distinctly culturally authoritarian, for the values of one group would control all others.[76] This suggests the truth of Robert Post's contention that "[e]fforts to establish pluralism will always shade, at one point or another, into [cultural authoritarianism]."[77] Moreover, since pluralism must inevitably edge into the domain of cultural authoritarianism, it is imperative that pluralist theory provide an answer to the vexed question of *what* community's standards should ultimately govern. Pluralist theory fails utterly in this effort.[78]

Hustler thus repudiates both pluralism and cultural authoritarianism as organizing principles for the free speech guarantee in the context of public discourse. The clear thrust of contemporary free speech cases involving public discourse—the speech essential to self-governance—is individualism. It is individual opinion that counts. Group opinions count only insofar as they are the harmonious massing of individual voices. To be sure, group opinions count at the ballot box, but when the Constitution curbs the ballot box in the interest of preserving free speech, it is the individual speaker who matters most.[79]

2. The Search for Truth

As early as 1644 John Milton defended free expression as an essential condition for the ascertainment of truth.[80] Milton was concerned with truth; free speech was only a useful means to its discovery. John Stuart Mill echoed this approach,[81] and through Justice Holmes's famous dissent in *Abrams v. United States*[82] it found its way into American constitutional law. Holmes declared "the theory of our Constitution," at least with respect to free speech, to be "that the best test of truth is the power of the thought to get itself accepted in the competition of the market."[83]

At bottom, the Holmesian defense rests on two assumptions: there is no conjecture so certain that it is immune from later refutation, and, in a reversal of Gresham's Law,[84] that true (or good) ideas will displace false (or bad) ones. The first assumption is most aptly applied to descriptive statements, scientific observations, and other empirically verifiable forms of speech. The latter assumption applies most strongly to speech that is laden with normative judgments, often ones incapable of verification. This is, of course, what hate speech is most often about. Thus, the statement "Professor Massey is scum" is wholly normative, and metaphorical as well. It can not easily be evaluated in empirical terms, because even though I am confident that an empirical case could be built to refute the assertion, the evidence would be ignored by the speaker, if only because it is irrelevant to the metaphorical statement. Holmes's point is that we need not concern ourselves unduly about conversion of the speaker; we need only be concerned that the polity be given access to the "true" data. This access occurs as a result of providing all speakers with the opportunity to present their opinions. In the Holmesian world, if enough opinions are voiced the polity will divine and adhere to the "truthful" ones.

There is an aspect of this view that is virtually indistinguishable from the self-governance rationale. If we assume that the Holmesian definition of a true opinion is one that has commanded a majority in the "marketplace of ideas," the function of the truth rationale becomes identical to the self- governance rationale. Just as the process of public discourse must be kept open to all individual voices in order to preserve democracy's claim to autonomy, the marketplace of ideas must be kept open to all individual opinions in order to provide the marketplace with the full spectrum of choices. Marketplace selection thus functions like majoritarian rule in the councils of self-government; the key to autonomy in either forum is the preservation of a process equally open to all individual members of the polity.[85]

The "marketplace of ideas" rationale has been justly criticized on several grounds. One criticism is that there is no guarantee that free speech will, in fact, lead to the truth.[86] Understanding truth, it is said, is at least as much a function of experience as of discussion, but since the free expression guarantee does not secure the full spectrum of experience, there can be no certainty that the limited scope of its protection will produce truthful understanding.[87] Moreover, the marketplace theory assumes that auditors will reject "[e]motional or 'irrational' appeals,"[88] but, in fact, they do not.[89] A related criticism is that, while truth may prevail in the long run, "the short run may be very long, [and during its course]. . .we may become overwhelmed by the inexhaustible supply of freshly minted, often very seductive, false ideas."[90]

Indeed, one need not search very far in our past to find abundant evidence that patently untrue ideas can prevail, at least in the short run. The Nazi idea that there is such a thing as a separate "Aryan" race and that "Aryans" are superior to others is the most obvious example. It may be that free expression provides no guarantee of the victory of truth, but the lack of free expression is surely no improvement. "The critical question is not how well truth will advance absolutely in conditions of freedom but how well it will advance in conditions of freedom as compared with some alternative set of conditions."[91] Societies that enforce official orthodoxies of speech and thought are characterized by their lack of imagination and creativity, and by their unwillingness to recognize and confront the real problems present in the society. By almost any measure, does anyone think that the coerced and policed speech of East Germany enabled it to address its societal needs over the last forty-five years better than its western counterpart?

The contention that the truth-seeking model is rooted in individualism has been derided as "nonsensical. . .when viewed through the lens of individualism's moral relativism and value skepticism."[92] If individualism holds that no person's conception of the good is intrinsically preferable to any other's, it is argued that individualism must necessarily "reject the plausibility of ascertainable truth,"[93] leaving "truth" to be "simply what the majority thinks it is at any given time."[94] This criticism fails because it does not account for the functional identity between truth-seeking and self-governance. In order to attack the individualistic premise of truth-seeking successfully, it is necessary to establish that self-governance is rooted in values other than individualism. But, as we have seen, attacks upon the individualistic basis of self-governance are flawed because they confuse majoritarianism with autonomy.[95]

It is also claimed that because experience may shape one's perception of truth more powerfully than speech, and because "most behavior, experiences, and lifestyle choices are fully subject to governmental influence and restriction[,]. . .individualism's image of persons freely choosing truth from among competing ideas"[96] is false. But this contention argues more strongly for greater preservation of individual autonomy to shape one's experiences than it demonstrates that the truth-seeking rationale for free expression is firmly rooted in non-individualistic values.

Nevertheless, the weight of all these criticisms may explain why the Holmesian model is not heavily relied upon as a principal rationale for the free expression guarantee. Perhaps another reason for its apparent intellectual eclipse is that, at least with respect to opinions incapable of verification, its function is essentially duplicative of the self-governance rationale.

Some have argued that the marketplace model justifies "free expression because of the aggregate benefits to society, and not because an individual speaker receives a particular benefit."[97] This observation is most trenchant with respect to statements capable of verification. For example, the value of collective acceptance of the Copernican, rather than the Ptolemaic, account of the solar system is undoubtedly greater to society than to the individual scientist urging acceptance of the Copernican model. With respect to opinions, however, this observation loses its vitality. Since unverifiable opinions can not be authoritatively invalidated, the value of their utterance is as much to the speaker as to the society. Indeed, the thoroughly wrong-headed opinion has far more value to the speaker than to society. Our tolerance of these opinions has much to do with the desire to preserve our social claim to autonomy and, in that narrow sense, we value free expression for its aggregate societal benefits. The key point, though, is that in our search for autonomy—whether couched in terms of self-governance or the marketplace of ideas—the social benefit we seek to obtain is the possibility of universal and equal individual access to the process.

3. The Development of Moral Virtue

John Milton's Areopagitica stands as the foremost reminder that moral choice—opting for the good rather than the bad—requires that actors be free to choose.[98] In order to make moral choices humans must be free to think and to express their thoughts, for often the process of moral deliberation involves an expression of views or thoughts, and subsequent reconsideration upon realization of the impact of the expressed sentiments upon others. Without this freedom, moral choice is not available; without moral choice, there can be no real moral virtue in the polity, only the withered and stifling ersatz morality that is the product of moral compulsion. In that relationship can be seen yet another connection with the self-governance rationale. Moral choice is valued in part for the development of moral virtue in individuals, and the development of moral virtue is both desirable in itself and as an aid to the development of civic virtue in the self-governing community.

It is partly for these reasons that Justice Brandeis condemned the notion that silence may be coerced by law, an idea he called "the argument of force in its worst form."[99] Brandeis made the claim in the course of an eloquent defense of the self-governance rationale, but entwined with that defense was clear recognition of the role of free speech in fostering moral virtue: "It is the function of speech to free men from the bondage of irrational fears."[100]

This rationale for free speech focuses primarily upon the moral and spiritual autonomy of each individual as speaker. But people both speak and hear. It is thus fair to ask whether a theory of free speech grounded in the development of moral virtue, but focused only upon the autonomy of speakers, is a complete theory of free speech. The advocates of prohibition of racist speech tell powerful and compelling stories of the spirit destruction visited upon individuals within racial and ethnic groups vilified by racist speech.[101] There is a price to be paid for the autonomy of speakers, and it is sometimes paid in the coin of the spirit of the auditors.[102]

The moral virtue defense of free speech appears to be a theory rooted almost entirely in an individualistic conception of law.[103] There is, however, a generally unrecognized way in that the moral virtue theory may seem to operate to enhance pluralist values but which, in the end, is but a further reinforcement of the individualistic paradigm. By tolerating abhorrent and hateful speech, we are able to see more clearly our societal biases and thereby hasten the process by which we purge ourselves of hidden intolerance. It may be that societal transformation is accomplished by the paradoxical process of tolerating the very sentiments we seek to extirpate.

To understand this paradox it is necessary to provide an example from humanistic psychology. Carl Jung contended that within every person resides a "shadow," a largely unconscious and morally uncontrollable collection of archetypal primitive emotions, judgments, and impulses that function as a dark side to every personality.[104] The shadow has a tendency to escape conscious recognition by its bearer because it is usually projected onto some other person. Hence, when a person loathes someone else it may well be that the loathing is really of one's own unrecognized evil.[105] It is the rare person who recognizes his projection for what it is, but once a person has done so—and faced "the relative evil of his nature"[106]—he has begun the process of transforming and transcending his inner demon. That process is ultimately one of facing the reality of oneself and controlling or altering the evil that resides within.

From a societal perspective, toleration of the individually unfocused racist epithet may be the avenue to recognition of our collective shadow, the first step in the transformative process of its eventual voluntary elimination or, at least, control. The intolerant impulse—banning such racist speech—may have counterproductive long-term results, for it enables the dominant society to tell itself (smugly and falsely) that, collectively, it has no problem; the problem lies wholly within those nasty racists whom we have righteously muzzled. Projection of our evil onto others in order to escape recognition of it in ourselves is as common to entire societies as the individuals who compose them. Thus, the nastiness of racist epithets serves to remind us all that there is a substantive nastiness in our society that we have yet to eradicate. Better that the truth of our condition be painfully revealed to us than we live in delusion that racial equality has been achieved by virtue of painting over the ugliness. In the honesty of the revelation we may ultimately create more real tolerance and respect for diverse groups than by pretending that silence passes for respect. The dangerous dog of racism is still a biter when muzzled. Real pluralism lies in a change of the dog's nature.

Even if I am correct that the moral virtue rationale for free expression is one that has a pluralist facet, that is an aspect of the rationale that is presently unrecognized. Like the back side of the moon, it is there but goes unobserved. Moreover, as the pluralist aspect of the moral virtue rationale is realized, it serves more to enhance the status of individual members of subordinated groups than to recognize the distinctive nature of the group. The societal transformation that is enhanced embodies a withering away of the importance of separateness as irrational prejudices and fears, projected onto subordinated groups, are recognized for what they are: fear of ourselves. Thus, to the extent that the moral virtue rationale has real bite in today's First Amendment doctrine, it continues to be hinged to the jawbone of individualism.

4. Tolerance

The unrecognized and somewhat pluralist aspect of the moral virtue rationale bears some resemblance to Dean Lee Bollinger's rationale for the existence of a guarantee of free expression.[107] Bollinger contends that the highest purpose of free speech is that it enables the society professing to protect it to cultivate the virtues of tolerance and self-restraint. "[F]ree speech involves a special act of carving out one area of social interaction for extraordinary self-restraint, the purpose of that is to develop and demonstrate a social capacity to control feelings evoked by a host of social encounters."[108] In order to accomplish these aims it is necessary to allow the most distasteful ideas to be aired, for that act of societal toleration is laden with heuristic value. Bollinger's insight is that "toleration of undesirable and unwanted behavior" operates as a method "to control and channel the impulses and capacities of" the societal members by "pointing up troublesome tendencies within those wishing to be intolerant, often by the community's engaging in self-restraint toward the very behavior it seeks to avoid."[109]

Justice Holmes admonished the nation that the principle of free thought does not embody "free thought for those who agree with us but freedom for the thought that we hate."[110] Justice Douglas thought that "a function of free speech. . .is to invite dispute. . . .Speech is often provocative and challenging. . . .That is why freedom of speech [is] protected."[111] Justice Brennan observed that we have a "profound national commitment to the principle that debate on public issues should be uninhibited, robust, and wide-open, and that it may well include vehement, caustic, and. . .unpleasantly sharp attacks."[112] All of these defenses of free speech were rooted more in self-governance or the market theory than in the ideal of tolerance. One of Bollinger's accomplishments is his ability to employ these highly individualistic defenses of free speech in the service of a more pluralist view of the value of free speech. For Bollinger, the value of free speech is in the communal lessons we learn from its existence, lessons in heterogenous cohabitation. But these lessons, while of considerable communal value, are not necessarily completely pluralist. Individual and group differences are equally well preserved by Bollinger's theory. As Bollinger's rationale succeeds, as a society we will ultimately treat each of our individual cohabitants with greater respect. In the end, both individualistic and pluralistic values are served.

5. The Pressure Release Theory

Thomas Emerson justified free expression on the grounds that:

> open discussion promotes greater cohesion in a society because people are more ready to accept decisions that go against them if they have a part in the decision-making process. . .[Free speech] thus provides a framework in that the conflict necessary to the progress of a society can take place without destroying the society. It is an essential mechanism for maintaining the balance between stability and change.[113]

Emerson's theory is a variant on the self-governance rationale, but with a less individualistic foundation in that it perceives the benefits of free discourse to inhere in social lubrication. At the same time, Emerson's theory is not particularly grounded in either culturally authoritarian or pluralist norms. Rather, it is a more frankly utilitarian theory. Social peace is to be had by free speech.

When Emerson's rationale is regarded as simply part of the extended family of self-governance it is possible to see that self-governance has a somewhat less individualistic cast than might first be supposed. Nevertheless, Emerson's pressure-release theory reinforces the core of self-governance—the maintenance of autonomy. It does this by its recognition that consensus is impossible, that every person is entitled to express her opinions, and that the very expression will ameliorate what might otherwise be destructive conflict. Emerson's theory explicitly recognizes and focuses upon the procedure by which free expression serves the value of autonomy rather than heteronomy. The heteronomical society courts destructive conflict by muzzling the despised viewpoint and then prevents eruption of that conflict by imposition of powerfully authoritarian controls. The autonomous society counts on the forum of unfettered public discourse to defuse conflict by providing to every individual the feeling that she has been heard, if not followed. The pressure-release theory is thus revealed as a logical corollary to the rationale of self-governance.

6. The Checking Value

Vincent Blasi coined the phrase and is most closely associated with the idea that free speech serves to:

> check[ ] the abuse of power by public officials.
>
> . . . .
>
> . . . .[T]he checking value grows out of democratic theory, but it is the democratic theory of John Locke. . ., not that of Alexander Meiklejohn. . . .[T]he role of the ordinary citizen is not so much to contribute on a continuing basis to the formation of public policy as to retain a veto power to be employed

> when the decisions of [public] officials pass certain bounds.[114]

The courts have accepted this idea most readily when engaged in grafting onto the free speech guarantee a right of press access to trials and other public judicial proceedings.[115] Part of the rationale for recognizing a right of public access to criminal trials in *Richmond Newspapers, Inc. v. Virginia*[116] was that such access "plays a particularly significant role in the functioning of the judicial process and the government as a whole."[117] Justice Brennan most clearly identified this role as that of the checking value when he noted that "public access to trials acts as an important check. . . .'The knowledge that every criminal trial is subject to contemporaneous review in the forum of public opinion is an effective restraint on possible abuse of judicial power.'" [118] Justice Brennan also noted that this checking function is but a part of the larger "*structural* role [free speech]. . .play[s] in securing and fostering our republican system of self-government."[119]

The checking value can thus be seen to be another variant upon the self-governance rationale. Yet, as Professor Blasi contends, this variant is a bit different from Alexander Meiklejohn's vision. The self-governance rationale, as Justice Brennan saw it, was to ensure both unfettered public discourse and informed public debate, one of the "indispensable conditions of meaningful communication."[120] Unfettered public discourse is the fork of the free speech stream that is most commonly associated with the self- governance rationale. It is informed public debate that is facilitated by the checking value. The checking value thus serves to protect "the antecedent assumption that. . .public debate. . .must be informed."[121] The checking value serves in a subsidiary, albeit important, role in relation to the self-governance rationale. If the root of self-governance is autonomy, achievable only by assiduous protection of individual entitlement to speak, its blossom is informed autonomy, achievable by delivery to individuals of the facts, opinions, and emotions upon which choice can be made. In that view, the checking value is itself unconnected to legal norms of individualism, pluralism, or cultural authoritarianism, but operates in the service of the individualistic conception of self-governance.

When the instrumental justifications for free expression are parsed it can be seen that they all partake, to some degree, of the rationale of self-governance. Self-governance is the most strongly individualistic of these justifications since its heart is the preservation of autonomous legal norms, an aspiration that can be realized only by preservation of an uninhibited individual right to speak. Although some of the instrumental justifications are seemingly unconnected directly to individualist norms, by their connection to the self-governance rationale they are revealed as subsidiary players in the highly individualistic drama of free expression as a means to the end of autonomous self-governance.

B. Free Expression as an End in Itself

While the instrumental justifications of free expression were the first to be advanced and continue to exert considerable sway over the development of free speech doctrine, a growing body of thought asserts that free expression is an end in itself, being an integral component of the larger idea that all persons are entitled to realize their full potential. In order to do so, they are entitled to express their opinions and beliefs without governmental censorship. Adherents to this view typically contend that the free speech guarantee "derives from the widely accepted premise of Western thought that the proper end of man is the realization of his character and potentialities as a human being."[122] From this premise readily follows the conclusion that every person has the right to form and express her beliefs and opinions. "[E]xpression is an integral part of the development of ideas, of mental exploration and of the affirmation of self."[123] In this view, the social utility of the speech is of no concern. "[I]t is not a general measure of the individual's right to freedom of expression that any particular exercise of the right may be thought to promote or retard other goals of the society."[124]

Illustrative of judicial acceptance of this rationale for free expression is Cohen v. California.[125] The Court gave constitutional protection to Paul Cohen's right to wear in public his jacket proclaiming "Fuck the Draft" not because it was persuaded that the sentiment expressed was an important contribution to public discourse; rather, the Court recognized that the value of

> putting the decision as to what views shall be voiced largely into the hands of each of us [lies] in the hope that use of such freedom will ultimately produce a more capable citizenry and more perfect polity and in the belief that no other approach would comport with the premise of individual dignity and choice upon which our political system rests.[126]

In its fixation upon the self-actualization of the speaker, this rationale plainly reveals itself as one firmly imbedded in the bedrock of individualism. But there are at least two problems with this rationale. First, it fails to explain why "expression should be deserving of special constitutional status, while other self-fulfilling activities are not."[127] In a sense, this criticism is aimed at the individualistic premise that the rationale is constructed upon, for it forces us to consider why the doctrine of constitutional protection for individual self-fulfillment should stop with the verbal or symbolic. Second, it focuses exclusively on the relationship of speech to the self-actualization of the speaker, ignoring completely the possibility that speech which aids one person's self-realization is destructive of the auditor's identical quest. What happens when, as in hate speech, there is a cost incurred by preserving the autonomy of speakers, and that cost is imposed in the form of spirit destruction visited upon the auditors?

Perhaps it is due to such limitations that some current scholars attempt to combine this rationale with the instrumental justifications.[128] Professor Tribe, for example, concludes that

> [t]hose who defend freedom of speech as an end in itself and as a constitutive part of personal or group autonomy at times err. . .by forgetting that freedom of speech is also central to the workings of a tolerably responsive and responsible democracy and that at least some of the first amendment's

> most convincing implications follow directly from this perspective. . . . Any adequate conception of freedom of speech must. . .draw upon several strands of theory in order to protect a rich variety of expressional modes.[129]

Professor Schauer prefers to evaluate the reasons why governments might seek to limit expression, rather than canvass the varying reasons why expression is worthy of protection. This approach offers Schauer a handy escape from the need to rely upon any particular theory or theories justifying free expression. Schauer describes the woeful record of governments in limiting expression and concludes that governments err because of their self-interest; they always desire to muffle public criticism of the government.[130] While Schauer's approach may assume that there is inherent as well as instrumental value in free expression, his conclusion—that government attempts to silence expression must be viewed with suspicion because of the inherent governmental interest in limiting expression—seems to highlight the force of the instrumental self-governance rationale in both its Meiklejohnian and Blasian forms: free speech acts to assure self-governance by providing both an unlimited forum for public discourse and a powerful check upon the stupidity, venality, or sheer obduracy of governments.

The striking fact that emerges is that, no matter what rationale is offered for free expression, the ultimate root of the guarantee can be traced to deeply individualistic premises. The actual development of free expression law, however, has not consistently relied on the theoretical rationales for a free expression guarantee. Some speech entirely evades constitutional protection, some speech may be suppressed without searching inquiry into the validity of the suppression, and other speech may only be suppressed under the most compelling of circumstances stringently examined. Brief examination of this application of theory is necessary to understand fully the foundational paradigms of free expression.

C. The Applied Theory of Free Expression

Not all speech is created equal. The constitutional law of free expression is rife with categories of speech, each receiving a differing quantum of constitutional protection from suppression depending on the Court's perception of the value of the speech involved and the harms that it inflicts. Even restrictions on the content of speech that generally bear a heavy presumption of constitutional invalidity[131] are not entirely immune from this inquiry. In assessing value and harm the Court must necessarily do so in reference to some principle, purpose, or ideal that is either furthered or hindered by the speech in question. Speech that furthers this ideal is deemed valuable; speech that hinders it is considered harmful. Thus, identification of the ideal ends served by free speech is critical to a coherent development of free speech law. Unfortunately, the categories created by the Court do not reflect a focus upon a single ideal; rather, the Court apparently sees free speech as serving multiple, and sometimes contradictory, ideals. There is nothing monotheistic about American free speech law, but it is also not a pantheistic pursuit. The best that can be said is that it is polytheistic, and the identity of the gods who dwell in free expression's Olympus is not always certain. Nevertheless, the paradigmatic roots of these multiple ideals may be seen by a quick review of some representative categories of speech that the Court has treated as undeserving of the highest quantum of constitutional protection.

The following discussion does not address fighting words—words "which by their very utterance inflict injury or tend to incite an immediate breach of the peace."[132] Prohibitions of hate speech are often defended as within the ambit of the fighting words doctrine and, thus, extended discussion of the concept is necessary. I have deferred that discussion until Part III(B), which deals with harm to specific individuals as a reason for suppression of hate speech, and Part V, which discusses R.A.V. v. City of St. Paul[133] and the future boundaries of protected public discourse and proscribable fighting words.

1. Obscenity and Pornography

Obscene speech is thought to serve no free expression ideal whatever because it is "utterly without redeeming social importance"[134] and is thus treated as proscribable from the free expression guarantee. This conclusion can not logically rest on the premise that obscenity is irrelevant to self-governance, for the Court has concluded that non-obscene entertainment and other speech marginally related to self-governance are entitled to fuller constitutional protection.[135] Rather, it must rest on some combination of the pluralist and culturally authoritarian paradigms.

The culturally authoritarian justification for suppression of obscenity may be seen in such cases as Paris Adult Theatre I v. Slaton,[136] in which the Court concluded that obscenity could be denied any constitutional protection because of "the interest of the public in the quality of life. . .[,] the total community environment, [and] the tone of commerce in the great city centers."[137] This interest is not generally one centered on the welfare of specific individual victims of obscenity, or specific groups (like women) who are arguably systematically oppressed by the existence of obscenity. Rather, "[o]bscenity is not suppressed primarily for the protection of others. Much of it is suppressed for the purity of the community. . . .Obscenity, at bottom, is not crime. Obscenity is sin."[138] In short, if the dominant sector of the community despises obscenity and considers it offensive and tasteless, it is entitled to enforce its cultural perspective through law.

The pluralist foundation for denying constitutional protection to obscenity may be seen in the argument that both obscenity and non-obscene pornography are deservedly lacking in constitutional protection because both "further[ ] the idea of the sexual inferiority of women."[139] The pluralist view of obscenity and pornography is that both should be suppressed because they degrade women and reinforce their subordinate status. Indeed, the pluralist view regards the very distinction between illicit obscenity and protected pornography as the product of a male consciousness and "proceed[ing] according to the interest of male power."[140] From the pluralist perspective, the culturally authoritarian argument for suppressing obscenity but providing some limited constitutional protection for pornography is simply another expression of male cultural authoritarianism. But the pluralist view of pornography and obscenity is no less culturally authoritarian; it is just that the authoritarian voice is, for a change, distinctly female.

As will be more completely developed in Part III, many of the arguments supporting suppression of hate speech are grounded in this same version of pluralism *cum* cultural authoritarianism. Professor Matsuda's argument for suppression of hate speech on the grounds that it is the agent of oppression of historically subordinated groups is revolutionary only in the sense that it is a demand that the authoritarian cultural voice come from a black or brown throat. The paradigm she employs for this purpose is, however, an utterly conventional one which has been virtually eliminated when the Court considers speech in the realm of public discourse. At bottom, egalitarian advocates of suppression of hate speech like Professor Matsuda employ a reactionary methodology—cultural author-itarianism—in the service of revolutionary goals. The twentieth century has amply demonstrated the abundant evil that can be produced in the service of culturally authoritarian visions. Nazi Germany, Stalin's Soviet Union, the Khmer Rouge in Cambodia, the apartheid regime in South Africa, and the Iranian theocracy provide five ready examples of the extreme evil that cultural authoritarianism has produced. Given this vivid recent history, one is entitled to wonder whether social change is best accomplished by employment of the reactionary tools most favored by tyrants.

Advocates of social transformation need not rely so heavily upon cultural authoritarianism, for there is also an individualistic component to the constitutional law of pornography that can be transported into the arena of hate speech. In 1982 the Supreme Court, in *New York v. Ferber*,[141] held that concededly non-obscene child pornography was a form of expression constitutionally susceptible to suppression. The process by which the Court in *Ferber* added child pornography—"'material that shows children engaged in sexual conduct, regardless of whether such material is obscene'"[142]—to the categories of unprotected speech is instructive in locating another paradigm that influences judicial selection of unprotected speech categories.

Ferber advanced several reasons for permitting the states to regulate "pornographic depictions of children."[143] The Court found that the "prevention of sexual exploitation and abuse of children constitutes a government objective of surpassing importance. . . .[and] that the use of children as subjects of pornographic materials is harmful to the physiological, emotional, and mental health of the child."[144] To prevent this harm from occurring the Court found that it was an indispensable necessity to prohibit the sale, advertising, or promotion of the photographs or films that record this sexual abuse. The Court found the governmental interest so compelling and the harm so significant that it rejected the *Miller v. California*[145] standard of obscenity in favor of inquiry into "whether a child has been physically or psychologically harmed in the production of the work."[146] Even when the Court balanced the governmental interest in suppression against the asserted expressive interests, it reached its conclusion that "the evil to be restricted . . .overwhelmingly outweighs the expressive interests"[147] because child pornography "bears so heavily and pervasively on the welfare of children *engaged in its production.*"[148]

The unifying thread of these reasons is that the pornographic speech in question has a close causal linkage to individualized injury to the children depicted. The thrust of the Court's rationale is not that the harm of child pornography is a more generalized one inflicted on viewers, or even the class of all children, but that it is imposed on identifiable individuals. To that extent, the Court's rationale meshes neatly with prior case law concerning other categories of speech, like defamation, that receive limited constitutional protection. The common trait that renders such speech of sufficiently "low value" to merit only limited immunity from suppression is that the speech inflicts a quite particularized and individualized injury by its very utterance. In *Ferber* the paradigmatic ideal that free expression was thought to serve was the primacy of the individual.

Application of the individualistic paradigm to the problem of hate speech suggests that hate speech is properly suppressed when it is focused upon a specific individual with the intent to inflict grievous injury. Suppression is most clearly justified where, in addition, it is the sole effective remedy to prevent or redress the injury. This approach, more fully developed in Parts III and V, is concededly less ambitious than other proposals for achieving the socially transformative goals desired by many advocates of suppression of hate speech. But, as is the case with so many things in life, the cost of using coercion as the vehicle for abrupt and thorough social renovation must be balanced against the benefits thereby obtained.[149] I cannot reduce that equation to mathematical proof, but I offer the history of the twentieth century as argument that the potential cost of using the culturally authoritarian voice ultimately outweighs the benefits of thorough suppression of hate speech under virtually all circumstances.

2. Speech in the Commission of the "Civility Torts"

The relationship of the free expression guarantee to the "civility torts"—defamation, invasion of privacy, and intentional infliction of emotional distress—illustrates two separate aspects of the individualistic paradigm. When the First Amendment was thought not to immunize speech uttered in the commission of the civility torts, the effect of the doctrine was to enable individual victims of such speech to obtain as complete a vindication of their individual injuries as tort law would permit. The constitutionalization of the civility torts might appear to be a repudiation of that paradigm but, in fact, merely represents another dimension of individualism in free expression law.

The Court's central rationale for establishing a constitutionally-mandated zone of immunity for speech that would otherwise trigger civility tort liability is to insure "that debate on public issues should be uninhibited, robust, and wide-open."[150] In so doing the Court explicitly recognized the centrality of the self-governance rationale to free expression and implicitly embraced the idea that self-governance is rooted in notions of autonomy. In order to preserve autonomy, and thus self-governance, the Court felt constitutionally compelled to immunize some speech invasive of individual reputational interests. The Court's "actual malice" test reflects its balancing of these two aspects of individualism—the direct individual interest in a vindicated reputation and the equally valuable individual interest in participation in autonomous self-governance. Similarly, the Court's creation of the "public figure" and "public concern" doctrines[151] are refinements of the same balance that the Court has sought to strike between two facets of individualism in tension. Although the Court *in Milkovich v. Lorain Journal Co.*[152] declined an opportunity to extend constitutional immunity to statements of opinion with factual implications, its decision not to do so was grounded on a belief that such immunity was unnecessary to autonomous self-governance and that it would, if recognized, cut even more deeply into the "'pervasive and strong interest in preventing and redressing attacks upon reputation.'"[153]

Hustler Magazine, Inc. v. Falwell,[154] rejected the idea that a similar balance could be struck with respect to speech inflicting individual emotional distress by employing "outrageousness" as the analogue to "actual malice," thus reinforcing the Court's commitment to unfettered public discourse as essential to autonomous self-governance. Using "outrageousness" as the measure of the limits of constitutional protection of speech that inflicts emotional injury would effectively assign to a single subcommunity the power to define those limits, for outrageousness can never be located other than by using a referent community.[155] Accordingly, the autonomous self-governance rationale for free expression was thought by the Court to require governments to refrain from endowing any particular referent community with a privileged status.

The constitutionalization of the civility torts has been actuated by an attempt to serve two aspects of individualism in tension with each other, but has not been driven by any conception of pluralism or cultural authoritarianism. This helps to explain the demise *of Beauharnais v. Illinois*,[156] that upheld an Illinois group libel statute against a free speech challenge. *Beauharnais* is often used as the starting point for a pluralist defense of suppression of hate speech that is aimed at, and injures, identifiable groups, but the case has been eclipsed as good law for three sound reasons.

First, the statute at issue in *Beauharnais* had been construed by the Illinois courts to prohibit only speech that had a "strong tendency. . .to cause violence and disorder."[157] Accordingly, the Court upheld the validity of a statute which, as construed, prohibited only hate speech that might plausibly result in a breach of the peace. It did not go so far as to uphold a more general prohibition upon hate speech. Today, thirty-four years after *Beauharnais*, we are entitled to question whether even that rationale would be sufficient, for now we have the benefit of such cases as *Brandenburg v. Ohio*,[158] that permits suppression of speech calculated to foment public disorder only if that result is "imminent," and *Cohen v. California*,[159] which holds that offensive speech may not be suppressed solely by reason of its offensiveness. In 1978, when American neo-Nazis wished to march through Skokie, Illinois for the purpose of expressing their hatred and contempt of that community's largely Jewish population, the Seventh Circuit regarded *Beauharnais* in precisely this jaundiced light in the course of invalidating a Skokie ordinance prohibiting speech "which promotes and incites hatred against persons by reason of their race, national origin, or religion, and is intended to do so."[160]

Second, the Court in *Beauharnais* assumed as correct *Chaplinsky*'s view that "libelous. . .utterances are no essential part of any exposition of ideas, and are of such slight social value as a step to truth that any benefit that may be derived from them is clearly outweighed by the social interest in order and morality."[161] From there the Court swiftly concluded that if "an utterance directed at an individual may be the object of criminal sanctions, we cannot deny to a State power to punish the same utterance directed at a defined group."[162] The Court thus embraced the notion that defamation is a species of speech outside the protective umbrella of the Free Speech Clause of the First Amendment. This rationale is plainly wrong after the devastating inroads on defamation's insulation from the speech guarantee worked by *New York Times Co. v. Sullivan*[163] and its progency.[164]

Finally, the Court accepted without question that speech which characterized the identifiable group of African-Americans as violent criminals and drug-users was defamatory if false.[165] The error in this was to suppose that an assertion of fact can be treated equally when made as to an individual and an entire group. To charge that "Professor Massey uses marijuana" is to assert a specific factual condition capable of empirical verification. The allegation that "law professors use marijuana" is quite dif-ferent. Within the group of law professors, it is entirely likely that some are and most are not. "The question is. . .not the existence of certain specific acts, but rather *whether those acts can appropriately be used to characterize the group.* The fundamental issue is the nature of the group's identity, *an issue that almost certainly ought to be characterized as one of evaluative opinion.*"[166] Evaluative opinions of all the things that instantiate culture—certainly including groups—would seem to be at the heart of the uninhibited, robust, and wide-open public discourse that the court in *New York Times Co. v. Sullivan* thought was demanded by a commitment to autonomous self-governance.

3. Speech in Schools

The foundational paradigm for defining the extent of free expression within schools has shifted over time. Prior to the Warren Court opinions of the 1960s, public schools from kindergartens to universities were thought to be invested with virtually plenary authority to regulate the speech of their students. Thus, university students could be and were dismissed for protesting university policies.[167] The justification for such complete control over student expression was rooted in the view that since "public education [is] an instrument of community life. . .[,] 'respect for constituted authority and obedience thereto is an essential lesson to qualify one for the duties of citizenship, and. . .the schoolroom is an appropriate place to teach that lesson.'"[168] This perspective was ardently culturally authoritarian, for it held that schools should "teach[] students the boundaries of socially appropriate behavior. . .[,] the shared values of a civilized social order. . .[and] the essential lessons of civil, mature conduct."[169] Under this view of the educational mission, control of hate speech within schools would be theoretically possible since at least the worst of the genre is neither "socially appropriate," consonant with "the shared values of a civilized social order," nor fairly within the description of "civil, mature conduct."[170] However, although the culturally authoritarian view of education continues to be recognized with respect to secondary and, presumably, elementary schools[171] it has been discarded for the university.

The culturally authoritarian perspective regarding education has been replaced by the related, and overlapping, conceptions that "[t]he classroom is peculiarly 'the marketplace of ideas'"[172] but also "the cradle of our democracy,"[173] a forum for students to be exposed to all sorts of ideas in the expectation that they will develop the intellectual "independence and vigor. . .[to] grow up and live in this relatively permissive, often disputatious, society."[174] The former conception of education is as an aid to the search for truth, the latter is as an instrument for developing the capacity of self-governance. Thus, the Court has begun to view education, particularly higher education, as having objectives that mimic highly individualistic rationales for free expression. The result is that, with respect to speech within universities, the Court has tended to apply the individualistic paradigm. By contrast, the Court's tendency to regard cultural inculcation as a significant component of the mission of elementary and secondary education has resulted in a distinctly culturally authoritarian cast to its understanding of the role of free expression within such schools.

It is thus hardly surprising that the Court has concluded that "the mere dissemination of ideas-no matter how offensive to good taste-on a state university campus may not be shut off in the name alone of 'conventions of decency.'"[175] Similarly, radical student groups may not be barred from public campuses simply because of antipathy to their message, or even generalized fear of disruption, but only in the event of their refusal to conform to, or actual violation of, valid conduct regulations.[176] Thus, speech that "materially disrupts classwork or involves substantial disorder or invasion of the rights of others" is not constitutionally immunized from regulation.[177] It is as plainly an uncontroversial regulation of speech to prohibit a student from chanting "Bullshit!" during my constitutional law class as it is to prohibit another student from using racial epithets in class. Both forms of speech materially and substantially disrupt the work of the class.

It is, however, quite another matter to prohibit the utterance of racist ideas, whether within or without the classroom. Admittedly, the distinction between the racist epithet and the racist idea is thin, highly contextual, and extraordinarily difficult to define with sufficient precision to overcome objections rooted in overbreadth and vagueness.[178] The operative distinction for free expression purposes within the university seems to be the point speech produces interference with the classroom, disorder or other breach of the peace, or interference with the rights of others. Thus, in *Papish v. Board of Curators*[179] the Court concluded that a public university could not control the choice of language employed by a student speaker, for that was part of the "content" of the speech; nor could the university prohibit expression "in the absence of any disruption of campus order or interference with the rights of others."[180]

The constitutional liquor to be distilled from this brew is not entirely clear. Taken at face value, *Papish* seems to suggest that all nondisruptive speech engaged in at a university is constitutionally protected. Yet, it is a virtual certainty that *Papish* intended to preserve a wide range of discretion to universities to judge the merits of speech uttered in connection with the educational program. It is surely ludicrous to suppose that *Papish* requires a public university to grant a Ph.D. to the author of a dissertation that consists of a single sentence: "This university is a cesspool of intellectual corruption." The author may be correct, but surely the university has a right to insist upon some demonstration of the supposed academic virtues as a precondition for award of academic honors. Thus, the central meaning of *Papish* is the more narrow proposition that a university has very little warrant to control speech uttered outside of the confined precincts of the classroom and the coursework derived therefrom. Indeed, this is evident from the fact that the *Papish* Court regarded the case as being controlled by *Cohen v. California*,[181] thus strongly indicating that the Court felt that the "university [possessed no] greater authority to regulate. . .speech than the state itself."[182] Once a student has left the classroom and its immediately ancillary demands, she is as free as any other citizen to speak, however offensive the content of her speech. *Papish*'s reliance on *Cohen* also suggests that the university's warrant to limit speech that "interfere[s] with the rights of others"[183] does not extend to speech that interferes merely by reason of its offensiveness.

But the conclusion that universities possess heightened authority to control speech in classrooms seems at odds with the conclusion of *Tinker v. Des Moines School District*[184] that student speech rights specifically include the classroom. The continued vitality of Tinker is partially undercut by such cases as *Bethel School District No. 403 v. Fraser*[185] and *Hazelwood School District v. Kuhlmeier*,[186] which permit educators to discipline offensive student-government speech and to entirely suppress "school-sponsored expressive activities so long as. . . [suppression is] reasonably related to legitimate pedagogical concerns."[187] But if *Tinker* remains alive, albeit crippled, it is difficult to rationalize doctrine that seems to permit expansive regulation of curricular speech only but simultaneously claims to preserve student speech rights within the classroom. The incoherence may be somewhat resolved by treating *Tinker* as standing for the proposition that speech which is not disruptive to the classroom or related coursework must be tolerated but is not entitled to exemption from the normal, and presumably objective, evaluation of the merits of speech that is central to the academic enterprise. In any case, in the university context cases like *Tinker*, *Bethel School District*, and *Hazelwood School District* are not particularly applicable. Far more relevant to the adult world of the university are cases such as *Papish*. Thus, within the classroom and in related curricular activities, universities would seem to possess the power to prohibit hate speech at the point that it becomes disruptive.

Whether this point is roughly coterminous with the *Brandenburg v. Ohio*[188] formulation, or whether it permits suppression of hate speech at some earlier point, is not entirely clear. Outside of the classroom, however, the university seems to be conceived by the Court as something virtually indistinguishable from the public forum, which typifies public discourse,[189] and with no more entitlement to regulate speech than any other governmental actor.

But, as will be developed in Part IV, this dichotomy may be too crude. There are places within the university community that seem outside the forum of public discourse, and thus more analogous to the privacy of the home. Living and eating spaces are surely public in a sense, but in the world beyond the university these locations are clearly the essence of private space. In dealing with the issue of hate speech within the university it is important to keep in mind that universities may be part of public discourse, but not for all purposes. The core function of the university may well be the search for truth and preparation of its students for self-governance, but that does not mean that every aspect of university life is equally public. Some sensitivity to the multiple functions of universities—as secure places to live as well as places to study and debate, perhaps rudely and contentiously—ought to be present when the constitutionality of university hate speech regulations are considered. The practical manifestation of this sensitivity within the prevailing paradigms pertaining to free expression is the subject of Part IV.

4. Speech in the Workplace

The issue of the extent that the free expression guarantee immunizes speech in the workplace has been explored most fully in the context of public employees. The prevailing conclusion is that "[w]hen employee expression cannot be fairly considered as relating to any matter of political, social, or other concern to the community, government officials should enjoy wide latitude in managing their offices, without intrusive oversight by the judiciary in the name of [free expression]."[190] Even when a government employee's speech is of public concern, the Court balances the employee's speech interests against the government's interest in efficient administration.[191] The former conclusion is founded in part upon a perception that, since private employers are generally immune from constitutional limits in proscribing employee speech in the interest of workplace efficiency, public employers ought to enjoy a similar latitude when the employee speech is unrelated to matters of public concern. The rationale for free expression that this conclusion seems based upon is that of self-governance, for matters of public concern are clearly the prototypical subject of speech that furthers self-governance. The ideal of speech in service of autonomous self-governance is, of course, an ideal informed by the individualistic paradigm. thus, the free expression guarantee enjoyed by public employees exists to serve individual expression upon matters germane to self-government. Since the scope of free speech of public employees seems initially driven by a desire to treat public and private employers equally in terms of maintaining an efficient workplace, it would be rational to assume that the constitutional limits applicable to governmental efforts to impose liability on private employers for their failure to muzzle the speech of their employees are at least as speech protective as those applicable to public employees.[192] This phenomenon occurs most markedly in the context of claims that employee speech which is sexually or racially harassing constitutes a breach by the employer of Title VII of the Civil Rights Act of 1964.[193] These claims break down into two broad categories: (1) abusive and offensive speech that is directed at an individual target, and (2) abusive and offensive speech that is not directed at any particular target. Although the Supreme Court has yet to address the limits that the free expression guarantee may impose upon congressional ability to mandate employer liability for employee speech, the Court has implicitly provided some answers to this question.[194]

In *Meritor Savings Bank v. Vinson*,[195] the Supreme Court held that speech which created a hostile work environment was actionable under Title VII of the Civil Rights Act of 1964.[196] Though the Court ruled only on a point of statutory interpretation, its decision that speech could be sufficiently injurious to warrant a Title VII claim carries with it the possible inference that there is no First Amendment barrier to the assertion of such a claim, at least under the egregious factual circumstances presented in *Meritor*.[197] It is critical to note that the Court identified a narrow category of speech as sufficiently injurious to trigger a Title VII claim: "Unwelcome sexual advances, requests for sexual favors, and other verbal or physical conduct of a sexual nature. . . .[which] has the purpose or effect of unreasonably interfering with an *individual's* work performance or creating an intimidating, hostile, or offensive working environment."[198] The pivot that Title VII liability turned upon was whether the abuse was sufficiently focused on an individual: "[f]or sexual harrassment to be actionable, it must be sufficiently severe or pervasive 'to alter the conditions of [the victim's] employment and create an abusive working environment.'"[199] The allegations of sexual harassment at issue in *Meritor* itself were of extremely individualized injury, being a combination of speech and action directed specifically to Mechelle Vinson and designed to coerce her into sexual intercourse. The Court underlined both its preoccupation with individual injury and its evident conclusion that the offensive speech at issue was wholly outside the circle of public discourse by noting that "'a requirement that a man or woman run a gauntlet of sexual abuse in return for the privilege of being allowed to work and make a living can be as demeaning and disconcerting as the harshest of racial epithets.'"[200] Thus, *Meritor* supports the proposition that speech which forms no part of public discourse and is directed at a targeted individual in an unbearably offensive manner may be suppressed.

While *Meritor* does not suggest that offensive speech that has no individualized target may be suppressed, there may well be circumstances where the offensive speech, though not directed toward any particular individual, is so pervasive in its effect and influence that it can be treated as directed toward a particular identifiable individual and thus capable of suppression. *Robinson v. Jacksonville Shipyards, Inc.*[201] may well be such a case. Lois Robinson was employed as a welder at Jacksonville Shipyards, engaged in dangerous ship repair work. She was one of a tiny number of women so employed and, in the course of her employment, was subjected to pervasive and repeated exposure to extremely offensive depictions of women as objects of male sexual pleasure,[202] as well as to sexually offensive commentary directed specifically to her.[203] The district court concluded that this employee speech supported employer liability for breach of Title VII and expressly rejected the argument that the free speech guarantee insulated the employer from Title VII liability.[204] Although the district judge was not clear on the point, his underlying rationale for the conclusion that the Constitution permits Title VII to impose liability upon employers for their toleration of a hostile work environment seems to be twofold: (1) the particular speech in the workplace that liability was premised upon formed no part of public discourse, and (2) the totality of the depictions and remarks suggested strongly that they were in considerable part directed toward Lois Robinson individually.

The free expression guarantee thus seems to protect (1) patently offensive workplace speech that is within public discourse, and (2) offensive speech that is not specifically directed toward a particular individual.[205] These two limitations derive their pedigree from the individualistic paradigm.

The first rationale is rooted in the idea that autonomous self-governance requires unfettered discourse, even to the point of offensive bruising of individual sensibilities. The limits of this rationale are either (1) the point that the individualized abuse no longer partakes of public discourse, or (2) the point that the individualized abuse is so focused and abusive that it threatens to rupture the social framework which permits individual autonomy to flourish. The first dividing line is fine, but can be glimpsed. An employee who derides the competence of his fellow employee in offensive and racially derogatory terms as exemplifying the reasons why affirmative action is bad public policy is speaking within public discourse. To say to an African-American fellow employee, "Hiring you less-qualified blacks lowers our company's productivity; you [racial epithet] can't drive a nail straight," is at the periphery of protected public discourse. Certainly the first part of the statement is protected; the second part, while offensive and repugnant, is protected only because it is uttered in a context of public discourse. By contrast, simple derision of one's fellow employee in the same racially offensive terms is surely no part of public discourse. To say to one's African-American fellow employee, "You [racial epithet] can't drive a nail straight," without elaboration, is simply to engage in private abuse. Although the difference is slight, in the context of public employees the Court has been able to distinguish between speech that touches upon private matters and that which is of public concern. There is no reason to think the task is measurably more difficult in the context of the private workplace. But simply because the offensive speech is private abuse does not mean that it is automatically without constitutional protection. Offensive speech which lacks the umbrella of public discourse may be suppressed only when the individualized abuse is so sharp that it threatens the social conditions that support the development of individual autonomy. This second dividing line is marked by the point that individually abusive speech is likely to erupt into immediate violence.

The second rationale is rooted in the individualistic notion that speech may be curbed when it is absolutely necessary to do so to protect another individual from harm, and when no overriding principle of public discourse argues against individual protection. The latter argument is strengthened by the contention that employees are a uniquely captive audience who may be protected from the unwilling infliction of offensive speech. As will be seen in the next subsection, the captive audience rationale serves to reinforce the individualistic paradigm that informs the law of free expression in the workplace.

5. Captive Audiences

While offensive speech generally may not be suppressed simply because of its offensiveness,[206] the Court has recognized that such speech may be regulated when it is delivered to a captive audience. In formulating the captive audience doctrine the Court has been driven by another facet of the individualistic paradigm—the perceived need to preserve individual privacy.[207] The Court has recognized the existence of a captive audience sufficient to support restrictions on offensive speech in the context of high-school students at a school assembly,[208] radio broadcasting during the hours in which children might be expected to be listening[209] as well as individuals in their homes.[210] In each case the Court acted upon "a belief that the recipients of the communication were somehow compelled to hear or see the message."[211]

Perhaps the clearest demonstration of the driving force of this view is *Frisby v. Schultz*,[212] where the Court concluded that a content-neutral municipal ordinance forbidding "focused picketing"—the practice of singling out an individual's home for public picketing—was valid even as applied to purely political speech. When forced to choose between speech at the heart of public discourse, and therefore most germane to ideals of autonomous self-governance, and individual interest in repose, the Court chose to protect the more direct individual interest. However, in *Carey v. Brown*[213] the Court invalidated a focused picketing statute as violative of the Equal Protection Clause because the statute permitted speech concerning labor disputes while prohibiting all other forms of focused picketing. Governments have the greatest ability to protect the individual held captive in her home from unwanted speech of others when the vehicle for doing so is content-neutral. Once the regulatory mechanism discriminates on the content of speech, *Carey* demands that, at least with respect to "high value" political speech,[214] governments sustain the burden of proving that content-based discrimination is narrowly tailored to serve a compelling governmental interest. In *Carey* itself the Court concluded that, although protection of the privacy of captive auditors was "surely an important value," the statute failed to advance "'that objective in a manner consistent with the. . . Equal Protection Clause'. . .because the statute discriminates among pickets based on the subject matter of their expression."[215]

Moreover, when the individual interest in repose is less immediately implicated the Court will not curb speech, even when the speech involved is at the edges of public discourse. *Erznoznick v. City of Jacksonville*,[216] finding that passers-by were not held captive by nudity displayed on an outdoor theatre screen, illustrates the unwillingness of the Court to slice too deeply into the individualistic rationales supporting free expression in order to protect individual sensibilities.[217] It would thus be a mistake to think that the concept of captivity is elastic enough to secure individual sensibilities in public. Rather, the burden normally falls upon the viewer to "avoid further bombardment of [his] sensibilities simply by averting [his] eyes."[218]

The key to the balance struck by the Court between the individualism of self-governance and the individualism of privacy is in the conclusion that an audience is not captive unless it "cannot practically avoid exposure" to the speech or if the speech intrudes on the audience in the privacy of the home.[219] To stretch the captive audience doctrine further, in order to protect the individual sensibilities of members of groups vilified in general terms, would grant to particular communities within the polity a power to censor the terms of public debate. And this "would largely undermine the entire freedom of speech fabric,"[220] woven as it is out of theoretical strands dyed in the belief that self-governance is only obtainable when every view may be expressed.

This is not to suggest that hate speech never runs afoul of the captive audience doctrine. As *Frisby v. Schultz* makes clear, hate speech targeted specifically at an individual in her home may be suppressed as part of a content-neutral prohibition of all such focused speech. But *Carey v. Brown* makes equally clear that *content-based* prohibitions of focused speech are not "finely tailored" enough to serve the very substantial state interest of protecting individuals in their homes from unwanted intrusive speech. The workplace may well present a similar category similar to the home, for "[f]ew audiences are more captive than the average worker,"[221] a fact recognized by our legal rules that interfere with labor relations on the grounds that the relationship is one infused by coercive submission of the employee to a working environment largely dictated by employers. Moreover, the captive nature of the employee in the workplace may serve to temper the *Chaplinsky* requirement that speech be specifically directed at an individual target in order to be susceptible of suppression. When hate speech is so pervasive and repetitive that it is incapable of evasion it is effectively identical to hate speech that is focused exclusively upon an individual target. Nevertheless, the legitimacy of governmental attempts to control such pointed offensive speech outside of *Chaplinsky*-type circumstances is problematic. As is the case with so many other applications of free expression theory, the legitimacy of suppression of hate speech under such circumstances is derived from the individualistic paradigm that weaves throughout the law of free expression.

* * *

ENDNOTES

43. WILLIAM G. LOCKHART ET AL., CONSTITUTIONAL LAW: CASES, COMMENTS, QUESTIONS 630 (6th ed. 1986).

44. Post, *supra* note 3, at 278.

45. The classic exposition of this view remains that formulated by Alexander Meiklejohn. *See* MEIKLEJOHN, *supra* note 37, at 15-16, 24-27, 39.

46. The classic American exposition is that of Justice Oliver Wendell Holmes, Jr.'s dissent in Abrams v. United States, 250 U.S. 616, 630 (1919). The rationale was first plainly enunciated by John Stuart Mill, who argued that unfettered discourse was more apt to produce true opinions and, by challenge, prevent an established truth from being treated as "dead dogma, not a living truth." JOHN STUART MILL, ON LIBERTY 34 (Elizabeth Rapaport ed., Hackett Publishing Co. 1978) (1859).

47. John Milton, Areopagitica, in 4 THE WORKS OF JOHN MILTON 294, 346 (speech to the English Parliament in 1644) (Frank A. Patterson gen. ed., William Haller speech ed., 1931-38) [hereinafter Areopagitica]. But see LEONARD LEVY, EMERGENCE OF A FREE PRESS 93-97 (1985), in which Professor Levy contends that Milton's "well-advertised tolerance did not extend to the thought that he hated." *Id.* at 94.

48. BOLLINGER, *supra* note 37, at 10 ("[F]ree speech involves a special act of carving out one area of social interaction for extraordinary self-restraint, the purpose of which is to develop and demonstrate a social capacity to control feelings evoked by a host of social encounters.").

49. THOMAS I. EMERSON, THE SYSTEM OF FREEDOM OF EXPRESSION 7 (1970) (Free speech "is a method of achieving. . .a more stable community. . . .It is an essential mechanism for maintaining the balance between stability and change.").

50. Vincent Blasi, *The Checking Value in First Amendment Theory*, 1977 AM. B. FOUND. RES. J. 521, 527-42 (free speech serves to check the abuse of power by public officials).

51. MEIKLEJOHN, *supra* note 37, at 26.

52. *See, e.g.*, FREDERICK SCHAUER, FREE SPEECH: A PHILOSOPHICAL ENQUIRY (1982). A free speech principle which restrains majority power "is by its nature anti-democratic, anti-majoritarian." *Id.* at 40. Thus "[t]he more we accept the premise of the argument from democracy [that free speech is protected in order to secure majoritarian rule], the less can we impinge on the right of self-government by restricting the power of the majority." *Id.* at 41.

53. Stanley Ingber, *Rediscovering the Communal Worth of Individual Rights: The First Amendment in Institutional Contexts*, 69 TEX. L. REV. 1, 17 (1990); *see also* Lee C. Bollinger, *Free Speech and Intellectual Values*, 92 YALE L. J. 438, 451-52 (1983) ("[I]t appears anomalous to restrict limitations on speech in the name of preserving self-government when the self-governing process has generated those very limitations.").

54. *See* HANS KELSEN, GENERAL THEORY OF LAW AND STATE 284-88 (Anders Wedberg trans., 1961). For an excellent summary of Kelsen's argument, skillfully applied to the free speech guarantee, see Post, *supra* note 3, at 280-83.

55. An example of this thought is Justice Scalia's observation that our assurance that legislation will not exceed "reasonable and humane limits. . .[is the requirement that] the democratic majority. . .accept for themselves and their loved ones what they impose on you and me." Cruzan v. Director, Mo. Dep't of Health, 110 S. Ct. 2841, 2863 (1990) (Scalia, J., concurring).

56. *See* Post, *supra* note 3, at 281.

57. *Id.* at 282.

58. The clearest examples of compelled speech are the two compulsory flag- salute cases: Minersville School District v. Gobitis, 310 U.S. 586 (1940) and West Virginia State Board of Education v. Barnette, 319 U.S. 624 (1943), which overruled *Minersville*. In Barnette, the Court described as the "fixed star in our constitutional constellation" the idea that "no official. . .can prescribe what shall be orthodox. . .[and] force citizens to confess by word or act their faith therein." 319 U.S. at 642.

59. 249 U.S. 211 (1919).

60. *Id.* at 216.

61. Harry Kalven, Jr., *Ernst Freund and the First Amendment Tradition*, 40 U. CHI. L. REV. 235, 237 (1973).

62. *Id.*

63. *Debs*, 249 U.S. at 215.

64. 249 U.S. 204 (1919).

65. 268 U.S. 652 (1925).

66. 274 U.S. 357 (1927), *overruled* by Brandenburg v. Ohio, 395 U.S. 444 (1969).

67. 395 U.S. 444 (1969).

68. *Id.* at 447.

69. *See* Post, *supra* note 3, at 286. Professor Post has done major work in this area. *See* Post, *supra* note 39; Robert C. Post, *The Social Foundations of Defamation Law: Reputation and the Constitution*, 74 CAL. L. REV. 691 (1986); Robert C. Post, T*he Social Foundations of Privacy: Community and Self in the Common Law Tort*, 77 CAL. L. REV. 957 (1989).

70. 376 U.S. 254 (1964).

71. *Id.* at 270.

72. 485 U.S. 46 (1988).

73. Post, *supra* note 39, at 631-32.

74. In Skyywalker Records, Inc. v. Navarro, 739 F. Supp. 578 (S.D. Fla. 1990), *rev'd*, 960 F.2d 134 (11th Cir. 1992), a federal district judge found 2 Live Crew's recording "As Nasty as They Wanna Be" obscene despite expert testimony that the album contained material of artistic value within the context of the urban African-American experience. *Id.* at 594-95.

75. Post, *supra* note 39, at 632.

76. This is essentially the quagmire created by the Court's attempts to excise obscenity from the free expression guarantee. Any definition of obscenity must be linked to the values of some community.

77. Post, *supra* note 8, at 314.

78. For an argument that pluralism's kin, communitarianism, fails to provide any basis for choosing between differing community standards in formulating law, see Paul W. Kahn, *Community in Contemporary Constitutional Theory*, 99 YALE L.J. 1, 80-81 (1989).

79. Indeed, even under the obverse condition—when free speech yields to the right to vote—the rationale is to protect the individual's right to vote. *See, e.g.*, Burson v. Freeman, 112 S. Ct. 1846, 1851 (1992) ("[T]he 'right to vote freely for the candidate of one's choice is of the essence of a democratic society."' (quoting Reynolds v. Sims, 377 U.S. 533, 555 (1964))). *Burson* upheld the validity of Tennessee's prohibition of election day political speech within 100 feet of polling places.

80. Areopagitica, *supra* note 47, at 347 ("Let [Truth] and Falsehood grapple; who ever knew Truth put to the wors[e], in a free and open encounter. Her confuting is the best and surest suppressing.").

81. *See supra* note 46.

82. 250 U.S. 616, 624 (1919).

83. *Id.* at 630.

84. Gresham's Law is the principle in economics that "bad money will drive out good money." The idea is that coin of less intrinsic value will displace more intrinsically valuable coin as a medium of circulation because people will hoard the more intrinsically valuable coin. *See* WEBSTER'S NEW INTERNATIONAL DICTIONARY OF THE ENGLISH LANGUAGE 1102 (2d ed. 1949); ALEXANDER GRAY, THE DEVELOPMENT OF ECONOMIC DOCTRINE 50 (1931).

85. This equation of truth-seeking with the process of self-governance effectively blunts the criticism that "[i]f truth is subjective. . .the concept of a marketplace of ideas intended to promote truth becomes meaningless." Pierre J. Schlag, *An Attack on Categorical Approaches to Freedom of Speech*, 30 UCLA L. REV. 671, 729 (1983).

86. *See, e.g.*, C. Edwin Baker, *Scope of the First Amendment Freedom of Speech*, 25 UCLA L. REV. 964, 974-78 (1978) (summarizing reasons why the marketplace of ideas will not inevitably produce truth); Ingber, *supra* note 53, at 11-15.

87. Baker, *supra* note 86, at 974-78; Ingber, *supra* note 53, at 14-15 (footnotes omitted) ("experiences, as much as any communication, bestow the knowledge. . .by which truth is often measured. The value and diversity of expression are necessarily limited by the range of experiences that are the subjects of the communication. Life experiences. . .probably have more influence on judgment than vice versa.").

88. Baker, *supra* note 86, at 976.

89. An objection to this criticism is that the emotional and irrational are not necessarily false. The emotive truth may be more powerful and important than the logical and rational. That is certainly part of the message of Cohen v. California, 403 U.S. 15 (1971):

> [M]uch linguistic expression serves a dual communicative function: it conveys not only ideas capable of relatively precise, detached explication, but otherwise inexpressible emotions as well. In fact, words are often chosen as much for their emotive as their cognitive force. We cannot sanction the view that the Constitution, while solicitous of the cognitive content of individual speech, has little or no regard for that emotive function which. . .may often be the more important element of the overall message sought to be communicated.

Id. at 26; *see also*, Karst, *supra* note 3 (describing the importance of emotional and symbolic speech to the empowerment of subordinated groups).

90. Harry H. Wellington, *On Freedom of Expression*, 88 YALE L.J. 1105, 1130

(1979).

91. Kent Greenawalt, *Free Speech Justifications*, 89 COLUM. L. REV. 119, 135 (1989) (footnote omitted).

92. Ingber, *supra* note 53, at 13.

93. *Id.*

94. *Id.* at 14 (footnote omitted).

95. *See supra* text accompanying notes 51-59.

96. Ingber, supra note 53, at 15.

97. Stanley Ingber, *The Marketplace of Ideas: A Legitimizing Myth*, 1984 DUKE L.J. 1, 4.

98. Areopagitica, *supra* note 47, at 346. *But see* LEVY, *supra* note 47, at 93- 97, in which Professor Levy contends that Milton's "well-advertised tolerance did not extend to the thought that he hated." *Id.* at 94.

99. Whitney v. California, 274 U.S. 357, 376 (1927) (Brandeis, J., concurring), *overruled by* Brandenburg v. Ohio 395 U.S. 444 (1969).

100. *Id.*

101. *See, e.g.*, Lawrence, *supra* note 3, at 431-34, 458-60; Matsuda, *supra* note 2, at 2326-40.

102. Patricia Williams apparently coined the phrase "spirit-murder" to capture this injury resulting from hate speech. *See* Patricia Williams, *Spirit-Murdering the Messenger: The Discourse of Fingerpointing as the Law's Response to Racism*, 42 U. MIAMI L. REV. 127, 151 (1987).

103. However, as noted above, the development of individual moral virtue is also prized because of its perceived social benefit—the hoped-for attainment of the civically virtuous community. Presumably, such a polity will have no problem with hate speech. This condition seems about as likely to me as the possibility that unfettered speech in the autonomous self-governing community will produce absolute unanimity on every question of policy.

104. CARL G. JUNG, THE PORTABLE JUNG 144-48 (Joseph Campbell ed. & R.F.C. Hull trans., 1971).

105. *See id.* at 146.

106. *Id.* at 148.

107. *See generally* BOLLINGER, *supra* note 37.

108. *Id.* at 10.

109. *Id.* at 238.

110. United States v. Schwimmer, 279 U.S. 644, 655 (1929) (Holmes, J., dissenting), *overruled by* Gironard v. United States, 328 U.S. 61 (1946).

111. Terminiello v. Chicago, 337 U.S. 1, 4 (1949) (citation omitted).

112. New York Times Co. v. Sullivan, 376 U.S. 254, 270 (1964).

113. EMERSON, *supra* note 49, at 7.

114. Blasi, *supra* note 50, at 527, 542 (footnote omitted).

115. *See, e.g.*, Richmond Newspapers, Inc. v. Virginia, 448 U.S. 555 (1980) (establishing the right of public and press to attend criminal trials); Press-Enterprise Co. v. Superior Court, 464 U.S. 501 (1984) (establishing right of access to voir dire proceedings in criminal trials); Press-Enterprise Co. v. Superior Court, 478 U.S. 1 (1986) (establishing right of access to transcript of preliminary hearings in criminal cases).

116. 448 U.S. 555 (1980).

117. Globe Newspaper Co. v. Superior Court, 457 U.S. 596, 606 (1982).

118. *Richmond Newspapers*, 448 U.S. at 596 (Brennan, J., concurring) (quoting *In re* Oliver, 333 U.S. 257, 270 (1948)).

119. *Id.* at 587.

120. *Id.* at 588.

121. *Id.* at 587.

122. Thomas J. Emerson, *Toward a General Theory of the First Amendment*, 72 YALE L.J. 877, 879 (1963).

123. *Id. See also* David A.J. Richards, *Free Speech and Obscenity Law: Toward a Moral

Theory of the First Amendment, 123 U. PA. L. REV. 45, 62 (1974) (clauses in the following quotation appear in different order at 62), who wrote:

> Freedom of expression permits and encourages the exercise of. . .the central human capacity to create and express symbolic systems, such as speech, writing, pictures and music[.]. . .In so doing, it nurtures and sustains the self-respect of the mature person.
>
> . . . .
>
> . . .[F]ree expression. . .rests on its deep relation to self-respect arising from autonomous self-determination without which the life of the spirit is meager and slavish.

Other defenses of free expression on the inherently desirable grounds of self-realization include RONALD DWORKIN, TAKING RIGHTS SERIOUSLY (1977); MARTIN H. REDISH, FREEDOM OF EXPRESSION: A CRITICAL ANALYSIS (1984); Baker, *supra* note 86; Martin H. Redish, *The Value of Free Speech*, 130 U. PA. L. REV. 591 (1982).

124. Emerson, *supra* note 122, at 880.

125. 403 U.S. 15 (1971).

126. *Id.* at 24 (emphasis added).

127. Regina v. Keegstra, [1990] 3 S.C.R. 697, 805 (McLachlin, J., dissenting). Frederick Schauer has also expressed this criticism. *See* SCHAUER, *supra* note 52; Frederick Schauer, *Must Speech Be Special?*, 78 NW. U. L. REV. 1284 (1983).

128. *See, e.g.*, SCHAUER, *supra* note 52; LAURENCE H. TRIBE, AMERICAN CONSTITUTIONAL LAW § 12-1, at 789 (2d ed. 1988); Steven Shiffrin, *The First Amendment and Economic Regulation: Away From a General Theory of the First Amendment*, 78 NW. U. L. REV. 1212 (1983).

129. TRIBE, *supra* note 128, s 12-1, at 788-89 (footnotes omitted).

130. *See generally* SCHAUER, *supra* note 52.

131. *See, e.g.*, Simon & Schuster, Inc. v. Members of the N.Y. State Crime Victims Bd., 112 S. Ct. 501, 508 (1991). There are, of course, certain categories like defamation of private figures that is not of public concern, obscenity, and "fighting words," in which this presumption is either greatly relaxed or not applicable. *But see* R.A.V. v. City of St. Paul, 112 S. Ct. 2538 (1992) (entire categories of speech may be proscribed but content-based discrimination within those cateogories is impermissible unless related to the reason for proscribing the entire category).

132. Chaplinsky v. New Hampshire, 315 U.S. 568, 571-72 (1942).

133. 112 S. Ct. 2538.

134. Roth v. United States, 354 U.S. 476, 484 (1957). Though Roth used obscenity's utter lack of redeeming social importance as the *rationale* for excluding it from the free speech guarantee, the Court has, of course, since dispensed with the requirement that material, to be proven obscence, must be "'*utterly* without redeeming social value."' Miller v. California, 413 U.S. 15, 24 (1973) (quoting Memoirs v. Massachusetts, 383 U.S. 413, 419 (1966), which *Miller* overruled).

135. *See, e.g.*, Winters v. New York, 333 U.S. 507, 510 (1948).

136. 413 U.S. 49 (1973).

137. *Id.* at 58.

138. Louis Henkin, *Morals and the Constitution: The Sin of Obscenity*, 63 COLUM. L. REV. 391, 395 (1963).

139. CATHARINE A. MACKINNON, FEMINISM UNMODIFIED: DISCOURSES ON LIFE AND LAW 154 (1987).

140. *Id.* at 150.

141. 458 U.S. 747 (1982).

142. *Id.* at 753.

143. *Id.* at 756.

144. *Id.* at 757-58.

145. 413 U.S. 15 (1973).

146. *Ferber*, 458 U.S. at 761.

147. *Id.* at 763-64.

148. *Id.* at 764 (emphasis added).

149. At this point, the obligatory citation is to Richard Posner's Economic Analysis of Law, or some similar legal economic treatise. *See, e.g.*, RICHARD A. POSNER, ECONOMIC ANALYSIS OF LAW 6 (3d ed. 1986). Instead, I refer the reader to Ursula, the octopus villain of The Little Mermaid, who informed Ariel that "Life's full of tough choices." THE LITTLE MERMAID (The Walt Disney Co. 1989).

150. New York Times Co. v. Sullivan, 376 U.S. 254, 270 (1964).

151. Curtis Publishing Co. v. Butts, 388 U.S. 130 (1967) (actual malice test applies to false speech concerning public figures); Gertz v. Robert Welch, Inc., 418 U.S. 323 (1974) (actual malice test applies to false speech concerning a private figure but which is of public concern); *see* Philadelphia Newspapers, Inc. v. Hepps, 475 U.S. 767, 775 (stating that a higher standard than common law applies to public figures when their speech is of public concern).

152. 110 S. Ct. 2695 (1990).

153. *Id.* at 2707 (quoting Rosenblatt v. Baer, 383 U.S. 75, 86 (1966)).

154. 485 U.S. 46 (1988).

155. *See supra* notes 71-77 and accompanying text; Post, *supra* note 39, at 632.

156. 343 U.S. 250 (1952).

157. Collin v. Smith, 578 F.2d 1197, 1204 (7th Cir. 1978), *cert. denied*, 439 U.S. 916 (1978).

158. 395 U.S. 444 (1969).

159. 403 U.S. 15 (1971).

160. *Collin*, 578 F.2d at 1199.

161. Beauharnais v. Illinois, 343 U.S. 250, 256-57 (1952) (quoting Chaplinsky v. New Hampshire, 315 U.S. 568, 572 (1942)).

162. *Id.* at 258.

163. 376 U.S. 254 (1964).

164. *See, e.g.*, Collin, 578 F.2d at 1205 (citing prior cases expressing "doubt, which we share, that Beauharnais remains good law at all after the constitutional libel cases"). This doubt is not confined to the courts. *See also* TRIBE, *supra* note 128, § 12-17, at 926-27 (The constitutional libel cases "seemed. . .to eclipse Beauharnais' sensitivity to group libel. . .claims—not only because *New York Times* sweepingly endorsed 'a profound national commitment to the principle that debate on public issues should be uninhibited, robust, and wide-open,' but also because *New York Times* required public officials bringing libel suits to prove that a defamatory statement was directed at the official personally, and not simply at a unit of government.").

Quite apart from its questionable status as good law, the group libel concept has been thoroughly discredited. *See, e.g.*, the four dissenting opinions in *Beauharnais*, 343 U.S. at 267 (Black, J., dissenting), at 277 (Reed, J., dissenting), at 284 (Douglas, J., dissenting), and at 287 (Jackson, J., dissenting); Post, *supra* note 3, at 298; Joseph Tanenhaus, *Group Libel*, 35 CORNELL L.Q. 261 (1950); Riesman, *Fair Comment I*, *supra* note 1, Riesman; *Fair Comment II*, *supra* note 1.

165. *Beauharnais*, 343 U.S. at 257-58.

166. Post, *supra* note 3, at 298 (emphasis added).

167. *See* Steir v. New York State Educ. Comm'r, 271 F.2d 13, 17-18 (2d Cir. 1959), *cert. denied*, 361 U.S. 966 (1960).

168. Post, *supra* note 3, at 319 (quoting Pugsley v. Sellmeyer, 250 S.W. 538, 539 (1923)).

169. Bethel Sch. Dist. No. 403 v. Fraser, 478 U.S. 675, 681, 683 (1986).

170. *Id.*

171. See *Bethel*, 478 U.S. at 678 (1986), in which the Court upheld discipline imposed upon a high school senior for his "offensive" and "indecent"

speech at a school assembly. The Court justified the school's curtailment of speech on the grounds that "public education. . .[contemplated that schools would] 'inculcat[e] fundamental values necessary to the maintenance of a democratic political system'. . .[including the] 'habits and manners of civility."' *Id.* at 681 (quoting Ambach v. Norwick, 441 U.S. 68, 76-77 (1979)); *see also* Hazelwood Sch. Dist. v. Kuhlmeier, 484 U.S. 260, 272 (1988) ("A school must also retain the authority to refuse to sponsor student speech that might reasonably be perceived to advocate. . . conduct. . .inconsistent with 'the shared values of a civilized social order,'. . . . Otherwise, the schools would be unduly constrained from fulfilling their role as 'a principal instrument in awakening the child to cultural values. . . ."') (quoting *Bethel*, 478 U.S. at 683 and Brown v. Board of Educ., 347 U.S. 483, 493 (1954), respectively); *cf. Hazelwood*, 484 U.S. at 273 ("[E]ducators do not offend the First Amendment by exercising editorial control over the style and content of student speech in school-sponsored expressive activities so long as their actions are reasonably related to legitimate pedagogical concerns.").

Some courts have permitted secondary and elementary schools to control hate speech on the ground that the culturally authoritarian view of education is constitutionally permissible at that educational level. *See, e.g.*, Clarke v. Board of Educ., 338 N.W.2d 272 (Neb. 1983).

172. Tinker v. Des Moines Sch. Dist., 393 U.S. 503, 512 (1969) (quoting Keyishian v. Board of Regents, 385 U.S. 589, 603 (1967)); *see also* Healy v. James, 408 U.S. 169, 180 (1972).

173. Adler v. Board of Educ., 342 U.S. 485, 508 (1952) (Douglas, J., dissenting), *overruled by* Keyishian v. Board of Regents, 385 U.S. 589 (1967); *see also* Abington Sch. Dist. v. Schempp, 374 U.S. 203, 241-42 (1963) (Brennan, J., concurring) ("public schools serve a uniquely *public* function: the training of American citizens in. . . .[our] uniquely democratic values").

174. *Tinker*, 393 U.S. at 509.

175. Papish v. Board of Curators, 410 U.S. 667, 670 (1973).

176. *See Healy*, 408 U.S. at 171-72.

177. *Tinker*, 393 U.S. at 513; *see also Healy*, 408 U.S. at 189; Burnside v. Byars, 363 F.2d 744, 749 (5th Cir. 1966) (speech which "materially and substantially interfere[s]" with educational concerns may be regulated), *quoted in Tinker* at 513.

178. *See, e.g.*, UWM Post, Inc. v. Board of Regents, 774 F. Supp. 1163 (E.D. Wis. 1991); Doe v. University of Michigan, 721 F. Supp. 852 (E.D. Mich. 1989) (striking down university hate speech regulations on grounds of overbreadth and vagueness).

179. 410 U.S. 667 (1973).

180. *Id.* at 671 n.6.

181. 403 U.S. 15 (1971).

182. Byrne, *supra* note 3, at 436 (discussing *Papish*).

183. *Papish*, 410 U.S. at 671 n.6.

184. 393 U.S. 503 (1969).

185. 478 U.S. 675 (1986).

186. 484 U.S. 260 (1988).

187. Id. at 273.

188. 395 U.S. 444 (1969).

189. See Widmar v. Vincent, 454 U.S. 263, 267 n.5 (1981) ("[T]he campus of a public university, at least for its students, possesses many of the characteristics of a public forum."); *see also id.* at 268-70. Even so, the Court in *Widmar* rejected the proposition that universities are public fora in every respect. *See infra* notes 308-311 and accompanying text.

190. Connick v. Myers, 461 U.S. 138, 146 (1983).

191. Rankin v. McPherson, 483 U.S. 378 (1987).

192. The governmental interest in regulating public employee speech in the interest of fulfilling its governmental responsibilities is arguably far stronger than the gov-

ernmental interest in penalizing private employers for their failure to suppress speech of their employees which the government finds obnoxious but the private employer does not. Thus, the free speech claims of private employees might be far stronger than those of public employees. At the very least, private employees are entitled to no less speech protection than their public counterparts.

193. 42 U.S.C.A. §§ 2000e to 2000e-17 (West 1981 & Supp. 1992).

194. The constitutionality of imposing Title VII liability upon employers for failing to curb the harassing speech of their employees has grasped the attention of commentators. *See* Browne, *Title VII as Censorship: Hostile-Environment Harassment and the First Amendment*, 52 OHIO ST. L.J. 481 (1991); Marcy Strauss, *Sexist Speech in the Workplace*, 25 HARV. C.R.-C.L. L. REV. 1 (1990); Volokh, *supra* note 3.

195. 477 U.S. 57 (1986).

196. 42 U.S.C.A. §§ 2000e to 2000e-17 (West 1981 & Supp. 1992).

197. *Cf.* R.A.V. v. City of St. Paul, 112 S. Ct. 2538, 2546 (1992) (suggesting, in dicta, that "sexually derogatory 'fighting words"' might constitutionally be punished under Title VII).

198. *Meritor*, 477 U.S. at 65 (emphasis added) (quoting Equal Employment Opportunity Commission Guidelines, 29 C.F.R. § 1604.11(a) (1985)).

199. *Id.* at 67 (second alteration in original) (emphasis added) (quoting Henson v. Dundee, 682 F.2d 897, 904 (11th Cir. 1982)).

200. *Id.* (quoting *Henson*, 682 F.2d at 902). *But cf.* United States v. Eichman, 496 U.S. 310, 318 (1990) (suggesting that the offensiveness of "virulent ethnic and religious epithets" might not suffice to justify their prohibition).

201. 760 F. Supp. 1486 (M.D. Fla. 1991).

202. See *id.* at 1494-98 for a depressing catalogue of the lewd depictions of women to which Robinson and her female co-workers were continually subjected.

203. See *id.* at 1498-1501 for a recitation of the verbal abuse directed specifically at Robinson and her female co-workers.

204. *Id.* at 1490-91, 1534-37.

205. *See, e.g.*, Strauss, *supra* note 194, at 20 (concluding that offensive speech which is not directed toward an individual victim is constitutionally incapable of suppression).

206. *See, e.g.*, Cohen v. California, 403 U.S. 15 (1971).

207. *See, e.g.*, Erznoznick v. City of Jacksonville, 422 U.S. 205 (1975); Daniel A. Farber, *Content Regulation and the First Amendment: A Revisionist View*, 68 GEO. L.J. 727, 741 n.71 (1980); Strauss, *supra* note 194, at 12.

208. Bethel Sch. Dist. No. 403 v. Fraser, 478 U.S. 675, 685 (1986).

209. FCC v. Pacifica Found., 438 U.S. 726 (1978).

210. Frisby v. Schultz, 487 U.S. 474, 484-85 (1988) (upholding the validity of a municipal ordinance prohibiting "focused picketing" and observing that "'privacy of the home is [of] the highest order in a free and civilized society,'. . . .that individuals are not required to welcome unwanted speech into their own homes and that the government may protect this freedom" (quoting Carey v. Brown, 447 U.S. 455, 471 (1980))); Rowan v. United States Post Office Dep't, 397 U.S. 728, 738 (1970) (upholding a statute permitting recipients of mail to instruct the Postmaster General to direct persons identified by the recipient to refrain from further mailings to the recipient, and observing that "[we] categorically reject the argument that [an individual] has a [constitutional] right. . .to send unwanted material into the home of another"). *Rowan* has been criticized because of the relative ease with which such offensive communications can be avoided. *See* MELVILLE B. NIMMER, NIMMER ON FREEDOM OF SPEECH § 1:02[F], at 1-25 n.58 (1984).

211. Strauss, *supra* note 194, at 13.

212. 487 U.S. 474 (1988).

213. 447 U.S. 455 (1980).

214. FCC v. Pacifica Found., 438 U.S. 726 (1978), upheld the use of content-based regulations which discriminated against "low value" indecent speech in the inter-

est of protecting captive auditors.

215. *Carey*, 447 U.S. at 471 (quoting Police Dep't v. Mosley, 408 U.S. 92, 99 (1972)).

216. 422 U.S. 205 (1975).

217. *See also* Cohen v. California, 403 U.S. 15 (1971) (holding that the public exhibition of a jacket emblazoned with the slogan "Fuck the Draft" did not hold public observers captive in any sense sufficient to warrant suppression).

218. *Id.* at 21.

219. Collin v. Smith, 578 F.2d 1197, 1206 (7th Cir.), *cert. denied*, 439 U.S. 916 (1978); FCC v. Pacifica Found., 438 U.S. 726 (1978); Rowan v. United States Post Office Dep't, 397 U.S. 728 (1970).

220. NIMMER, *supra* note 210, § 1.02[F], at 1-33.

221. Balkin, *supra* note 3, at 423.

CHAPTER 4

THE UNIQUENESS OF THE UNIVERSITY

"Problems in Implementing University Speech Restrictions: The University as a Special Environment"*

*David F. McGowan*** and Ragesh K. Tangri****

*   *   *

> [S]tudents who support universities through tuition and who are encouraged to think of the university as their home are involuntarily forced into a position of complicity with racism when their campus is offered to hate groups as a forum.[365] —Mari Matsuda

> In a university knowledge is its own end, not merely a means to an end. A university ceases to be true to its own nature if it becomes the tool of Church or State or any sectional interest. A university is characterized by the spirit of free inquiry, its ideal being the ideal of Socrates—"to

---

*The complete article from which the following is excerpted, entitled "A Libertarian Critique of University Restrictions of Offensive Speech," appears at 79 California Law Review 825 (1991). Footnotes have been changed to endnotes and are numbered as in the original. Reprinted with permission.

** Law clerk, Judge A. Raymond Randolph, United States Court of Appeals for the District of columbia Circuit. B.A. 1986, University of California, Los Angeles; J.D. 1990, Boalt Hall School of Law, University of California, Berkeley. The views expressed here are the author's alone, and do not necessarily represent the views of Judge Randolph or any other person.

***B.A. 1986, University of California, Berkeley; J.D. candidate 1991, Boalt Hall School of Law, University of California, Berkeley.

The authors wish to thank Professors Paul J. Mishkin and Robert C. Post for their efforts to educate us about the first amendment. We would also like to thank Ms. Laura M. Craska and Mr. Michael Mundaca for their efforts to bring clarity ans support to our arguments. Failings that remain in any of those areas are ours alone. Finally, we would like to thank Messrs. Page and Goldberg for their heroic efforts to reduce this Comment to one final, printed, and timely form.

> follow the argument where it leads." This implies the right to examine, question, modify or reject traditional ideas and beliefs. Dogma and hypothesis are incompatible, and the concept of an immutable doctrine is repugnant to the spirit of a university.[366]

The discussion to this point has addressed speech regulations in the abstract. The regulations are, however, designed to operate in a university setting, which is both undeniably and mercifully different from a park or factory or Congress. We need to address two questions about the setting. First, how are universities different, for free speech purposes, from the world at large, and second, do those differences matter?

Before we begin, we will explore one broader issue, that of state action. Although state universities are state actors in that they are created by the state government and receive state funds, their mission is not simply to enforce the general laws of the state. Their mission, stated most broadly, is education, and so a somewhat more sophisticated analysis is needed to appraise the constitutionality of university action than to analyze the deprivation Wilson suffered on his picket line.[367] The issue may be analyzed as an unconstitutional conditions problem. Universities claim an exemption from the first amendment based on their educational mission. When a university regulates a student's speech, it claims that that restriction is necessary to effectuate its goal. For example, a university may not grade meaningfully a series of papers, assigning some A's and some F's, without engaging in what in other circumstances would be impermissible content discrimination. The inquiry thus is twofold: whether the goal the university has chosen is a legitimate one for it to pursue as a market participant and whether the restriction of speech is related to that goal in some sufficiently close way as to pass constitutional muster.[368] The second inquiry may proceed in the same way as it does in other areas where the fit between a regulation and its stated purpose is of constitutional importance.[369]

The former inquiry, however, is more difficult. It is not enough simply to assert, as Professor Byrne does,[370] that university officials are more trustworthy than other sorts of state actors in regulating speech. There is no a priori reason to believe that this is true, and the practice under the Michigan regulation should give us long pause before we place uncritical reliance upon university administrators to be relatively more benign despots than are politicians. We need a theory, grounded in the first amendment, constraining the purposes for which a state university may claim an exemption for its speech regulations. An easy example would be a university that sought to teach only doctrines espoused by the Republican or Democratic party. Such a program would be unjustifiable on purely pedagogical grounds, and would be a clear violation of the content-neutrality generally mandated by the first amendment.[371]

One could make a similar argument for restrictions designed to ensure civility on campus. After all, *Cohen* seems to foreclose state control of the civility of speech,[372] and there are relatively few cases in which such a regulation seems necessary to facilitate the goal for which a university claims exemption from the first amendment—education. Where the fit between civility regulations and education is sufficiently tight, for example in the classroom, there would be no constitutional problem. Outside the classroom, however, the fit seems too loose to withstand Cohen. This argument is not necessarily compelling, however, as universities may choose among several competing conceptions of their mission.[373] There is no *constitutional* reason that any of these choices is compelled. We see no reason, for example, why the first amendment necessarily prohibits a state from establishing a small university designed to comfort and nurture its students in a close, communal environment. We believe, however, that some choices are better than others, and that the university best realizes the true conception of its purpose when it maximizes the speech that is exchanged within its confines by reference to marketplace principles. The arguments set out above seek to establish the superiority of marketplace theory generally. Those below seek to establish that superiority with specific reference to the university.

A. The Argument From Student Vulnerability

The argument regarding how we should treat universities

for free speech purposes revolves around two ideas that arise from diametrically opposed premises. The first premise holds that the university should maintain at least a minimal level of civility so that its students will not feel threatened and so be unable effectively to pursue their studies. This premise rests upon an empirical assumption that college students require such protection because, as Professor Matsuda puts it, "[m]any of the new adults who come to live and study at the major universities are away from home for the first time, and at a vulnerable stage of psychological development. Students are particularly dependent on the university for community, for intellectual development, and for self-definition."[374]

The assumption and premise together support viewing the campus as a special environment in which racist speech should not be tolerated. Matsuda asserts:

> Official tolerance of racist speech in this setting is more harmful than generalized tolerance in the community-at-large. It is harmful to student perpetrators in that it is a lesson in getting-away-with-it that will have lifelong repercussions. It is harmful to targets, who perceive the university as taking sides through inaction, and who are left to their own resources in coping with the damage wrought. Finally, it is a harm to the goals of inclusion, education, development of knowledge, and ethics that universities exist and stand for.[375]

Matsuda believes that minority group students are especially harmed because they "often come to the university at risk academically, socially, and psychologically."[376] This argument covers a wide range of psychological and jurisprudential turf, but it ultimately fails to justify treating the campus as a special environment in which speech may be regulated to protect students.[377] The argument's empirical assumption about the nature of college students is at best a very broad generalization, with limited applicability to many large universities which typically enroll a substantial number of graduate students, older, returning students, and other less vulnerable sorts.

We need not contest the empirical validity of Professor

Matsuda's assumption, however, to resist her conclusion. First, students in general may well be extremely vulnerable when they arrive at college and, therefore, more easily traumatized by racist speech. That fact alone, however, merely describes individualized vulnerabilities that may exist in a wide array of places—it fails to distinguish the campus from other fora except by asserting that the concentration of vulnerable people is higher on campus than in society generally. Because it fails uniquely to justify restricting speech on campus, Professor Matsuda's assumption is largely irrelevant to her conclusion.

The same may be said of Professor Matsuda's harm-based arguments. Matsuda first argues that the harm from racist speech on campus is more severe because perpetrators learn that they can "get away with it," presumably meaning that they can engage in racist speech without official penalty.[378] Of course, persons speaking off campus learn the same lesson, and the argument is circular to the extent that it assumes that racist speakers should be subject to official regulation—the very point at issue. Professor Matsuda next argues that the targets of racist speech will perceive the university as taking sides against them through inaction.[379] This argument claims, at least to some extent, that students will engage in a paradigm example of the fallacy of the false opposite, and there is really no good reason that speech should be regulated to prevent such indulgence. If we are to regulate speech because a prospective audience may interpret it through a logical fallacy, there will be little speech left at all. Additionally, it advocates the questionable tactic of preparing students to deal with what she describes as a largely racist world by shielding them from racism. We are thus left with the question of what to do with vulnerable students offended by racist speech. The alternative to insulating them from racist viewpoints through the mechanism of speech restrictions is to inculcate the values of tolerance and intellectual self-reliance by preserving a vigorous and widely varied university marketplace. From both a normative and a pragmatic perspective, the latter result is preferable.

Moreover, as Justice Powell has written in a somewhat different context, "University students are, of course, young adults. They are less impressionable than younger students and should be able to appreciate that the University's policy is one of neutrality. . . ."[380] Finally, the argument from student vulnerability is difficult to cabin in anything remotely resembling a principled fashion. In essence, the argument advocates a revival of the vision of the university *in loco parentis* for the narrow case of racist speech. The argument, however, takes a familiar form: Racist speech harms students at level X, and thus may be regulated for the students' own good. All external stimuli harming students at level X may be regulated under this principle, and we must now differentiate among such stimuli, a quest similar in form and difficulty to our prior search for constitutive elements of personhood. The question now is why racist speech and not obscenity or speech advocating communism or some other doctrine offensive to a given board of regents?

The problem is not chimerical, as the University of Missouri's efforts to deny recognition to a homosexual student group demonstrate. The university's rationale was precisely Matsuda's—the university first found that "[t]here are potential or latent homosexuals. . .who come into adolescence or young adulthood unaware that they have homosexual tendencies."[381] The university further found that "homosexuality is an illness and should and could be treated as such and is clearly abnormal behavior."[382] From such a base, it was only a short analytical journey to denying recognition to the student group on the ground that formal recognition would "tend to reinforce the personal identities of the homosexual members of those organizations and will perpetuate and expand an abnormal way of life."[383] Worse yet, and more pertinent to the present discussion, formal recognition would "tend to cause latent or potential homosexuals who become members to become overt homosexuals."[384]

This form of refutation itself should appear familiar, for it is precisely the form of argument we saw in demonstrating that process-based theories of truth are untenable.[385] The conclusion there applies here as well: Because we cannot agree upon what is true, or what should be deemed to reach the threshold of harm X, we should prevent the government from making that decision for fear that it might get it wrong. The concept of normative truth is simply replaced with the concept of a normative level of harm justifying the exercise of power *in loco parentis*. Not surprisingly, the argument from student vulnerability also runs afoul of the principles we saw in discussing offense-based regulations—we are protecting the students from ideas, which are by definition neither true nor false. Our earlier discussion does not decide the question of the university as a special environment, however. For Matsuda makes one final argument, best treated as a particular vision of the university as a special marketplace of ideas.

B. The University Marketplace

Traditional first amendment doctrine holds that the university is "peculiarly the 'marketplace of ideas,'"[386] and that the skepticism underlying marketplace theory is at its strongest on campus. Chief Justice Warren put it best, if somewhat dramatically:

> To impose any strait jacket upon the intellectual leaders in our colleges and universities would imperil the future of our Nation. No field of education is so thoroughly comprehended by man that new discoveries cannot yet be made. Particularly is that true in the social sciences, where few, if any, principles are accepted as absolutes. Scholarship cannot flourish in an atmosphere of suspicion and distrust. Teachers and students must always remain free to inquire, to study and to evaluate...otherwise our civilization will stagnate and die.[387]

The unique strength of marketplace skepticism on campus is reflected in the Court's application of that skepticism to offense-based regulations, holding that "the mere dissemination of ideas—no matter how offensive to good taste—on a state university campus may not be shut off in the name alone of 'conventions of decency.'"[388]

This view is opposed by what Professor Matsuda refers to as "the goals of inclusion, education, development of knowledge and ethics that universities stand for."[389] These "goals" lead Matsuda to conclude not only that racist speech generally may be regulated, but also that certain ideas should be denied even a classroom forum. She argues that "[p]oorly documented, racially biased work does not meet the professional standards required of academic writing."[390] These competing visions are difficult to reconcile. Professor Matsuda's marketplace argument obviously runs headlong into the problems with stigma-based regulations that we discussed above. Still, there is a strong intuitive pull in the notion that the campus is *different* from society at large, and that we should preserve that difference. We believe, however, that Professor Matsuda mistakes the way in which universities are, and should be, different from the rest of society.

The university marketplace is different from the marketplace in society at large because the university community exists to consider a much wider range of ideas in much greater depth. These differences separate the university from political debate, workplace debates, and mass media.[391] The animating features of the university community are the mutually reinforcing values of tolerance and skepticism. They alternatively allow and inspire investigation and intellectual innovation; where they are constrained, the community is to that extent weakened. This view comports with the Court's current view of the university—and probably with the aspirations of most university communities. We also believe that it is a desirable vision, and we may see this by returning to Professor Matsuda's vulnerable students. When a student confronts a highly offensive, degrading instance of speech, what is she to do? The marketplace theory we advocate here tells her, in essence, to listen to the speech and formulate rational, compelling responses. She must then place those responses in the same marketplace and fight for them until they are accepted.[392]

The campus debate over offensive speech has not been

limited to the speech of students or outside speakers, but has come to include questions of professorial classroom speech as well. Two recent incidents from the Berkeley campus of the University of California should serve to frame the problem. The Fall 1990 class reader for Environmental Design I contained excerpts from a work by Wallace Stegner.[393] The passage included the word "wetback," used as a reference to Mexicans who had entered the United States in apparent violation of applicable immigration laws.[394] Some students in the class (and later students not in the class) were offended by the use of the term and criticized the instructor for his insensitivity for including them in the first place.[395]

Later that same term, a group of approximately fifty students held a demonstration during an anthropology class taught by Professor Vincent Sarich.[396] Many, if not most, of the students apparently were not enrolled in Professor Sarich's class at the time.[397] The students objected to statements published by Professor Sarich (and related information taught in the course) which attempted to draw a statistical correlation between differential male/female cranial volume and differential male/female performance on standardized tests.[398] The demonstration succeeded in preventing further instruction that day, in spite of vociferous objection to the demonstrators voiced by at least some of the students enrolled in the class.[399]

Between them, these incidents implicate two of the core concerns of academic freedom: freedom of research and freedom of teaching.[400] If offensive speech restrictions (or equivalent standards adopted by faculty review panels)[401] are read to cover the classroom speech or research publications of professors, the implications for the university could go beyond even those flowing from restrictions on student speech. Bearing in mind John Searle's warning that many supposedly dire campus trends are merely silly, not catastrophic,[402] this Section will nevertheless examine what limitations, if any, academic freedom places upon restrictions of professorial speech. In order to do so, we must examine the primary justifications for, and implementations of, academic freedom in

American universities.

It is important to note at the outset that there are two operational conceptions of academic freedom in the United States. The first is the conception held within the academy, and enforced primarily within a given university or within the profession as a whole, which tends to focus on the rights of the individual academic.[403] The second is the conception adopted by the courts, which focuses upon the freedom of the institution against other societal actors, including courts themselves.[404] We will refer to the former as the professional conception, the latter as the legal conception. Academic freedom in the United States initially derived from the model that flourished in Germany during the nineteenth century.[405] The German model covered two primary activities: research and teaching. The concern was that the development and dissemination of knowledge not be limited by social forces (usually the government or the church) external to the university.[406]

As American universities began to spring up in ever-increasing numbers during the nineteenth century, they generally were structured on a corporate model: Established by a charter or trust, they were managed by a President who was appointed by, and in turn ultimately answerable to, a board of trustees. Professors formally were the employees of the institution, and so were subject to the same legal rules as the employees of any other firm. Most importantly, they could be fired at will.[407]

Against this background, it is apparent why the first formal effort to define and implement a coherent and nationwide policy on academic freedom in the United States took pains to put forth an alternate view of the relation between the university and the individual professor. The American Association of University Professors (AAUP) issued its first Principles of Academic Freedom in 1915, and the conception there articulated was and remains the foundational and most eloquent (if not most recent) statement of the professional conception of academic freedom.[408] The AAUP put forth the idea that even private universities were not, for the most part, truly private concerns.[409] Instead, the Declaration argued, they were entrusted with a public mission: the advancement of knowledge in all its forms, and through that advance the advancement of the republic as a whole.[410] In short, universities were to carry out the project of the Enlightenment. This, however, required that the profession make a decision as to how such an advance was best to be achieved.

The 1915 Declaration clearly commits the AAUP to what was in essence the marketplace theory of truth.[411] The Declaration is for the most part phrased in the language of science, reflecting the prevailing view of the day that most disciplines were "sciences" of one sort or another.[412] In such disciplines, the goal was to move ever closer to a single, objective, and ultimately knowable truth.[413] With knowledge so conceptualized, the profession's commitment to marketplace theory is readily understood: As long as the search for truth proceeds according to commonly agreed on principles, such as standards of verifiability, ability to be reproduced, and rules of proof, error can be detected, and corrected, in a relatively efficient way. The consequence is that the AAUP rejected any attempt institutionally to define truth.[414] Truth is, of course, never considered conclusively established. It is always open to challenge and possible refutation.

The individual freedom required by the marketplace model was clearly inconsistent with a relationship based on master-servant principles. Instead, the university administration and the board of trustees were viewed as trustees in a much stronger sense: holders of a trust from the public as a whole, a trust dedicated to the idea of free inquiry into the truth.[415] Professors, in turn, were viewed not as employees in the traditional sense, but rather as appointees, who should hold their appointments during good behavior.[416] The academy had come to conceive of itself as a profession, properly subject only to self-regulation.

Self-regulation[417] was and remains one of the keys to the implementation of the professional view of academic freedom.

Decisions as to hiring, promotion, and evaluation are to be made by faculty committees.[418] While those decisions are subject to approval by various levels of the university administration,[419] culminating in the board of trustees, the professional view of academic freedom contemplates that such actors should only rarely, in the most extreme of circumstances, overturn the decisions of the peer review committee.[420]

The legal conception of academic freedom is generally stated in terms of the "four freedoms" of universities, from a statement by South African universities quoted by Justice Frankfurter in his concurrence in *Sweezy v. New Hampshire*:[421] The right of the university "to determine for itself on academic grounds who may teach, what may be taught, how it shall be taught, and who may be admitted to study."[422] The relationship between the academic mission and the university's restrictions on speech is what justifies its claim of exemption from the strictures of the first amendment.[423] The values underlying this freedom are that universities are the prime players in the disinterested (that is, unbiased) search for knowledge, that they foster a method of thought and discourse conducive to that search, and that they instill such capabilities in others, who in turn carry those values into society.

The necessary consequence of this is that the legal conception of academic freedom does relatively little to protect the interests of individual professors, as opposed to institutions. [424] If the goal is to maximize institutional autonomy and minimize intrusion by the government, the fact that courts are part of the government limits the extent to which they can substitute their judgement for the choices of the institution. Thus, courts generally do not characterize the claims of individual professors as "academic freedom" claims, preferring instead to resolve such claims under general first amendment analysis. [425]

Applying the different conceptions of academic freedom to the problem of potentially offensive professorial speech yields differing results. The legal conception probably would prohibit certain express limitations imposed by a board of regents or president, but quite possibly only if imposed on the subject matter of a class or course of research. In any case, such restrictions imposed by an administration normally would be opposed vigorously by the faculty and peer review organs within a university. The real problem occurs when precisely those organs, usually the guarantors of the rights of individual professors, become the actors who either initiate or acquiesce in the restriction on faculty speech. If, as was the case with the situation involving Professor Sarich, there was a possibility not only of disciplinary action against a professor, but disciplinary action taken by a faculty committee,[426] there is little that courts would be willing to do to intervene. The issue thus collapses to a normative one: how ought peer review committees judge cases involving allegations of offensive speech on the one hand, and academic freedom on the other?

The issue in large measure returns to the goals of the university, the preferred method for achieving those goals, and so to marketplace theory. There is little we can add here to the discussion of marketplace theory given above. A peer review committee should be mindful of its role as the internal guarantor of professional autonomy. Thus, when faced with a case involving what Professor Matsuda has termed "[p]oorly documented racially biased work,"[427] a peer review committee should take care to ensure that its judgment is based solely on the first, and not the second, set of objectives.

C. The University as a Public Forum

Public forum doctrine is relatively recent, and has been characterized by confusion regarding both its foundations and application.[428] The doctrine states that certain places and resources controlled by the government are public fora, where speech will receive the full protection of the first amendment, whereas other places and resources controlled by the government are not. These latter places are more analogous to private property[429] where speech may be restricted.[430]

The doctrine was born in *Hague v. CIO*,[431] in which the Court struck down an ordinance requiring a permit for public parades or meetings in streets and parks.[432] Acknowledging that the government owned the land in question, and that a private landowner could restrict speech on his property at will, the Court concluded that the government held public streets and parks in trust for the people, and that these streets and parks have been devoted to expressive activity from time immemorial.[433] Such a simple formulation quickly ran into trouble,[434] however, and in recent years the Court has refined the forum inquiry to focus on the primary purpose of the government institution at issue and on the compatibility of first amendment activity with that purpose.

In *Cornelius v. NAACP Legal Defense and Educational Fund, Inc.*,[435] for example, the federal government sought to exclude all advocacy organizations from the Combined Federal Campaign, or CFC.[436] The Court concluded that although the CFC took place in a public office, the government intended to facilitate the raising of charitable donations, while minimizing the accompanying disruption of the federal workplace.[437] Finding that both goals would be thwarted by allowing advocacy organizations to join the CFC, and finding no intent on the part of the government to open the federal workplace to all speech, the Court held that the CFC was not a public forum.[438] Thus, the public forum doctrine examines the primary mission of the government institution, and only permits regulation of speech that is fundamentally incompatible with that mission.[439] If we use this approach to inquire whether universities are public fora, we must look first to the traditional role the university has played. The language the Court has chosen in the past indicates that it views campuses as crucially involved in the marketplace of ideas.[440] This view supports the conclusion that a university campus is in fact a public forum.

The language of past holdings on campus speech suggests that the Court has traditionally viewed universities as unique locations where speech plays a heightened role and thus where the interchange of ideas, even offensive ideas, receives full first amendment protection.[441] The Court has spoken of "the. . .significant interest in the widest latitude for free expression and debate consonant with the maintenance of order."[442] Moreover, the Court emphasized that the first amendment does not allow for standards based upon the content of speech.[443] Instead, the Court stated, the first amendment was particularly committed to protecting academic freedom,[444] for the classroom "is the peculiarly 'marketplace of ideas.'"[445]

The Court provided a final gloss on the question of the university as a public forum in *Widmar v. Vincent.*[446] In *Widmar*, the Court was faced with a challenge to a University of Missouri policy that denied use of campus facilities to groups meeting for religious purposes while allowing their use by secular campus groups.[447] The Court held that the university had created a public forum "open for use by student groups" by opening its facilities generally to such groups.[448] The campus' status as a public forum in turn subjected to first amendment scrutiny any university policy that restricted use.[449] Thus, the Court's holding linked a marketplace model of the university with content-based constitutional standards. It therefore appears that even managerial authority[450] has limits when that authority seeks to restrict speech because of the ideas the speech contains. The exercise of such authority is valid only insofar as it serves to facilitate the marketplace.[451]

The analysis is clearest when the area in question is a campus plaza, commons, or quad. Such a space closely resembles the traditional "speaker's corner" of a public park. More importantly, it is a speaker's corner for a community whose primary mission is best carried out through maximizing the exchange, discussion, and investigation of ideas. The physical characteristics of such an area are another important factor in determining whether it is a public forum. Such open spaces allow students to move freely from one conversation to another, or to avoid debates altogether. Speakers and listeners are not subjected to speech they cannot avoid.[452] Such characteristics, as well as the voluntary participation of the speakers and listeners involved, provide the sort of "buffer zone" that makes it likely that different sensibilities and points of view can be accommodated.[453]

To limit[454] speech in such a location would run counter to both the traditional physical conception of a public forum and the educational mission of a university.

While the analysis may appear more complicated in the classroom, neither forum analysis nor marketplace theory ultimately supports a conclusion different from the one we reached above. Although the physical characteristics of a classroom certainly differ from some traditional public fora, they by no means preclude the conclusion that the classroom is also one. The classroom is at the core of the educational mission of the university. It is where ideas are not merely exchanged, but are subjected to reasoned inquiry. Appeals to emotion have less place there than on a soapbox. This means that an erroneous idea expressed in class is likely to meet searching scrutiny and be effectively disproved. Moreover, the classroom is the primary place for students to acquire the tools necessary to disprove, as opposed merely to disagree with, racist assumptions. The success of this endeavor may be less certain, and certainly less fully tested, if those in the classroom cannot dissect offensive assumptions out loud.

Most of the objections to "free speech" in a classroom can in fact be expressed as time, place, and manner limits. When a professor decides which students to recognize, and in what order, she simply is using a precedence system that varies only slightly from the "first come, first served" method. The fact that students are expected not to conduct an argument by screaming at one another reflects a straightforward manner limitation on volume.[455] The key is that a professor could not consistently refuse to call on a student because she disagreed with the student's views, or allow some students to yell while requiring others to whisper. In such an event the professor would be imposing speech restrictions unrelated to the academic mission, and thus would forfeit the university's claim to be exempt from the first amendment. These traditional understandings of the proper functioning of a classroom reflect the classroom's purpose as a forum for the interchange of ideas. The classroom resembles a market under perfect conditions—it exists for the introduction and exchange of ideas, not for their inculcation.

The most complicated situation is presented by residence halls. The university is generally the owner, but residence halls are also, at least in part, private living spaces for the students who occupy them. Traditionally, private homes have been viewed as enclaves which to some extent displace the first amendment.[456] This means that, at the very least, a university could restrict the right of one student to enter another's room. The university most likely could also discipline a student who posted material on another student's door, since such speech would be directed at the personal residence of the affected student.[457] The common living spaces of a dormitory (for example, the lounges, restrooms, and recreation halls) present a more difficult problem, but one that ultimately can be solved through an examination of the physical characteristics and purposes of the specific areas. Lounges in which students hold open discussions, meetings, and the like are probably public fora, while dormitory study halls devoted to solitary reading probably are not. Even in those spaces that are not traditional public fora, restrictions on speech must conform to the limits of viewpoint-neutrality.[458]

The determination that the vast majority of space on a university campus is a public forum is consistent with the general rationale of the "marketplace of ideas." Marketplace theory works best where inquiry can be full and where values of rationality apply.[459] To the extent that our society is committed to the argument from truth, the university is "peculiarly" the marketplace of ideas in part of necessity: If reason cannot be expected to prevail in such a setting, it cannot be expected to prevail anywhere.

This view of the role of the campus clashes with Professor Matsuda's view that the campus has a special obligation to restrict racist speech because its students are especially vulnerable. First, because the structure of classroom debate makes it more likely that no opinion will go unchallenged, if we are confident that racist ideas are insupportable, then the university would seem the ideal place to have them aired and disproved. Second, if, as Professor Matsuda says, education and the development of knowledge are among the goals of the university, then it seems anomalous to adopt a policy that is both at odds with that development through the marketplace of ideas and stifling to the education of persons who hold false views—who, at least in Professor Matsuda's eyes, are presumably in the most desperate need of education. If the university is a public forum, the main conclusion we can draw is that the first amendment applies with full force on campus. This serves to negate arguments by proponents of offensive speech regulations that the campus should adopt special measures against offensive speech. It does not prevent the campus from taking action consistent with the first amendment, however, to limit nonpublic discourse that would not otherwise qualify for first amendment protection.[460]

*　　　*　　　*

Endnotes

365. Matsuda, *supra* note 21, at 2372-73.

366. The Open Universities in South Africa 10-12 (statement of a conference of senior scholars from the University of Cape Town and the University of the Witwatersrand, including A.v.D.S. Centlivres and Richard Feetham, chancellors of the respective universities), *quoted in* Sweezy v. New Hampshire, 354 U.S. 234, 263 (1957) (Frankfurter, J., concurring).

367. *See* Gooding v. Wilson, 405 U.S. 518 (1972).

368. This approach is similar to the approach suggested by Professor Sunstein for unconstitutional conditions cases generally. *See* Sunstein, *Why the Unconstitutional Conditions Doctrine is an Anachronism (With Particular Reference to Religion, Speech, and Abortion)*, 70 B.U.L. Rev. 593, 621 (1990).

369. *See* Tussman & tenBroek, *supra* note 222.

370. *See* Byrne, *supra* note 21, at 418 ("[w]hen the university proscribes a manner of speech, it is more likely that the step is taken to further valid goals of education or scholarship rather than to maintain favor with the majority who may dismiss the censor").

371. *See* Texas v. Johnson, 491 U.S. 397, 414 (1989).

372 . Cohen v. California, 403 U.S. 15, 22-23 (1971).

373. *See* Post [Racist Speech, Democracy, and the First Amendment, 32 William and Mary Law Review 267 (1991)], *supra* note 76, at 319.

374. Matsuda, *supra* note 21, at 2370-71. Matsuda expounds upon the vulnerability of students as follows:

> The typical university student is emotionally vulnerable for several reasons. College is a time of emancipation from a preexisting home or community, of development of identity, of dependence-independence conflict, of major decision making, and formulation of future plans. The move to college often in-

> volves geographic relocation—a major life-stress event—and the forging of new peer ties to replace old ones. . . . A negative environmental response during this period of experimentation could mar for life an individual's ability to remain open, creative, and risk-taking.

Id. at 2370 n.249.

375. *Id.* at 2371.

376. *Id.* Professor Matsuda bases her assertion upon statistics indicating that minorities are underrepresented in the professions and underenrolled in colleges, and suffer from higher drop-out rates than majority group students. *Id.* at 2371 n.253. She then mentions, presumably as part of her causal assertion, that minorities are not represented on law faculties in proportion to their percentage of society at large. These assertions are subject to the same objections that apply to Professor Matsuda's use of racism's relative market share.

First, if faculty composition is an alternative or additional cause of minority discomfort at universities, increasing minority discomfort by some amount, then restrictions on racist speech will not solve the problem completely, falling short by precisely this amount. Moreover, Matsuda presents no evidence that restrictions on speech will *solve* problems of campus racism and minority discomfort. Such regulations are both drastically underinclusive and overinclusive for that task, at levels that simply cannot pass first amendment scrutiny. At a minimum, there is no reason to believe that regulating speech will alter the utility of holding racist beliefs and therefore no reason to believe that regulations will address the problem underlying the injuries Professor Matsuda seeks to remedy. See *supra* note 252 (arguing that the suppression of racist speech will not lower the utility of holding racist beliefs).

377. But *see* Comment, *supra* note 133, at 952-55 (universities particularly justified in protecting students because they as a practical matter cannot leave the campus). We find the increasingly frequent attempts to analogize the university to the workplace deeply disturbing. The argument, which was made in Doe v. University of Michigan, 721 F.Supp. 852, 856 (E.D. Mich. 1989), and has been around for some time in the journals, *see, e.g.*, Note, *Campus Conduct Policies*, *supra* note 21, at 226; Note, *Title VII Solution*, *supra*, note 21, at 125, is premised on the notion that a college education is an economic necessity in this day and age. This premise is, however, plainly false. While it is true that college graduates earn more than those without degrees, this fact is, of course, a function of the relative scarcity of college graduates. If everyone went to college, there would be no income gap. Yet if only a relatively few people go to college, and a college degree is *necessary* to prosperity, then what are we to say of the millions of people in this country who do not have degrees? It is more than a little demeaning to the overwhelming majority of people who have not finished college to say that they lack the "necessities" presumed to inhere in a college degree. That average incomes of college graduates exceed the average for nongraduates tells us precisely the opposite of what the premise claims: a college degree is not necessary, in any meaningful sense, to get along in this country. A degree may, of course, be *necessary* if by necessity one means relative economic wealth—a solidly upper-middle class lifestyle. One should not wreak such linguistic havoc, however, in the name of proving something that is clearly false.

This point leads to a second, more disturbing point. The analogy assumes that people seek to maximize wealth rather than utility. This, again, is simply false. People do not inevitably seek the employment that gives them the biggest paycheck. In employment, as in everything else, they seek those things that have the greatest utility for them, which may or may not be the most remunerative. There are plenty of law professors who could be millionaires but who prefer a more reflective life. Such decisions are not economically irrational. By assuming people are motivated only by money, the analogy necessarily posits a purely money-based view of education. We go to college, on the analogy's account, because we want to make money. There are plenty of people, however, for whom education is its own reward, and who would attend school even without any economic incentive. Students who go into social work, public interest law, and the like, evidence similar nonmonetary motivations. The analogy between work and school cannot explain this phenomenon. (Even if some people work because they love what they do, if economic *necessity* is to be equated with maximizing one's salary, as in the analogy, a worker would leave a job she loved for a less satisfying but more remunerative position.) (The Managing Editor of this law review led a life of profitable debauchery as a tour manager for rock bands, a life he gave up to work on this Comment. Only such extreme examples may be considered prima facie irrational.)

Finally, the analogy distorts the first amendment beyond all recognition. Speech in the workplace is controlled in part because work is compelled for the majority of people—workers are a true captive audience. If they leave their posts to avoid offensive speech, they will either literally be leaving their jobs or they will be fired. At this level, the analogy collapses because the economic necessity premise is patently false. At a minimum, one can graduate college without spending much time in public areas where offensive speech is likely to be found. And, as noted at *infra* notes 453-55, regulation of epithets in the classroom (all that is "necessary" to get a degree in the strict sense) poses few first amendment problems. More to the point, however, speech regulations in the workplace serve, at least in part, to allow workers to concentrate on the job at hand without distraction. And upon closer examination, this aspect of workplace regulations clearly differentiates the office and the classroom, at least with respect to first amendment theory.

Workplace speech restrictions, especially those mandated (as interpreted by the courts) by title VII, clearly refect a normative judgment that certain types of speech are simply too hurtfull to be vented at work. These restrictions are designed, however, essentially to make the workplace safe (psychologically and otherwise) for workers who might be verbally persecuted by virtue of minority status. Title VII exists to help people get work by prohibiting discrimination in hiring, and it helps them to keep their jobs by prohibiting discrimination once they are hired. A worker who is unable to do the job may be fired, and title VII does not apply to such a situation, even if the reason the worker cannot do the job is that she was traumatized by offensive speech on the way to the factory. (A worker traumatized by, say, racist speech at the factory might well have a claim, which is of course the source of the analogy.)

Ultimately, therefore, title VII keeps the workplace safe from speech that will inhibit an employee's ability to work. That is why the Equal Employment Opportunity Commission's guidelines on the statute (which, after all, does not itself mention speech) speak in terms of harassment that "unreasonably [interferes] with an individual's work performance." 29 C.F.R. § 1606.8 (1990). This whole structure assumes, however, that the employee's job is something other than to consider and analyze ideas that may be expressed in potentially offensive remarks. Otherwise the utilitarian structure of title VII folds into itself and falls apart. As argued extensively above, however, the "job" of university students (at least from the university's perspective) is precisely to confront and analyze new ideas. If those ideas are deeply offensive to the student, the university gives him the freedom to formulate a response and reject the idea. Offensiveness alone changes neither the student's mission nor the university's. The idea of restricting speech to allow a student to do his or her "job" is incoherent.

More generally, the "captive audience" rationale is of little utility in constructing a "civility zone" around potential victims moving in public places. First, the citizens who stood to be offended by Cohen's jacket were in a courthouse hallway, Cohen v. California, 403 U.S. 15 (1971), and literally may have been compelled to be there by virtue of an arrest warrant or subpoena. As such they were far more "captive" than a college student with access to all parts of a campus. Second, such restrictions are not content neutral: they turn on what is offensive to the listener. *See* Boos v. Barry, 485 U.S. 312, 320- 24 (1988) (rejecting justifications of preventing offense to foreign government in striking regulations prohibiting picketing in form of embassies). To enact such restrictions would result in a least-common-denominator level of civility for everyone to protect the "individual" interest of the most sensitive listener whose "civility zone" might overlap with such speech.

378. Matsuda, *supra* note 21, at 2371.

379. *Id.*

380. Widmar v. Vincent, 454 U.S. 263, 274 n.14 (1981). *Widmar* struck down the University of Missouri's policy prohibiting religious groups from using campus facilities.

381. Board of Curators of the University of Missouri, Resolution (Nov. 16, 1973), *quoted in* Gay Lib v. University of Mo., 416 F.Supp. 1350, 1359 (W.D. Mo. 1976), *rev'd*, 558 F.2d 848 (8th Cir. 1977), *cert. denied*, 434 U.S. 1080 (1978).

382. *Id.*

383. C. Coil, Hearing Officer's Recommended Findings of Fact (adopted by the Board of Curators of the University of Missouri, Nov. 16, 1973), *quoted in Gay Lib*, 416 F.Supp. at 1358.

384. *Id.*

385. *See supra* text accompanying notes 56-58.

386. Keyishian v. Board of Regents, 385 U.S. 589, 603 (1967).

387. Sweezy v. New Hampshire, 354 U.S. 234, 250 (1956).

388. Papish v. University of Mo., 410 U.S. 667, 670 (1973) (citing Healy v. James, 408 U.S. 169, 192-93 (1972)).

389. Matsuda, *supra* note 21, at 2371.

390. *Id.* at 2365.

391. Geraldo on Habermas is an experience we will undoubtedly (and mercifully) be spared.

392. A corollary of this argument is that the best way to combat racism in society as a whole is to disprove its premises through open discussion. The argument applies analogously to racist speech and invective. As Professor Farber puts it:

> [O]ffensiveness is often an important part of the speaker's message. Use of offensive language reveals the existence of something offensive and ugly, whether in the situation described by the speaker or in the speaker's mind itself. . . . Suppressing this language violates a cardinal principal of a free society, that truths are better confronted than repressed.

Farber, *Civilizing Public Discourse: An Essay On Professor Bickel, Justice Harlan, and the Enduring Significance of* Cohen v. California, 1980 DUKE L.J. 283, 302.

393. Jennings, *Racial Slur Found in Course Reader*, Daily Californian, Oct. 23, 1990, at 1, col. 3. The excerpts were from Stegner, *Striking the Rock*, THE AMERICAN WEST AS LIVING SPACE (1987).

394. Jennings, *supra* note 393, at 1, col. 3.

395. *Id.* at 7, col. 3-4.

396. Miller, *Students Clash in Anthro*, Daily Californian, Nov. 8, 1990, at 1, col. 1.

397. Finseth, *Sarich an Eclectic by Nature*, Daily Californian, Dec. 7, 1990, at 3, col. 1.

398. Miller, *supra* note 396, at 11, col. 1.

399. *Id.* at 1, col. 1, 11, col. 1.

400. Metzger, *Profession and Constitution: Two Definitions of Academic Freedom in America*, 66 TEX. L. REV. 1265, 1269 (1988).

401. *See infra* text accompanying notes 419-20.

402. Searle, *The Storm Over the University*, N.Y. Rev. of Books, Dec. 6, 1990, at 34, col. 2.

403. *See generally* Metzger, *supra* note 400, at 1276-77; Byrne, Academic Freedom: A "Special Concern of the First Amendment," 99 YALE L.J. 251, 255 (1989); see infra notes 408-20.

404. See Byrne, supra note 403, at 255 (academic freedom sometimes used to refer to the freedom of the university as corporate entity against the state).

405. Metzger, *supra* note 400, at 1270-71. The German conception included

three freedoms: for the university, the professors, and the students. For reasons that are beyond the scope of this Comment, only the first two survived the journey to our shores, and the rights of students have never been included in any working definition of "academic freedom" as used in this country. *Id.* at 1269-72.

406. *Id.* at 1269-72.

407. Rabban, *Does Academic Freedom Limit Faculty Autonomy?*, 66 TEX. L. REV. 1405, 1413 (1988).

408. The most recent comprehensive AAUP statement is the 1940 declaration of principles. Both statements are reprinted in ACADEMIC FREEDOM AND TENURE (L. Joughin ed. 1967) [hereinafter ACADEMIC FREEDOM], with the 1915 version at page 155 and the 1940 version at page 33.

409. *Id.* at 160.

410. *Id.* at 161; *see also* Rabban, *supra* note 407, at 1409.

411. *See supra* text accompanying notes 49-68.

412. ACADEMIC FREEDOM, *supra* note 408, at 164-65.

413. *Id.* at 164.

414. Metzger, *supra* note 400, at 1274, 1320.

415. *Id.* at 1279.

416. ACADEMIC FREEDOM, *supra* note 408, at 156. The 1915 Declaration draws an explicit analogy to federal judges. *Id.*

417. This is generally known in the trade as peer review.

418. Rabban, *supra* note 407, at 1410-11.

419. *Id.* at 1411. It is important to remember that most members of the administration will also be academics in their own right, and so should have professional interests partially balancing their institutional ones.

420. *Id.* at 1412. Even Marxist critics of the American implementation of academic freedom seem to agree that peer review is a tolerable device. *See e.g.*, Piven, *Academic Freedom and Intellectual Dissent*, in REGULATING THE INTELLECTUALS 21 (C. Kaplan & E. Schrecker eds. 1983).

421. 354 U.S. 234 (1957).

422. *Id.* at 263 (Frankfurter, J., concurring) (emphasis added).

423. *See supra* notes 365-70 and accompanying text.

424. *Cf.* Metzger, *supra* note 400, at 1291 ("the. . .1915 report did not find a close friend in the first amendment"); *see also* Byrne, *supra* note 403, at 255 (arguing that while the "non-legal tradition of academic freedom has been directed at protecting. . . the individual professor," the legal conception "should primarily insulate the university from interference by the state").

425. Metzger, *supra* note 400, at 1319.

426. Finseth, *supra* note 397, at 3, col. 1.

427. Matsuda, *supra* note 21, at 2365.

428. *See* Post, *Between Governance and Management: The History and Theory of the Public Forum*, 34 UCLA L. REV. 1713, 1715-16 (1987).

429. *See id.* at 1758-64 (describing in detail the state of the doctrine). A refinement of the doctrine, stating that in some circumstances private property will be considered to have become a public forum, would be relevant to the treatment of private universities. In an attempt to preserve the unitary treatment of public and private campuses, we will not pursue that distinction here.

430. If the government property is found to be a public forum, any content- based restriction on speech will be subject to strict scrutiny. United States v. Kokinda, 110 S.Ct. 3115, 3119 (1990) (plurality opinion) (holding sidewalk outside post office not traditional public forum). Even if the Court finds the property a nonpublic forum, the state is still limited to imposing restrictions in a viewpoint-neutral manner. Cornelius v. NAACP Legal Defense & Educ. Fund, Inc., 473 U.S. 788, 806 (1985) (remanding for inquiry into viewpoint-neutrality of otherwise permissible regulation in a nonpublic forum).

431. 307 U.S. 496 (1939) (plurality opinion).

432. *Id.* at 516 (ordinance requiring permit for public parade or meeting void on its face because it allows for "arbitrary suppression of free expression of views on national affairs").

433. *Id.* at 515.

434. *Compare* United States v. Grace, 461 U.S. 171, 178-80 (1983) (finding public sidewalk in front of Supreme Court to be a public forum) *with* Greer v. Spock, 424 U.S. 828, 835-37 (1976) (finding public streets and sidewalks within military base not a public forum).

435. 473 U.S. 788 (1985).

436. *Id.* at 790. The CFC is the annual charitable fundraising drive within federal government offices; it is carried out by government employees on government time. *Id.*

437. *Id.* at 805.

438. *Id.* at 804-06. Similarly, in Perry Education Association v. Perry Local Educators' Association, 460 U.S. 37 (1983), the Court found that by providing an interoffice mail system for its teachers, the school district had not created a public forum compelling it to allow all groups to use the mail system. *Id.* at 46-47. Furthermore, the Court found that such access would be inconsistent with the purpose of the system. *Id.* at 49-52.

439. Note that this does not displace completely the inquiry into the traditional use of the government institution. Where the institution has long been used for speech purposes, for instance, a government claim that speech is suddenly incompatible with the institution properly may be viewed with skepticism. Similarly, we may consider the Court's "limited" or "designated" public forum doctrine as a subset of the overall purpose inquiry. "Limited" or "designated" public forums are those which traditionally have not been used for free speech purposes, but which the government is found intentionally to have opened to speech. *Cornelius*, 473 U.S. at 802; *Perry*, 460 U.S. at 45. Government regulation of speech in a limited or designated forum is subject to the same constraints as regulation in a traditional public forum. *Perry*, 460 U.S. at 46. That the government intentionally opened an institution for speech can best be seen as creating a presumption that speech is not incompatible with the institution's purpose. Should this presumption prove inaccurate, the government can close the institution to speech, but it must do so on a reasonable basis. *See* United States v. Kokinda, 110 S.Ct. 3115, 3119-20 (1990) (plurality opinion) (regulation of speech on property that government has not dedicated to speech tested under the rule).

440. The special role of the university was first discussed in Sweezy v. New Hampshire, 354 U.S. 234 (1957). Although the case involved a professor who challenged questions put to him at a loyalty hearing, and the case was decided on due process grounds, the plurality opinion included a paragraph-long encomium on the virtues of the university. *Id.* at 250. The concurring opinion, quoting from a South African plea for academic freedom, was similarly impressed with the importance of unfettered speech on college campuses. *Id.* at 262-63.

441. *See, e.g.*, Papish v. University of Mo., 410 U.S. 667 (1973) (student on campus distributed newspaper containing offensive headline and cartoon); Healy v. James, 408 U.S. 169 (1972) (students wishing to organize local chapter of Students for a Democratic Society (SDS) denied recognition and access to campus facilities); Keyishian v. Board of Regents, 385 U.S. 589 (1967) (professors sued to enjoin application of state statute requiring dismissal of any employee who was member of "subversive" organization, whether or not employee intended to carry out aims of organization).

442. *Healy*, 408 U.S. at 171.

443. *Papish*, 410 U.S. at 671 ("the First Amendment leaves no room for the operation of a dual standard in the academic community with respect to the content of speech").

444. *Keyishian*, 385 U.S. at 603 ("Our Nation is deeply committed to safeguarding academic freedom [which is] a special concern of the First Amendment, which does not tolerate laws that cast a pall of orthodoxy over the classroom.").

445. *Id.*

446. 454 U.S. 263 (1981).

447. *Id.* at 265.

448. *Id.* at 267.

449. *Id.* at 267 n.5 (quoting Healy v. James, 408 U.S. 169, 180 (1972)).

450. Professor Post uses the term "managerial authority" to describe the exercise of the government of its power to limit speech inconsistent with the primary purpose of an institution. Post, *supra* note 428, at 1717 (stating that government's managerial authority allows it "constitutionally [to] regulate speech as necessary to achieve instrumental objectives").

451. *See id.* at 1799 ("government action within organizational domains is at times designed for the specific purpose of facilitating symbolic interaction, as occurs. . .in. . . universities"); *id.* at 1834 n.402 ("Special environments like universities may constitute an exception to this generalization, since in such environments the culture of academic freedom might instrumentally connect a tradition of public access for expressive purposes with the achievement of educational objectives.").

452. *See* Cohen v. California, 403 U.S. 15, 21 (1971) (dismissing argument that state has interest in protecting sensitive viewers in courthouse hallway when the viewers could "avert[ ] their eyes" or move away).

453. *See generally* Post, *supra* note 294; *see also supra* notes 49-68 and accompanying text.

454. By "limit" we mean a content-based limitation. We assume that a true time, place, and manner limitation (for example, limiting the times of day that amplification equipment can be used, or initiating a precedence system) would be as valid on a university campus as anywhere else.

455. *See* Ward v. Rock Against Racism, 491 U.S. 781 (1989) (upholding sound amplification restrictions on concerts in New York City's Central Park as valid place and manner restrictions).

456. *See, e.g.*, Frisby v. Schulz, 487 U.S. 474, 483-84 (1988) (upholding local ordinance limiting demonstrations on public sidewalks outside private homes in part because of the privacy interests inherent in the home); FCC v. Pacifica Found., 438 U.S. 726, 748 (1978) (allowing limits on indecent radio broadcasts in part because they reach into private homes).

457. *See Pacifica*, 438 U.S. at 748 (upholding limit on speech uttered in a public forum but directed at a private home).

458. Cornelius v. NAACP Legal Defense & Educ. Fund, Inc., 473 U.S. 788, 806 (1985) (holding that in regulating access to a nonpublic forum, government may not distinguish on the basis of viewpoint).

459. F. SCHAUER, *supra* note 59, at 26 ("In systems of scientific and academic discourse, the argument from truth has substantial validity.").

460. As Professor Charles Wright stated in his landmark article, "I fully share the view. . .that the life of a university depends on 'the pursuit of truth and knowledge solely through reason and civility,' and that lack of civility leads only to a harmful polarization of opinion, but it is perfectly clear that the first amendment did not enact Mrs. Emily Post's book of etiquette." Wright, *The Constitution on the Campus*, 22 VAND L. REV. 1027, 1057 (1969) (quoting CRISIS AT COLUMBIA: REPORT OF THE FACT-FINDING COMMISSION APPOINTED TO INVESTIGATE THE DISTURBANCES AT COLUMBIA UNIVERSITY IN APRIL AND MAY, 1968, at 196 (1968)).

CHAPTER 5

THE CONSTITUTIONAL ANSWER

"The Unconstitutionality of Campus Bans on 'Racist Speech': The View from Without and Within"*

*Robert A. Sedler***

I. INTRODUCTION

"Racist speech" is a generic term, which refers primarily to speech that denigrates persons on the basis of their race or ethnic origin, but also includes speech that denigrates on the basis of gender or sexual orientation. Many universities have enacted regulations restricting racist speech in response to a disturbing number of overtly racist incidents on university campuses, as well as hostile incidents directed against women and against gay and lesbian persons. The justification for restricting racist speech on campus is that racist speech by its very nature causes discrete and serious harm to racial minorities, women, gay and lesbian persons, and other victim groups, and so creates an "intimidating hostile, or demeaning environment"[1] that "interfere[s] with an individual's academic efforts,. . .[and] participation in University sponsored extra-curricular activities."[2]

---

*The complete article from which the following is excerpted appears at 53 University of Pittsburgh Law review 631 (1992). Footnotes have been changed to endnotes and are numbered as in the original. Reprinted with permission.

** Professor of Law, Wayne State University. A.B. 1956, J.D. 1959, University of Pittsburgh. Valuable research assistance in the preparation of this article was provided by Ms. Barbara Chupa, a member of the Michigan Bar, when she was a third-year law student at Wayne State University Law School.

Proponents of these bans argue that the universities must restrict racist speech in order to provide equality of educational opportunity for racial minorities and other victim groups.[3]

The prevalence of university racist speech policies and other proposals to sanction racist speech has prompted an enormous amount of academic literature on the subject. It is fair to say that most of the academic commentators advocate some form of restriction on racist speech on the university campus, emphasizing the harm that it causes to racial minorities and other victim groups and what commentators contend is the resulting denial of equal educational opportunity. While all of the advocates of campus restrictions on racist speech recognize that such restrictions interfere with freedom of expression, they insist that the value of free expression must be balanced against the harm caused by racist speech and against the equality value of the Fourteenth Amendment.[4]

Much of the discussion about the First Amendment in this context, like much of the academic commentary about the First Amendment generally, tends to be somewhat theoretical and philosophical. Academic commentators frequently attempt to demonstrate that restrictions on racist speech are not inconsistent with and may actually advance First Amendment values, and therefore, such restrictions should be constitutionally permissible.[5] The contrary view—a distinctly minority one—is that campus bans on racist speech will inhibit the discussion of controversial ideas and therefore, are inconsistent with the unfettered freedom of inquiry to which a university should be committed.[6]

In this article my approach to the question of the constitutionality of campus bans on racist speech is quite different and very narrowly focused. The perspective that I hope to contribute to the debate over campus bans on racist speech is that of the *litigating lawyer*, operating within the framework of what I call the "law of the First Amendment."[7] The law of the First Amendment is that body of concepts, principles, and specific doctrines that has emerged over the years from the Supreme Court's First Amendment decisions. In First Amendment cases, it is the law of the First Amendment which controls the result, or at least sets the parameters for the resolution of the question at issue.

In this article I will demonstrate that under the law of the First Amendment, virtually any campus ban on racist speech imposed by a public university will be found to be unconstitutional.[8] My purpose in adding the litigation perspective to the academic debate over campus bans on racist speech is in no sense an attempt to trump the debate or make it irrelevant. Quite to the contrary, academic debate over what the First Amendment should mean, and over whether racist speech on campus should be protected under the First Amendment is quite valuable. The exploration of these questions goes to the heart of academic inquiry and is an important function of commentary. It may be that at some time in the future, the views of academic commentators on this very controversial question may reach the Justices on the Supreme Court and will be embodied in the law of the First Amendment, although I think that this is highly unlikely.[9]

My purpose in analyzing campus bans on racist speech under the law of the First Amendment is to make it clear that regardless of whether or not such bans should be constitutionally permissible, the stark reality is that they are not.[10] When they are challenged in court, the court will declare them unconstitutional, just as the court did in *Doe v. University of Michigan*,[11] and *The UMW Post v. Board of Regents of the University of Wisconsin System*,[12] the only two campus racist speech cases to come before the courts thus far. It is my hope to persuade public universities to abandon this unconstitutional enterprise, and turn their attention to more productive and effective ways of providing equality of educational opportunity for their students.

As the title indicates, this discussion will proceed from "without and within"—from the dual perspectives of an academic commentator and of a lawyer who was lead counsel for the ACLU in the challenge to the University of Michiga"s racist speech policy. I have approached legal questions in this manner previously,[13] and believe that such an approach has much to commend it. To the extent that the impartial and dispassionate perspective of a pure legal scholar is a virtue, this perspective is admittedly lacking.[14] However, participation as an advocate yields insights that detached scholarly observation can not provide. My involvement in *Doe v. University of Michigan* has provided special insights for me, and they form a very important part of this article.[15]

Part II presents the controversy over racist speech on campus. This involves an understanding and acknowledgement of the harm to individuals and to the educational environment that commentators have identified as being caused by racist speech and the other reasons why universities may be imposing campus bans on it today. I will also discuss the University of Michigan's policy and how that policy operated in practice.[16] Part III details the law of the First Amendment as it applies to restrictions on racist speech. In Part IV, from a constitutional standpoint the most important part of the article, I will discuss the constitutionality of campus bans on racist speech under the law of the First Amendment. Here I will present the components of the law of the First Amendment that are applicable to determine the constitutionality of campus bans on racist speech and that were dispositive in the *Doe* and *UWM Post* cases. I will also explain why virtually any campus ban on racist speech imposed by a public university will be found unconstitutional. In Part V, I will discuss the actions that public universities can and should take to protect the rights of racial minorities and other victim groups, to ensure that all students enjoy equality of educational opportunity on the university campus.

II. THE CONTROVERSY OVER RACIST SPEECH ON CAMPUS

The primary effort to restrict racist speech in American society is taking place on university campuses today. Campus bans have been enacted in response to a disturbing number of overtly racist incidents on university campuses, as well as hostile incidents directed against women and against gay and lesbian persons. Most of the recent overtly racist incidents have been directed against black-American students at traditionally all-white universities, to which blacks are now being admitted in more than token numbers.[17] Notions of racial supremacy, which unfortunately still lurk just below the surface in the thinking of many Americans, become legitimatized in the minds of some white students when black students are admitted under "affirmative action" programs with lower "paper credentials" than white students who are denied admission.[18] A white student thus can legitimatize an underlying racist belief in terms of purported opposition to affirmative action. White students with racist beliefs apparently feel less restrained today in openly expressing them through degrading "racial epithets." Because of an increase in reported incidents, universities often feel a strong need to provide a degree of protection for their minority students.

There is also increased sensitivity on university campuses, as elsewhere, to claims of verbal and physical sexual harassment against women, which sometimes involve "date rape." The concept of sexual harassment has been expanded, perhaps in light of the concerns raised by aggressive sexual behavior by men, to include not only the traditional forms of sexual harassment— unwanted sexual touching, persistent demands for a sexual relationship, "obscene phone calls"—but also to the expressed view of women as sexual objects, and the dissemination of pornography and other materials depicting the sexual subordination of women. This expanded notion of sexual harassment has led to a willingness on the part of universities to protect female students from being subjected to "sexual speech" in a variety of circumstances.

Homosexuals are a third group targeted by those who engage in racist speech. The societal hostility toward persons of same-sex orientation, particularly male homosexuals, which the Supreme Court itself has recognized and to an extent legitimized,[19] is readily expressed by some male college students as they try to establish their own male identity. As a result, incidents of "gay-bashing" which occur on college campuses, as well as in the larger society, sometimes involve physical violence. Most academics and university administrators, however, unlike the larger society, are sensitive to the needs of individuals living non-traditional lifestyles, and want to protect gay and lesbian students from hostility directed against them by other students because of their different sexual orientation.

The primary and most frequently articulated justification for restricting racist speech on campus is that it causes discrete and serious harm to racial minorities and other victim groups, and as a result denies them equality of educational opportunity.[20] As Professor Matsuda has put it: "The negative effects of hate messages are real and immediate for the victims. Victims of vicious hate propaganda have experienced physiological symptoms and emotional distress ranging from fear in the gut, rapid pulse rate and difficulty in breathing, nightmares, post-traumatic stress disorder, hypertension, psychosis, and suicide."[21] Racist speech is also said to promote the "ideology of racial supremacy"[22] and is a "mechanism[] for keeping selected victim groups in subordinated positions."[23] When the racist speech takes the form of an insult directed against a particular person, it can "inflict injury by [its] very utterance"[24] and can cause that person to doubt her or his self-worth as a human being.[25]

Some academics further contend that on the university campus, racist speech causes harm both to the interchange of ideas and to the educational environment by: injecting "irrationality" into the interchange; silencing minority students and other victim groups due to the visceral shock and preemptive effect of racist words on further speech; and devaluing the speech of minorities and other victim groups.[26] Finally, it is said that racist speech can interfere with a university's educational mission, insofar as that mission includes promoting diversity and teaching respect for human dignity and individual self-worth.[27]

It cannot be denied that racist speech may cause discrete and serious harm to racial minorities, other victim groups and to the educational environment. It may be assumed that campus bans on racist speech are motivated by a genuine concern for the personal and educational welfare of racial minorities, women, gay and lesbian persons, and other victim groups, and for the educational environment on the university campus. However, these reasons for restricting racist speech interact with another phenomenon that goes beyond the personal and educational welfare of the students who suffer harm from the effects of racist speech.

This phenomenon is the growing emergence of a new *secular orthodoxy* on the campuses of many American universities today. The existence of this secular orthodoxy is at the heart of the debate over "politically correct thinking," or "P.C." Many faculty members and administrators today are products of the sixties, and are trying to implement on the campus the values that came to the fore in the sixties: values of racial equality, gender equality, and respect for individual differences and alternative life styles. Other aspects of this secular orthodoxy are that homosexuality is a morally acceptable and legitimate lifestyle, that the tenets of feminism are superior to the traditional view of women, and that male-oriented sexuality is a form of discrimination against women.

While the proponents of these values in the university community deny that they are trying to impose politically correct thinking on students and colleagues, there is clearly the danger that the efforts to implement these values in the academic setting will give rise to a new officially-imposed secular orthodoxy, in which ideas that are seemingly inconsistent with these values are deemed to be illegitimate. One such illegitimate idea, for example, is that there are biological differences among racial groups which contribute to cognitive and other differences among the races. A related idea is that biological differences between men and women cause men and women to behave differently in some respects, so that men are biologically more suited to perform certain kinds of tasks while women are biologically more suited to perform other kinds of tasks.

Universities' efforts to restrict racist speech, while legitimately motivated by a genuine concern for the personal and educational welfare of minority students and other victim groups, may also reflect the new secular orthodoxy that is emerging in much of the university world today. Just as the universities in the 1950's and the 1960's all too often tried to establish a *political orthodoxy* by restricting the expression of controversial political ideas and prohibiting "anti-establishment" political activity, today we see the universities trying to implement a new secular orthodoxy, one component of which is the imposition of restrictions on racist speech.[28]

This is exactly what happened with respect to the operation of the University of Michigan's racist speech policy invalidated in *Doe v. University of Michigan.*[29] I will concentrate on demonstrating three salient points that have emerged from the "empirical study" of the operation of one university's racist speech policy.

The first and most significant point is that the University's policy was directed against the expression of *racist ideas* and was intended by those who administered it to implement a new secular orthodoxy on the university campus. That this was the thrust of the policy and the intention of those administering it is demonstrated both by the "interpretive guide"[30] that was issued by the University and by the way that the policy was administered in practice.

The guide "purported to be an authoritative interpretation of the Policy and provided [fourteen] examples of sanctionable conduct."[31] The plaintiff contended that, "[e]very single example prohibit[ed] acts of expression or association that are absolutely or in all but very limited circumstances protected by the First Amendment."[32] The following example, which was the basis for the plaintiff's standing in *Doe*,[33] and which was a major point of reference for the overbreadth challenge, clearly illustrates how the policy was directed against the expression of racist ideas and was intended to impose a secular orthodoxy on the campus: "[a] male student makes remarks in class like 'Women just aren't as good in this field as men,' thus creating a hostile learning atmosphere for female classmates."[34] This example would serve to implement that aspect of the secular orthodoxy which maintains that the tenets of feminism are superior to the traditional view of women, specifically that aspect which maintains that there are no biological differences between the sexes which would make members of each sex biologically more suited than the other to engage in particular kinds of activity. Under the policy, as this example indicates, whenever a male student expressed an idea that was contrary to these aspects of the secular orthodoxy, he would be deemed to have created "a hostile learning atmosphere for female classmates."[35]

Even more telling in regard to the advancement of the secular orthodoxy and the impact of the policy on the expression of ideas was the matter of how the policy was administered in practice. Through discovery, we obtained all of the cases in which complaints of a violation of the policy were filed.[36] The district court relied on three of the cases involving expression in the classroom in support of its conclusion that, "as applied by the University over the past year, the Policy was consistently applied to reach protected speech."[37] I will use two of these cases to illustrate how the policy was applied to implement the prevailing secular orthodoxy with respect to homosexuality.

In one of the cases, a graduate student in Social Work (who we later discovered was black) was charged with harassment on the basis of sexual orientation in that he had "repeatedly said that homosexuality is an illness that needs to be cured,"[38] and that he had "developed a model to change gay men and lesbians to a heterosexual orientation."[39] He also had discussed efforts to apply this model in his field placement. The student contested the charge, and the case went to a formal hearing.[40] A divided hearing panel held that the student's discussion of "homosexuality as an illness" did not violate the policy. However, the panel stated gratuitously that the finding should not be constructed as "condoning the actions or statements of [the student],"[41] and that what he was accused of doing "should be reviewed by the appropriate social work professionals in considering [the student's] suitability as a professional social worker."[42]

In a second case, in a business school class a student read a limerick which poked fun at alleged homosexual acts of a well-known athlete. After class, another student, apparently gay, read him the policy and accused him of having engaged in intimidating behavior.[43] Although the offending student immediately apologized, the offended student filed a complaint. The offending student agreed to an informal resolution, under which he published a letter of apology in the campus newspaper and agreed to attend a "Gay Rap" session.[44] As these two cases demonstrate, the policy was perceived by the officials administering it and the students filing complaints under it as embodying the prevailing secular orthodoxy, here that aspect pertaining to homosexuality.[45]

Another series of cases involved enforcement of the prevailing secular orthodoxy with respect to sexual harassment and attitudes about sexuality. In one of them a male student had put up a poster "'depicting a monster attacking a woman sexually,' and a caption reading, '[d]ate rape is not rape.'"[46] The charge was that the poster constituted sexual harassment against "female residents of 76 corridor square."[47] The student entered into a "behavior contract" with the resident advisor and the building director, under which he agreed among other things to "refrain from placing any offensive or harassing materials on his door,[48]. . .[to] attend a Sexual Assault Prevention program at a specified time [and to] write no less than a two page analysis of the presentation. . . ."[49] In another, a student had posted signs in a residence hall advertising for a roommate. The sign "was headed 'SEX.' and referred to an 'active Co-Ed hall with many lean and hungry women.'"[50] The charge was that "the sign constituted sexual harassment against 'any female resident, staff member, or visitor.'"[51] The student was given a verbal reprimand by a member of the Housing Staff.[52] Again, these examples indicate that the policy was perceived by the officials administering it and the students filing complaints under it as embodying that aspect of the secular orthodoxy dealing with sexual harassment and sexuality.

The second point that has emerged from the "empirical study" reflected in the *Doe* litigation is that the university officials were using a form of "mind control" to enforce the policy: they required offending students to write humiliating letters of apology, to undergo "re-education" and "sensitivity training," and to enter into "behavior contracts."[53] In the case of the business student whose limerick offended a gay classmate, the University required the student to publish a letter of apology in the campus newspaper and to attend a Gay Rap session. The University required the student who put up the "Date rape is not rape" poster to enter into a behavior contract and attend a Sexual Assault Prevention program.[54]

A third case involved a black law student, who during the course of an argument with a white law student in the Law Building, "used the term 'white trash' and said, '[i]t would be in your best interest not to be indignant to me or four o'clock will be more than quitting time.'"[55] The black student complied with the white student's demand for a letter of apology. The letter of apology was very humiliating and could not help but adversely affect the black student's self-esteem—the very thing that a racist speech policy is supposedly designed to prevent.[56] In another case, where a guest in a student's dormitory room was overheard making the remark, "Its just a nigger fighting," the conduct of the guest was "imputed" to the student, and the accused student agreed to attend a seminar or workshop on "diversity."[57] As stated in the plaintiff's brief in *Doe*, this kind of activity on the part of the university officials administering the policy was "something that might more appropriately be found at the University of Beijing than on the campus of one of America's great universities."[58]

The third point that emerges from experience with the operation of the University of Michigan's racist speech policy is that contrary to popular belief, racist speech is not a matter of straight white males versus minorities, women, gays and other victim groups: complaints were filed against black students for racist and homophobic speech. A complaint was filed against a white student for asserting that a minority faculty member had discriminated against blacks.[59] A number of the complaints were filed by women students on the ground that male students, sometimes unidentified, had put up posters or pictures of a sexual nature. Other complaints were on the basis of overheard remarks that were not addressed to the complainant. In short, it was everybody complaining about everybody else about everything.

As the above discussion makes clear, the policy was intended to advance a new secular orthodoxy and was administered in such a way as to reach any form of expression that was deemed to be offensive or to run counter to the prevailing secular orthodoxy. Proponents of campus bans on racist speech insist that there is no inconsistency between such bans and the function of a university as a place for free and unfettered inquiry and expression. The empirical study of how one major university's campus ban on racist speech was administered and operated in practice raises some concern about this contention.

Academic commentators tend to dismiss *Doe v. University of Michigan* as a case involving no more than one university's poorly drafted racist speech policy.[60] In arguing for more carefully drafted campus speech bans, they imply that such bans would not have the same kind of impact on the free expression of ideas as did the University of Michigan's policy. Although I think that the way that the University of Michigan administered its policy is symptomatic of the way that most universities would administer such a policy,[61] this is largely beside the point. *It is my submission that campus bans on racist speech, no matter how narrowly-framed and no matter how justified, are directed primarily against the expression of racist ideas.* Since, as I will demonstrate in the next section of the article, a public university cannot *for any reason* prohibit the expression of racist ideas on campus, virtually any campus ban on racist speech will be found to violate the First Amendment.

III. THE LAW OF THE FIRST AMENDMENT AND CAMPUS BANS ON RACIST SPEECH

The Law of the First Amendment

As stated at the outset, this article discusses the constitutionality of bans on racist speech on campus from the perspective of the litigating lawyer and with reference to what I have called the law of the First Amendment.[62] It is this law that is applicable in actual First Amendment litigation. It consists in large part of *concepts, principles and specific doctrines* that the

Court has developed over the years in the process of deciding First Amendment cases. These concepts, principles and specific doctrines are supplemented by a residually applicable balancing approach, which to a degree consists of a number of subsidiary doctrines. In the context of actual litigation, First Amendment analysis is very much a matter of *identification* and *application*. In many cases, once the Court identifies the appropriate concept, principle or specific doctrine, the parameters for the resolution of the constitutional question at issue have been established and the result is often fairly clear.

The point to be emphasized in this regard is that the result in litigation is controlled by the Court's application of the law of the First Amendment and not by a general "balancing" approach or by some "theory" about the meaning of the First Amendment. It is sometimes said that when governmental regulation is directed at the non-communicative impact of expression, as opposed to the specific message or viewpoint expressed, the Court follows an *ad hoc* balancing approach: balancing the interest in freedom of expression against other societal interests as these interests appear in the context of particular limitations on expression.[63] However, as an explanation of how First Amendment analysis operates in litigation, the balancing approach explanation, even as to regulation directed at the non-communicative impact of expression, is somewhat misleading.

Often the result in a First Amendment case is controlled by the application of the appropriate concept, principle or specific doctrine. When this is so, no balancing takes place at all, and the application of the concept, principle or specific doctrine either renders the particular limitation on expression unconstitutional or at least sets the parameters for the resolution of the constitutional question.[64] Moreover, even when there is no controlling concept, principle or specific doctrine, the Court's application of the residual balancing approach is qualified by the Court's precedents dealing with a particular kind of restriction or interference with expression. To this extent, the Court is applying "subsidiary doctrine" to determine the constitutionality of the particular restriction or interference in issue rather than engaging in a general balancing approach.[65]

The constitutionality of campus bans on racist speech then will be determined with reference to the law of the First Amendment. The courts will not engage in some general balancing—balancing the harm caused to the victims by racist speech against the resulting interference with freedom of expression, or balancing the "equality value" of the Fourteenth Amendment against the "freedom of expression value" of the First Amendment. Rather, they will be applying the law of the First Amendment.

Any significant campus ban on racist speech will conflict with three very important First Amendment principles: content neutrality, the protection of offensive speech, and the heightened protection of expression in the academic context, and will therefore invariably be held unconstitutional. This was the fate of the very broad University of Michigan ban in *Doe v. University of Michigan*, and of the much narrower University of Wisconsin ban in the *UWM Post* case.

Since I have discussed these principles at length elsewhere, I will only summarize that discussion here, and I will then discuss the application of these principles in the *Doe* and *UWM* cases. Under the principle of content neutrality, the government may not proscribe any expression because of its content, and an otherwise valid regulation violates the First Amendment if it differentiates between expression based on content.[66] Analytically, there are two aspects to the principle of content neutrality: viewpoint neutrality and categorical neutrality. Under the viewpoint neutrality aspect of the principle, to which the Court has never recognized any exceptions, the government cannot regulate expression in such a way as to favor one viewpoint over another. The requirement of viewpoint neutrality was the basis for the Court's invalidation of state and federal bans on flag desecration.[67] The majority took the position that the asserted governmental interest in preserving the flag as a "symbol of nationhood and national unity"[68] violated this requirement, emphasizing that the government had authorized burning as a proper means of disposing of a torn or soiled flag, so that the thrust of the ban was directed toward the content of the message conveyed by the burning.[69]

The requirement of viewpoint neutrality also resulted in the invalidation of a District of Columbia law that prohibited the display of any sign within 500 feet of a foreign embassy that would "tend[] to bring a foreign government into public odium or public disrepute. . . ."[70] The law by its terms only prohibited displays that were critical of the foreign government; displays that were favorable to the foreign government were not prohibited. The law in effect ordained an officially approved viewpoint about the foreign government whose embassy was being picketed.[71] Likewise, the requirement of viewpoint neutrality was violated by a federal law that allowed the wearing of U.S. military uniforms in a portrayal only if the portrayal does not "'tend to discredit' the military."[72] Still another example of the application of this aspect of the principle of content neutrality is found in the invalidation of the civil rights anti-pornography law that defined proscribed pornography as the "graphic sexually explicit subordination of women."[73] The law was invalidated because it favored one view of the role of men and women in sexual encounters—equality between men and women—over another—the sexual subordination of women by men.[74]

Under the second aspect of the principle of content neutrality, categorical neutrality, the government generally cannot regulate in such a way as to differentiate between categories of expression.[75] Recently, the Court strongly affirmed this aspect of the principle when it struck down New York's "Son of Sam" law, because that law only applied to a criminal's proceeds from "storytelling" about the crime and not to other assets.[76]

As the above demonstrates, the principle of content neutrality is a very powerful one, and if it applies to a challenge of a particular restriction of expression, it controls the outcome of that challenge.[77] The First Amendment, as the Court has said, requires "equality of status in the field of ideas,"[78] and the principle of content neutrality is the doctrinal vehicle by which such "equality of status" is achieved.

The second applicable First Amendment principle, protection of offensive speech, forecloses any justification for a restriction on expression on the ground that the expression is offensive. As the Supreme Court stated in *Johnson v. Texas* when striking down the Texas flag desecration laws: "[i]f there is a bedrock principle underlying the First Amendment, it is that the government may not prohibit the expression of an idea simply because society finds the idea itself offensive or disagreeable."[79] Nor may the government prohibit the expression of an idea in a particular manner that is highly offensive, such as by the use of an "unseemly expletive."[80] Under this principle the government cannot prohibit the expression of an idea on the ground that the idea itself or the manner in which the idea is expressed is highly offensive to many people. Therefore, any time the government tries to justify a restriction on expression on the ground of its "offensiveness," the justification is necessarily improper.

The third principle, heightened protection of expression in the academic context, emerged from the constitutional challenges of governmental efforts in the fifties and sixties to impose a political orthodoxy on university campuses and in the public schools. As the Court in a number of cases invalidated loyalty oath requirements for public employees and legislative inquiries into the beliefs and associations of teachers, it emphasized the importance of free inquiry in the academic context. For example, as Justice Brennan stated in *Keyishian v. Board of Regents*:

> Our Nation is deeply committed to safeguarding academic freedom, which is of transcendent value to all of us and not merely to the teachers concerned. That freedom is therefore a special concern of the First Amendment, which does not tolerate laws that cast a pall of orthodoxy over the classroom. . . .The classroom is peculiarly the "marketplace of ideas."[81] The Nation's future depends upon leaders trained through wide exposure to that robust exchange of ideas which discovers truth "out of a multitude of tongues, [rather] than

through any kind of authoritative selection."[82]

It is on the basis of this kind of language in the Court's opinions and its actions in protecting freedom of academic inquiry against governmental interference that we can find a principle of heightened protection of expression in the academic context.

This principle was also involved in cases arising in the late sixties and early seventies when public universities tried to restrict "anti-establishment" speech and association on campus. In *Healy v. James*[83] the Court held that a public university could not refuse to grant official recognition to a student group, here the local chapter of the Students for a Democratic Society, because of disagreement with the group's philosophy or because of an unsubstantiated fear that the group would be a "disruptive influence."[84] The Court also held that a public university could not constitutionally expel a student for distributing on campus a newspaper which contained a cartoon "depicting policemen raping the Statue of Liberty and the Goddess of Justice,"[85] and an article with the headline, "'M_____ f_____ Acquitted,' which discussed the trial and acquittal of a New York City youth who was a member of an organization know as 'Up Against the Wall, M_____ f_____.'"[86]

In the context of campus bans on racist speech, these First Amendment principles interact with each other, and operate in conjunction with the void on its face doctrine. The void on its face doctrine, which is extremely important in actual First Amendment litigation, is one of those doctrines that is derived from the fundamental First Amendment concept of chilling effect.[87] Under this doctrine, a law regulating or applicable to expression may be challenged on its face for substantial overbreadth or vagueness.[88] The doctrine is extremely powerful in practice, not only because the challenged law can be invalidated without regard to whether the activity of the party challenging it is constitutionally protected,[89] but also because the constitutional analysis does not go beyond the terms of the law itself. Moreover, once a law is invalidated on its face, it is as if the law literally has been excised from the statute books: it cannot be enforced against any person in any circumstances.[90]

In practice, however, the void on its face doctrine, while perhaps applied "sparingly and only as a last resort"[91] to laws that have as their primary purpose the regulation of conduct and have only an incidental effect on expression,[92] is readily applied to invalidate laws that by their terms are directed against expressive activity. Thus, in *Houston v. Hill*,[93] the Court invalidated on its face a Houston ordinance making it unlawful for a person to "in any manner oppose, molest, abuse or interrupt any policeman in the execution of his duty."[94]

In the context of campus bans on racist speech then, the principles of content neutrality, protection of offensive speech, and heightened protection of expression in the academic context interact with each other, and in conjunction with the void on its face doctrine operate to impose an insuperable constitutional obstacle to a public university's efforts to ban racist speech on campus.

* * *

Addendum

While this article was in press and shortly before its publication, the Supreme Court rendered its decision in *R.A.V. v. City of St. Paul, Minnesota*,[178] where the Court unanimously, although in two separate and differing opinions, struck down a St. Paul ordinance banning the display of a symbol which one knows or has reason to know arouses anger, alarm or resentment in others on the basis of race, color, creed, religion or gender.[179] Although serious time constraints prevent an extended analysis of the case and its ramifications, there can be no doubt that the Court's holding makes authoritative the thesis of the present article: "[t]hat under the law of the First Amendment, virtually any campus ban on racist speech imposed by a public university will be found to be unconstitutional."[180] Indeed, in view of the Court's holding, it is now possible to eliminate the use of "virtually" as a qualification.

The Minnesota Supreme Court attempted to give the obviously overbroad ordinance a narrowing construction by limiting it to "fighting words."[181] The concurring opinion of Justice White, joined in this respect by Justices Blackmun, Stevens and O'Connor, found that the narrowing construction was insufficient to avoid the unconstitutional overbreadth, because the narrowing construction defined "fighting words" to include speech that causes anger, alarm or resentment based on racial, ethnic, gender or religious bias.[182] As Justice White stated, "[t]he mere fact that expressive activity causes hurt feelings, offense, or resentment does not render the expression unprotected,"[183] and since the ordinance, as purportedly narrowly construed, reached that kind of expression, it was "fatally overbroad and invalid on its face."[184] The rationale of Justice White's opinion makes it absolutely clear, as I have contended, that the fighting words exception is extremely narrow and cannot be expanded to include functional equivalents of fighting words or to provide a psychic harm justification for campus bans on racist speech.[185]

The Court majority, however, in an opinion written by Justice Scalia, and joined in by Chief Justice Rehnquist, and Justices Kennedy, Souter and Thomas, went even further. Without considering the effect of the Minnesota Supreme Court's purported narrowing construction of the ordinance, the majority held that the ordinance was unconstitutional because it violated the principle of content neutrality. Over the strong disagreement of the concurring Justices, the majority held that the principle of content neutrality applied to unprotected speech, such as "fighting words." Since the ordinance, as interpreted, prohibited only a particular category of fighting words—those dealing with race, ethnicity, gender, and religion—while not restricting at all other kinds of fighting words, it violated the principle of content neutrality. As Justice Scalia stated:

> Displays containing abusive invective, no matter how vicious or severe, are permissible un-

> less they are addressed to none of the specific disfavored topics. Those who wish to use "fighting words" in connection with other ideas—to express hostility, for example, on the basis of political affiliation, union membership, or homosexuality—are not covered. The First Amendment does not permit St. Paul to impose special prohibition on those speakers who express views on disfavored subjects.[186]

In this article I stated: "[A]s *Doe v. University of Michigan* and the *UWM Post* case make clear, any campus ban on racist speech, no matter how purportedly limited, that reaches the expression of racist ideas violates the First Amendment. Under the principle of content neutrality, a public university cannot ban the expression of racist ideas in any circumstance or for any purpose."[187] In *R.A.V.*, the Supreme Court majority applied the principle of content neutrality to invalidate a ban on racist speech that was limited to unprotected "fighting words." This being so, it is beyond contravention that the principle of content neutrality protects the expression of racist ideas without qualification, and renders unconstitutional that "narrowest possible" campus ban that would restrict such expression.

R.A.V. then sounds the death knell for campus bans on racist speech. As a result of that decision, I am thus more optimistic that "public universities will now decide to turn away from this unconstitutional enterprise and instead direct their efforts to bringing about a meaningful equality of educational opportunity on campus."[188]

Endnotes

1. The above language is taken from the University of Michigan's Policy on Discrimination and Discriminatory Harassment by Students in the University Environment, which was invalidated in Doe v. University of Mich., 721 F.Supp. 852 (E.D.Mich. 1989).

2. *Id.*

3. *See, e.g.*, Charles R. Lawrence, III, *If He Hollers Let Him Go: Regulating Racist Speech on Campus*, 1990 Duke L.J. 431, 446-48, 462-66.

4. *See, e.g.*, Alan E. Brownstein, *Regulating Hate Speech at Public Universities: Are First Amendment Values Functionally Incompatible with Equal Protection Principles*, 39 Buff. L. Rev. 1 (1991); Richard Delgado, *Campus Antiracism Rules: Constitutional Narratives in Collision*, 85 Nw. U. L. Rev. 343 (1991); Charles H. Jones, *Equality, Dignity, and Harm: The Constitutionality of Regulating American Campus Ethnoviolence*,

37 WAYNE L. REV. 1383 (1991); Lawrence, *supra* note 3; Mari J. Matsuda, *Public Response to Racist Speech: Considering the Victim's Story*, 87 *Mich. L. Rev.* 2320 (1989); Rodney A. Smolla, *Rethinking First Amendment Assumptions About Racist and Sexist Speech*, 47 WASH. & LEE L. REV. 171 (1990).

5. It is contended, for example, that "racist speech" distorts the debate in the "marketplace of ideas," particularly by devaluing the speech of victim groups. Lawrence, *supra* note 3, at 468-70. It may also be noted that the kind of restrictions they propose are usually stated in terms of general propositions rather than in terms of specific regulations.

6. The constitutional and policy arguments against campus bans on "racist speech" are cogently set forth in Nadine Strossen, *Regulating Racist Speech on Campus: A Modest Proposal*, 1990 DUKE L. J. 484.

7. Robert A. Sedler, *The First Amendment in Litigation: The "Law of the First Amendment,"* 48 WASH. & LEE L. REV. 457 (1990) [hereinafter *Law of the First Amendment*].

8. The scope of constitutionally permissible regulation of "racist speech" on the campus of a public university is so limited that any ban that would be able to withstand constitutional challenge would have no more than symbolic significance, and would not stop "racist speech" at all.

9. Although it may be "heresay"[sic] to say so, I do not think that the Supreme Court pays very much attention to "grand theories" posited by academic commentators or to their proposals for "sweeping changes" in constitutional interpretation. In fact, I do not think that it pays much attention to their views at all. *See* Robert A. Sedler, Book Review, 8 CONST. COMMENTARY 265, 268-69 (1991).

10. We are speaking, of course, only of bans imposed by public universities, where the Constitution comes into play. As to proposals to extend constitutional requirements to private universities, see Henry J. Hyde & George M. Fishman, *The Collegiate Speech Protection Act of 1991; A Response to the New Intolerance in the Academy*, 37 WAYNE L. REV. 1469 (1991).

11. 721 F. Supp. 852 (E.D.Mich. 1989).

12. 774 F. Supp. 1163 (E.D.Wis. 1991).

13. *See, e.g.*, Robert A. Sedler, *The Summary Contempt Power and the Constitution: The View from Without and Within*, 51 N.Y.U. L. REV. 34 (1976); Robert A. Sedler, *Metropolitan Desegregation in the Wake of* Milliken*: On Losing Big Battles and Winning Small Wars: The View Largely from Within*, 1975 WASH. U. L.Q. 535; Robert A. Sedler, *The Procedural Defense in Selective Service Prosecutions: The View from Without and Within*, 56 IOWA L. REV. 1121 (1971).

14. On the other hand, it would not appear that this kind of perspective is found in most of the academic writings on "racist speech." Most of the authors are quite "passionate" in their advocacy of restrictions on "racist speech."

15. There was also extensive discovery in *Doe*, which produced the "legislative history" leading up to the adoption of the policy and all of the cases in which complaints of a violation of the policy were filed. The complaints of violation and their disposition by the university officials administering the policy can serve as an "empirical study" of how a "racist speech" policy has operated in practice. I will discuss the results of this "empirical study" to some extent in this writing to demonstrate the impact that a ban on "racist speech" can have on the free expression of ideas on a university campus.

16. *See infra* notes 64-97 and accompanying text.

17. For some examples of these incidents, see Lawrence, *supra* note 3, at 431- 34.

18. One of the most enduring consequences of the long and tragic history of racial discrimination in this Nation is an enormous educational gap between blacks as a group and whites as a group. *See* Robert A. Sedler, *The Constitution, Racial Preference, and the Equal Participation Objective, in* SLAVERY AND ITS CONSEQUENCES: THE CONSTITUTION, EQUALITY AND RACE 123, 125 n.18 (Robert Goldwin & Art Kaufman eds., 1988) [hereinafter Sedler, *The Constitution*]. Because of this enormous "educational gap," the determination of admission to a university primarily on the basis of "comparative objective

academic indicators," such as grades and test scores, ordinarily will result in the admission of few, if any, blacks. *See* Robert A. Sedler, *Racial Preference, Reality and the Constitution:* Bakke v. Regents of the University of California, 17 SANTA CLARA L. REV. 329, 349-55 (1977). It is only by affirmatively taking race into account in the admission process and admitting black students with significantly lower "comparative objective academic indicators" than white students that the traditionally all-white universities can hope to enroll more than token numbers of black students. The same educational gap exists for hispanic students, and the same need for "affirmative action" applies to them.

19. *See* Bowers v. Hardwick, 478 U.S. 186 (1986).

20. For a summary of the different categories of harm caused by "racist speech," see Robert C. Post, *Racist Speech, Democracy, and the First Amendment*, 32 WM. & MARY L. REV. 267, 271-77 (1991).

21. Matsuda, *supra* note 4, at 2336.

22. *Id.* at 2332.

23. *Id.*

24. Richard Delgado, *Words That Wound: A Tort Action for Racial Insults, Epithets and Name-Calling*, 17 HARV. C.R.-C.L. L. REV. 133, 173-74.

25. *Id.* at 136-37.

26. *See* Post, *supra* note 20, at 275.

27. *Id.* at 275-77.

28. In the late 1960's and early 1970's, while on the law faculty of the University of Kentucky, I was much involved with the "New Left," as I defended young men in draft resistance cases and students and others engaged in anti-war protest activity. In reviewing THOMAS I. EMERSON, THE SYSTEM OF FREEDOM OF EXPRESSION (1970), I drew on that involvement to suggest that the "New Left," like the "Establishment" then in power, would not hesitate to suppress ideas with which it disagreed:

> While the present social-economic-political system has brought to power persons whose values are likely to be wealth-oriented and essentially conservative, I do not think that the attitude toward dissent and social change would necessarily be different if a "peaceful revolution" were to take place and the reins of power were transferred to those whose values are socialistic and radical. . . .In short, if the dissent and social change objective is to be protected, it is necessary to take account of the attitudes toward dissent and social change on the part of those administering the legal system, and those attitudes cannot be expected to be favorable no matter what the social-economic-political complexion of the society may be. While my "input" in this regard comes from observing the system as administered by the "Establishment right," I am willing to assume—and believe I must if my goal is to maximize the freedom to dissent and work for social change—that the same problem will exist if the system is administered by an "Establishment left."

Robert A. Sedler, *The First Amendment in Theory and Practice*, 80 YALE L. J. 1070, 1082 (1971) (reviewing THOMAS I. EMERSON, THE SYSTEM OF FREEDOM OF EXPRESSION (1970)).

And in regard to the "younger" "New Left" people, who are well-represented among university faculty members and administrators today, I made the following observation:

> My own discussions with younger "New Left" people—and I should add that politically I consider myself a part of the "New Left"—about freedom of expression have caused me some dismay, particularly when they make arguments such a "certain kinds of expression (support of the Vietnam War)

> are so immoral that they cannot be tolerated," and "repression by definition exists only in a capitalistic system," so that the imprisoning of "counterrevolutionary" writers in the Soviet Union does not constitute repression.

Id. at 1082 n.54. The new officially-imposed secular orthodoxy on some university campuses today indicates just how prophetic these observations have turned out to be.

29. In the planning stage of the present article, I had intended to discuss in detail the substance of the University's racist speech policy and how it operated in practice. In the interim, however, there have been a number of other discussions of this matter, *see, e.g.*, Joseph D. Grano, *Free Speech v. the University of Michigan*, ACADEMIC QUESTIONS, Spring 1990, at 7; Peter Linzer, *White Liberal Looks at Racist Speech*, 65 ST. JOHN'S L. REV. 187, 194- 196, 211-14 (1991), including my own, Robert A. Sedler, Doe v. University of Michigan *and Campus Bans on "Racist Speech": The View from Within*, 37 WAYNE L. REV. 1325, 1331-36 (1991), so I will not belabor the present writing with another detailed discussion.

30. The "interpretive guide," was issued after concerns were expressed by the Board of Regents about the vagueness of the terms of the policy. A copy of the policy and the guide were sent by mail to all registered students in the University for the 1988-89 academic year.

31. 721 F.Supp. at 857-58.

32. Brief in Support of Plaintiff's Motion for Preliminary Injunction, at 16 (Doe v. University of Michigan, 721 F.Supp. 852 (E.D.Mich. 1989) (No. 89-CV-71683-DT)).

33. *See infra* note 99.

34. Affirmative Action Office, University of Mich., What Students Should Know About Discriminatory Harassment [hereinafter Guide] (booklet distributed to students concurrently with the University's promulgation of Policy).

35. *Id.* That ensuring conformity to the secular orthodoxy was at least one purpose of the Policy is further illustrated by the comments in the guide on classroom discussion. "*What about classroom discussion?* The University encourages open and vigorous intellectual discussion in the classroom. To reach this goal students must be free to participate in class discussion without feeling harassed or intimidated by others' comments." *Id.*

To say the least, these comments turn freedom of academic inquiry on its head. Freedom of speech and inquiry is restricted if the expression of certain ideas would be perceived as "harassing or injuring others." And students must refrain from making comments that could cause other students to feel "harassed or intimidated." Students must thus "learn the secular orthodoxy" so that they will not be accused of making "harassing or intimidating" comments.

Another example, directed against the expression of offensive ideas, was: "[y]ou comment in a derogatory way about a particular person or group's physical appearance or sexual orientation, or their cultural origins, or religious beliefs." *Id.* The number of viewpoints that would be prescribed under this example is simply staggering. As the plaintiff stated in his affidavit:

> Rather than encourage her maturing students to question each other's beliefs on such diverse and controversial issues such as the proper role of women in society, the merits of particular religions, or the moral propriety of homosexuality, the University has decided that it must protect its students from what it considers to be "unenlightened" ideas.

Affidavit of John Doe in Support of Plaintiff's Motion for Preliminary Injunction, at 8-9, *Doe* (No. 89-CV-71683-DT).

Still another example was: "[Y]ou display a confederate flag on the door of your room in the residence hall," *id.* notwithstanding that the expression of ideas by means of a display of a flag has been considered protected by the First Amendment ever since Stromberg v. California, 283 U.S. 359 (1931). Four other examples involved offensive jokes: "[You] tell jokes about gay men and lesbians;" "[y]ou laugh at and joke about someone in your class who stutters;" "[y]our student organization sponsors entertainment that includes a comedian who slurs Hispanics;" "[m]ale students leave pornographic pictures and jokes on the desk of a female graduate student." Affidavit of John Doe in support of Plaintiff's Motion for Preliminary Injunction, at 8-9, *Doe* (No. 89- CV-71683-DT). Offensive jokes and parody are fully protected by the First Amendment, regardless of their outrageousness or the real injury they may cause to a person's feelings. Hustler Magazine v. Falwell, 485 U.S. 46 (1988).

36. As we had requested, all the names of the complaining and offending students were deleted from the files. After sifting through the cases, and discarding the large number of obscene phone call complaints and most of the cases where no action was taken, we settled on 20 representative cases, and submitted them with a summary of each case and the complete file as an exhibit. *See* Plaintiff's Exhibit submitted in Support of Motion for Preliminary Injunction, *Doe* (No. 89-CV-71683-DT) [hereinafter Exhibit].

In UWM Post v. Board of Regents of the Univ. of Wis. Sys., 774 F. Supp. 1163 (E.D.Wis. 1991) where the court invalidated the University of Wisconsin's "racist speech" ban, the court discussed nine cases where students at various campuses in the University of Wisconsin System had been sanctioned under the ban. Except for the fact that these cases did not involve classroom discussion (classroom discussion was specifically exempted from the ban), the cases bear a striking similarity to the University of Michigan cases, and we will refer to some of them in the discussion following.

37. 721 F. Supp. at 865. This was in response to the university's argument that "the Policy did not apply to speech that is protected by the First Amendment," and its urging the court "to disregard the Guide as 'inacurrate' and look instead to 'the manner in which the Policy has been interpreted and applied by those charged with its enforcement.'" *Id.* at 864-65. As the district court went on to say:

> The manner in which these three complaints were handled demonstrated that the University considered serious comments made in the context of classroom discussion to be santionable under the Policy. . . .There is no evidence in the record that the Administrator ever declined to pursue a complaint through attempted mediation because the alleged harassing conduct was protected by the First Amendment. . . . The University could not seriously argue that the policy was never interpreted to reach protected conduct. It is clear that the policy was overbroad both on its face and as applied.

Id. at 866.

38. Exhibit, *supra* note 36, at 5-6.

39. *Id.* at 6.

40. This was the only case that went to a formal hearing. The hearing panel was to consist of four students and a tenured faculty member.

41. *Id.*

42. *Id.* The case is discussed at 721 F. Supp. at 865. The student was also found guilty of sexual harassment against particular women, a charge that was clearly supported by the evidence.

43. *Id.* at 7.

44. Exhibit, *supra* note 36, at 7. The case is discussed at 721 F.Supp. at 865.

The third case involved statements made by a white dental student at the orientation session of a preclinical dentistry class. The was widely regarded as one of the most difficult for second year dentistry students. In the orientation session, where the class was broken up into small groups, the student stated that "he had heard that minorities have a difficult time in the course and that he had heard that they were not treated fairly." Exhibit, *supra* note 36, at 5. The faculty member teaching the course, herself a minority person, filed a complaint on the ground that the comment was unfair and hurt her chances for tenure. The student was then counseled about the existence of the policy, and he agreed to write a letter apologizing for making the statement without adequately verifying the allegation, which he said he had heard from his roommate, a black former dentistry student. 721 F. Supp. at 865.

45. In another case where a complaint was filed, but no action was indicated in the file, presumably because the identity of the offending student or students was not known, the charge was that students had put up a poster announcing an "End of Art Fair" party, which used the word "fag" several times. Exhibit, *supra* note 36, at 2.

46. *Id.* at 4.

47. *Id.*

48. *Id.*

49. Exhibit, *supra* note 36, at 4. Another student sent a female student a computer message in which he described an apparently fictionalized case of date rape. The complaint only requested that the Administrator send the student the letter. The Administrator informed the student that his action was in violation of the policy and that "his message 'reflects an insensitive and dangerous attitude toward date rape, which is a serious and significant problem on this campus and in our society."' *Id.* at 7.

50. *Id.* at 3-4.

51. *Id.* at 4.

52. *Id.* at 4. Other cases of this nature where complaints were filed, but where no action was indicated in the file, presumably because the identity of the offending student or students was not known, included the following: (1) "[a] student distributed a flyer headed, '25 Good Reasons Why Beer is Better Than Women,"' which contained mostly sexual references, *id.* at 6; (2) a note was placed on the door of a female student's room saying "Q. How many men does it take to mop a floor? A. None, it's a woman's job," *id.* at 8; (3) "[a] student posted a "Myth of the Month" poster on a residence hall bulletin board [and] [t]he 'fact' in [it] was that, 'In certain situations, women ask for rape,"' *id.* at 8; (4) "[m]agazine pictures of nude women were posted over the stalls in the men's bathroom, *id.*

53. *See generally id.* at 1-9.

54. Two similar cases occurred under the operation of the University of Wisconsin's ban. In one a student at the University of Wisconsin-Eau Claire was engaged in an argument with a female student about statements she made in the University newspaper, and during the course of the ten minute argument, he called her a "fucking bitch" and a "fucking cunt." UMW Post v. Board of Regents of the Univ. of Wis. Sys., 774 F.Supp. 1163, 1167 (E.D.Wis. 1991). The offending student was placed on probation for a semester and was required to perform 20 hours of community service at a shelter for abused women. *Id.* In the other, a student at the University of Wisconsin-River Falls yelled at a female student in public, "you've got nice tits." *Id.* at 1168. The offending student was placed on probation for the remainder of his enrollment at the university and was required to apologize to the female student, to refrain from further contact with her and to obtain psychological counselling. *Id.*

55. Exhibit, *supra* note 36, at 1.

56. *Id.*

The "mirror image" of this case was presented in a case arising under the University of Wisconsin ban, where during an argument with a black female student, a white female student referred to her as a "fat-ass nigger." *UMW Post*, 774 F. Supp. at 1168. The offending student, who was already on probation, was required to write a letter of apology, to view a video on racism and write an essay on the video, and was also reassigned to another residence hall. *Id.*

In another case, a student who had called another student "Shakazulu," in addition to being placed on probation and being required to consult with an alcohol abuse counselor, was required to "plan a project in conjunction with the Center for Education and Cultural Advancement to help sensitize [himself] to the issues of diversity." *Id.* at 1167.

57. Exhibit, *supra* note 36, at 8.

58. Reply Brief in Support of Plaintiff's Motion for Preliminary Injunction, at 4-5 n.3, *Doe* (No. 89-CV-71683-DT).

59. *See supra* note 44.

60. *See. e.g.*, Lawrence, *supra* note 3, at 477-78 n.161; Smolla, *supra* note 4, at 208 ("the University failed to confine sufficiently its definition of covered speech").

61. This is demonstrated by the way in which the University of Wisconsin ban, which was more narrowly crafted than the University of Michigan ban, had been administered in practice. We have previously given some examples of that administration. A particularly egregious interference with the expression of ideas under the Wisconsin ban was the disciplining of a student for angrily saying to an Asian-American student: "Its people like you—that's the reason this country is screwed up," and that, "[w]hites are always getting screwed by minorities and some day the Whites will take over." UMW Post v. Board of Regents of the Univ. of Wis. Sys., 774 F. Supp. 1163, 1167 (E.D.Wis. 1991).

62. My thesis with respect to the "law of the First Amendment" is developed fully in *Law of the First Amendment, supra* note 7. In the present writing, I will reference that article frequently, but will try to avoid needless repetition.

63. *See, e.g.*, LAURENCE H. TRIBE, AMERICAN CONSTITUTIONAL LAW (2d ed. 1988). As Professor Tribe puts it: "the 'balance' between the values of freedom of expression and government's regulatory interest is struck on a case-by-case basis, guided by whatever unifying principles may be articulated." *Id.* at 792.

64. *See Law of the First Amendment, supra* note 7, at 460-61. In this regard, it may be noted that the Court's application of a general "balancing" approach over the years has resulted in some specific doctrines that reflect "balancing" considerations, such as the "clear and present danger" doctrine, the "commercial speech" doctrine, and the "symbolic speech" doctrine. These doctrines now control where applicable and make any further balancing in a particular case unnecessary.

65. See *id.* at 461, 481-83.

66. *Id.* at 466.

67. United States v. Eichman, 110 S.Ct. 2404 (1990); Texas v. Johnson, 491 U.S. 397 (1989).

68. *Eichman*, 110 S.Ct. at 2407; *Johnson*, 491 U.S. at 420.

69. *Eichman*, 110 S.Ct. at 2409; *Johnson*, 491 U.S. at 410-418. The dissenting Justices, by contrast, took the position that the defendant's flag burning in these cases did not involve the expression of ideas, and that it was the "use of this particular symbol and not the idea that he sought to convey by it" which was being prescribed. *Johnson*, 491 U.S. at 432. Thus, in their view, the laws did not implicate the principle of viewpoint neutrality. *Johnson*, 491 U.S. at 432-33, 438-39.

70. Boos v. Barry, 485 U.S. 312, 316 (1988).

71. *Id.*

72. Schacht v. United States, 398 U.S. 58, 62 (1970).

73. American Booksellers Ass'n v. Hudnut, 771 F.2d 323, 324 (7th Cir.1985), *aff'd mem.*, 475 U.S. 1001 (1986).

74. Id. As the Seventh Circuit stated:

> Under the ordinance graphic sexually explicit speech is "pornography" or not depending on the perspective the author adopts. Speech that "subordinates" women and also, for example, presents women as enjoying pain, humiliation, or rape, or even simply presents women in "positions of servility or submission or display" is forbidden, no matter how great the literary or political value of the work taken as a whole. Speech that portrays women in positions of equality is lawful, no

> matter how graphic the sexual content. This is thought control. It establishes an "approved" view of women, of how they may react to sexual encounters, of how the sexes may relate to each other. Those who espouse the approved view may use sexual images; those who do not, may not.

Id. at 328.

75. Under this aspect of the principle, the Court has invalidated a variety of laws distinguishing between categories of expression. See the discussion and review of cases in *Law of the First Amendment, supra* note 7, at 468-70.

The requirement of category neutrality is built into the doctrine applicable to governmental licensing of expression, in that the licensing criteria cannot distinguish between categories of expression. So, a "parade permit" law not only cannot distinguish between viewpoints, but also cannot distinguish between parades based on the subject matter of the parade. If a city allows an organization to sponsor a Thanksgiving Day parade, for example, it cannot refuse to allow another organization to have a rally protesting abortion.

The Court has recognized two limited exceptions to the requirement of category neutrality in governmental regulation, both involving the regulation of particular lower level speech. In order to deal with the secondary consequences resulting from the concentration of businesses purveying sexually explicit materials, a city can enact zoning regulations requiring such businesses to spread out. Young v. American Mini Theatres, Inc., 427 U.S. 50 (1976). And because commercial speech receives less constitutional protection than non-commercial speech, a billboard regulation does not violate the First Amendment when it exempts some billboards from the regulation, although it does violate the First Amendment when it exempts some non-commercial billboards from the regulation. Metromedia, Inc. v. San Diego, 453 U.S. 490 (1981).

76. Simon & Schuster, Inc. v. Members of N.Y. Crime Control Bd., 112 S.Ct. 501 (1991).

77. Recall that the question that divided the Court in the flag desecration cases was the application of the principle to the challenged restrictions in question. Where the terms of a flag desecration law expressly violate the principle of content neutrality, such as a law prohibiting "casting contempt" on the flag, the law clearly is unconstitutional. *See* Smith v. Goguen, 415 U.S. 566 (1974).

78. Police Dep't of Chicago v. Mosley, 408 U.S. 92, 96 (1972).

79. Texas v. Johnson, 491 U.S. 397, 414 (1989). In that case, the Court refused to recognize an exception to this principle "even where our flag has been involved." *Id.* The principle of protection of offensive speech even applies to commercial speech. Thus the government cannot prohibit product advertising, such as an advertisement for contraceptives, on the ground that such advertising would be offensive to many persons. Bolger v. Youngs Drug Prods. Corp., 463 U.S. 60 (1983).

80. Cohen v. California, 403 U.S. 15, 23 (1971) (public display of jacket with the message, "Fuck the Draft").

81. The concept of the "marketplace of ideas" was long ago expressed by Justice Holmes in Abrams v. United States, 250 U.S. 616, 630 (1919) (Holmes, J., dissenting):

> But when men have realized that time has upset many fighting faiths, they may come to believe even more than they believe the very foundations of their own conduct that the ultimate good desired is better reached by free trade in ideas—that the best test of truth is the power of the thought to get itself accepted in the competition of the market, and that truth is the only ground upon which their wishes safely can be carried out. That at any rate is the theory of our Constitution.

82. 385 U.S. 589, 603 (1967) (alteration in original) (quoting United States v. Associated Press, 52 F.Supp. 362, 372 (1943)). Similarly, as Chief Justice Warren

stated in Sweezy v. New Hampshire, 354 U.S. 234, 250 (1957) (plurality opinion):

> The essentiality of freedom in the community of American universities is almost self-evident. No one should underestimate the vital role in a democracy that is played by those who guide and train our youth. To impose any strait jacket upon the intellectual leaders in our colleges and universities would imperil the future of our Nation. . . .Teachers and students must always remain free to inquire, to study and to evaluate, to gain new maturity and understanding; otherwise our civilization will stagnate and die.

83. 408 U.S. 169 (1972).

84. The Court, citing *Keyishian*, observed that "[t]he college classroom with its surrounding environs is peculiarly the 'marketplace of ideas,' and we break no new constitutional ground in reaffirming this Nation's dedication to safeguarding academic freedom." *Id.* at 180-81.

85. *Id.* at 667-68.

86. Papish v. Board of Curators of Univ. of Mo., 410 U.S. 667 (1973). The university's justification that the expulsion was necessary to uphold its interest in maintaining "conventions of decency" on campus was summarily rejected, the Court observing that, "the mere dissemination of ideas—no matter how offensive to good taste—on a state university campus may not be shut off in the name alone of 'conventions of decency."' *Id.* at 670. As this discussion indicates, for this reason the expulsion also violated the principle of protection of offensive speech. And the university's attempt to justify its action as a reasonable time, place and manner limitation foundered on the principle of content neutrality, since the undisputed facts showed that the student was "expelled because of the disapproved *content* of the newspaper rather than the time, place or manner of its distribution." *Id.* at 670 (alteration in original).

87. See the discussion of the "chilling effect" concept in *Law of the First Amendment, supra* note 7, at 462-64.

88. Analytically, a law is overbroad when it includes within its terms constitutionally protected expression, and is vague when the terms are such that it could reasonably be construed to include within its prohibitions constitutionally protected expression. A law can be overbroad without being vague, such as a law prohibiting all peaceful picketing. Thornhill v. Alabama, 310 U.S. 88 (1940). Usually, however, overbreadth and vagueness merge, and the Court has stated that it has "traditionally viewed vagueness and overbreadth as logically related and similar doctrines." Kolender v. Lawson, 461 U.S. 352, 358 n.8 (1983). In practice, the challenge ordinarily is that the law on its face, is substantially vague and overbroad, in violation of the First Amendment.

89. *See* Robert A. Sedler, *The Assertion of Constitutional Jus Tertii: A Substantive Approach*, 70 CAL. L. REV. 1308, 1326-27 (1982).

90. As Justice White, who is no great fan of the void on its face doctrine, has stated, it is "strong medicine" and should be applied "sparingly and only as a last resort." Broadrick v. Oklahoma, 413 U.S. 601, 613 (1973).

91. *Id.*

92. An example is a law prohibiting the dissemination of child pornography, to which the void on its face doctrine was held inapplicable. New York v. Ferber, 458 U.S. 747 (1982). In cases where the law contains a severability clause and the severable part of the law could operate independently, the Court will not invalidate the law in its entirety, but will only strike down the "facially invalid" part of the law. *See, e.g.*, Brockett v. Spokane Arcades, Inc., 472 U.S. 491 (1985).

93. 482 U.S. 451 (1987).

94. *Id.* at 455. The ordinance was overbroad because it prohibited persons from criticizing and insulting police officers, which is constitutionally protected expression. The overbreadth here was real and substantial in relation to the law's plainly legiti-

mate sweep. *Id.* at 460-65. Other examples of regulations of expression found to be void on its face include regulations prohibiting: "opprobrious words or abusive language tending to cause a breach of the peace," Gooding v. Wilson, 405 U.S. 518, 519 (1972) (quoting GA. CODE ANN. s 26-6303), "[people to] assemble. . .on any of the sidewalks. . .and there conduct themselves in a manner annoying to persons passing by," Coates v. City of Cincinnati, 402 U.S. 611 (1971) (quoting CINCINNATI, OHIO, CODE OF ORDINANCES § 901-L6), and "wantonly to curse or revile or to use obscene or opprobrious language toward or with reference to any member of the city police while in the actual performance of his duty." Lewis v. New Orleans, 415 U.S. 430 (1974) (quoting NEW ORLEANS, LA., NEW ORLEANS ORDINANCE 828 M.C.S. § 49-7). In the *Lewis* case the Louisiana Supreme Court tried to "rewrite" the statute to limit it to constitutionally unprotected "fighting words," as defined in Chaplinsky v. New Hampshire, 315 U.S. 568 (1942), but the effort failed, since the language of the statute "plainly has a broader sweep than the constitutional definition of 'fighting words,'" 415 U.S. at 132, and so remained "susceptible of application to protected speech." *Id.* at 134. For an additional discussion of the void on its face doctrine see *Law of the First Amendment*, *supra* note 7, at 464-66.

* * *

178. 60 U.S.L.W. 4667 (U.S. June 22, 1992) (No. 90-7675).

179. ST. PAUL, MINN., LEGIS. CODE § 292.02 (1990). The case arose out of a prosecution against a group of teenagers who burned a crudely-made cross on the lawn of a black family that had moved into a previously all-white neighborhood. Instead of prosecuting them only for a trespass on the property of the black family—which would not, of course, have raised any First Amendment question—the city chose to prosecute them also under the ordinance, which would apply even if they had burned the cross on their own lawn.

180. *See supra* note 8 and accompanying text.

181. *In re* Welfare of R.A.V., 464 N.W.2d 507, 510 (Minn. 1991).

182. *R.A.V.*, 60 U.S.L.W. at 4677. In effect, the Minnesota Supreme Court was trying to invoke the "words which by their very utterance inflict injury" part of *Chaplinsky*, just as the University of Wisconsin did in the *UWM Post* case. As the district court found in that case and as I have contended, that part of *Chaplinsky* has never been followed by the Supreme Court. *See supra* notes 129-43 and accompanying text.

183. *R.A.V.*, 60 U.S.L.W. at 4677.

184. *Id.*

185. *See supra* notes 124-55 and accompanying text.

186. *R.A.V.*, 60 U.S.L.W. at 4671. The above discussion refers to a violation of the category aspect of the content neutrality principle. Justice Scalia also said that the ordinance violated the viewpoint neutrality aspect of the principle, since it actually discriminated on the basis of viewpoint, "fighting words" expressing a message of racial tolerance, for example, were not prohibited, while "fighting words" expressing a message of racial hatred were.

> One could hold up a sign saying, for example, that all "anti-Catholic bigots" are misbegotten; but not that all "papists" are, for that would insult and provoke violence "on the basis of religion." St. Paul has no such authority to license one side of a debate to fight freestyle, while requiring the other to follow Marquis of Queensbury Rules.

Id.

The four concurring Justices strongly disagreed with the majority's position on this issue, saying that the First Amendment permitted content distinctions with respect to unprotected speech, and that, using an equal protection rational basis analysis, the city could conclude that the prohibited kinds of "fighting words" were more harmful than other kinds of "fighting words." As Justice White put it:

> It is inconsistent to hold that the government may proscribe

> an entire category of speech because the content of that speech is evil [citing New York v. Ferber, 458 U.S. 747, 763-64 (1982) (child pornography)]; but that the government may not treat a subset of that category differently without violating the First Amendment; the content of the subset is by definition worthless and undeserving of constitutional protection. . . .The ordinance proscribes a subset of "fighting words," those that injure "on the basis of race, color, creed, religion or gender." This selective regulation reflects the City's judgment that harms based on race, color, creed, religion, or gender are more pressing public concerns than the harms caused by other fighting words. In light of our Nation's long and painful experience with discrimination, this determination is plainly reasonable.

Id. at 4674-75.

187. *See supra* note 144.

188. *See supra* note 180.

CHAPTER 6

THE SUPREME COURT ON HATE SPEECH:

*R.A.V. v. CITY OF ST. PAUL, MINNESOTA**

Justice SCALIA delivered the opinion of the Court.

In the predawn hours of June 21, 1990, petitioner and several other teenagers allegedly assembled a crudely made cross by taping together broken chair legs. They then allegedly burned the cross inside the fenced yard of a black family that lived across the street from the house where petitioner was staying. Although this conduct could have been punished under any of a number of laws,[1] one of the two provisions under which respondent city of St. Paul chose to charge petitioner (then a juvenile) was the St. Paul Bias-Motivated Crime Ordinance, St. Paul, Minn.Legis.Code § 292.02 (1990), which provides:

> "Whoever places on public or private property a symbol, object, appellation, characterization or graffiti, including, but not limited to, a burning cross or Nazi swastika, which one knows or has reasonable grounds to know arouses anger, alarm or resentment in others on the basis of race, color, creed, religion or gender commits disorderly conduct and shall be guilty of a misdemeanor."

Petitioner moved to dismiss this count on the ground that the St. Paul ordinance was substantially overbroad and impermissibly content based and therefore facially invalid under the First Amendment.[2] The trial court granted this motion, but the

*This opinion appears at __ U.S. __, 112 S. Ct. 2 (1992). Footnotes have been changed to endnotes and are numbered as in the original.

Minnesota Supreme Court reversed. That court rejected petitioner's overbreadth claim because, as construed in prior Minnesota cases, see, e.g., In re Welfare of S.L.J., 263 N.W.2d 412 (Minn.1978), the modifying phrase "arouses anger, alarm or resentment in others" limited the reach of the ordinance to conduct that amounts to "fighting words," i.e., "conduct that itself inflicts injury or tends to incite immediate violence ...," In re Welfare of R.A.V., 464 N.W.2d 507, 510 (Minn.1991) (citing Chaplinsky v. New Hampshire, 315 U.S. 568, 572, 62 S.Ct. 766, 769, 86 L.Ed. 1031 (1942)), and therefore the ordinance reached only expression "that the first amendment does not protect." 464 N.W.2d, at 511. The court also concluded that the ordinance was not impermissibly content based because, in its view, "the ordinance is a narrowly tailored means toward accomplishing the compelling governmental interest in protecting the community against bias motivated threats to public safety and order." Ibid. We granted certiorari. . .111 S.Ct. 2795, 115 L.Ed.2d 969 (1991).

I

In construing the St. Paul ordinance, we are bound by the construction given to it by the Minnesota court. Posadas de Puerto Rico Associates v. Tourism Co. of Puerto Rico, 478 U.S. 328, 339, 106 S.Ct. 2968, 2975-2976, 92 L.Ed.2d 266 (1986); New York v. Ferber, 458 U.S. 747, 769, n. 24, 102 S.Ct. 3348, 3361, n. 24, 73 L.Ed.2d 1113 (1982); Terminiello v. Chicago, 337 U.S. 1, 4, 69 S.Ct. 894, 895-896, 93 L.Ed. 1131 (1949). Accordingly, we accept the Minnesota Supreme Court's authoritative statement that the ordinance reaches only those expressions that constitute "fighting words" within the meaning of Chaplinsky. 464 N.W.2d, at 510-511. Petitioner and his amici urge us to modify the scope of the Chaplinsky formulation, thereby invalidating the ordinance as "substantially overbroad," Broadrick v. Oklahoma, 413 U.S. 601, 610, 93 S.Ct. 2908, 2914-2915, 37 L.Ed.2d 830 (1973). We find it unnecessary to consider this issue. Assuming, arguendo, that all of the expression reached by the ordinance is proscribable under the "fighting words" doctrine, we nonetheless conclude that the ordinance is facially unconstitutional in that it prohibits otherwise permitted speech solely on the basis of the subjects the speech addresses. [3]

The First Amendment generally prevents government from proscribing speech, see, e.g., Cantwell v. Connecticut, 310 U.S. 296, 309-311, 60 S.Ct. 900, 905-906, 84 L.Ed. 1213 (1940), or even expressive conduct, see, e.g., Texas v. Johnson, 491 U.S. 397, 406, 109 S.Ct. 2533, 2540, 105 L.Ed.2d 342 (1989), because of disapproval of the ideas expressed. Content based regulations are presumptively invalid. Simon & Schuster, Inc. v. Members of N.Y. State Crime Victims Bd. . . .(KENNEDY, J., concurring in judgment); Consolidated Edison Co. of N.Y. v. Public Serv. Comm'n of N.Y., 447 U.S. 530, 536, 100 S.Ct. 2326, 2332-2333, 65 L.Ed.2d 319 (1980); Police Dept. of Chicago v. Mosley, 408 U.S. 92, 95, 92 S.Ct. 2286, 2289-2290, 33 L.Ed.2d 212 (1972). From 1791 to the present, however, our society, like other free but civilized societies, has permitted restrictions upon the content of speech in a few limited areas, which are "of such slight social value as a step to truth that any benefit that may be derived from them is clearly outweighed by the social interest in order and morality." Chaplinsky, supra, 315 U.S., at 572, 62 S.Ct. at 762. We have recognized that "the freedom of speech" referred to by the First Amendment does not include a freedom to disregard these traditional limitations. See, e.g., Roth v. United States, 354 U.S. 476, 77 S.Ct. 1304, 1 L.Ed.2d 1498 (1957) (obscenity); Beauharnais v. Illinois, 343 U.S. 250, 72 S.Ct. 725, 96 L.Ed. 919 (1952) (defamation); Chaplinsky v. New Hampshire, supra, ("fighting words"); see generally Simon & Schuster, supra. . . (KENNEDY, J., concurring in judgment). Our decisions since the 1960's have narrowed the scope of the traditional categorical exceptions for defamation, see New York Times Co. v. Sullivan, 376 U.S. 254, 84 S.Ct. 710, 11 L.Ed.2d 686 (1964); Gertz v. Robert Welch, Inc., 418 U.S. 323, 94 S.Ct. 2997, 41 L.Ed.2d 789 (1974); see generally Milkovich v. Lorain Journal Co., 497 U.S. 1, 13-17. . . and for obscenity, see Miller v. California, 413 U.S. 15, 93

S.Ct. 2607, 37 L.Ed.2d 419 (1973), but a limited categorical approach has remained an important part of our First Amendment jurisprudence.

We have sometimes said that these categories of expression are "not within the area of constitutionally protected speech," Roth, supra, 354 U.S., at 483, 77 S.Ct., at 1308; Beauharnais, supra, 343 U.S., at 266, 72 S.Ct., at 735; Chaplinsky, supra, 315 U.S., at 571-572, 62 S.Ct., at 768 769; or that the "protection of the First Amendment does not extend" to them, Bose Corp. v. Consumers Union of United States, Inc., 466 U.S. 485, 504, 104 S.Ct. 1949, 1961, 80 L.Ed.2d 502 (1984); Sable Communications of Cal., Inc. v. FCC, 492 U.S. 115, 124, 109 S.Ct. 2829, 2835, 106 L.Ed.2d 93 (1989). Such statements must be taken in context, however, and are no more literally true than is the occasionally repeated shorthand characterizing obscenity "as not being speech at all," Sunstein, Pornography and the First Amendment, 1986 Duke L.J. 589, 615, n. 146. What they mean is that these areas of speech can, consistently with the First Amendment, be regulated because of their constitutionally proscribable content (obscenity, defamation, etc.) not that they are categories of speech entirely invisible to the Constitution, so that they may be made the vehicles for content discrimination unrelated to their distinctively proscribable content. Thus, the government may proscribe libel; but it may not make the further content discrimination of proscribing only libel critical of the government. We recently acknowledged this distinction in Ferber, 458 U.S., at 763, 102 S.Ct., at 3357-3358, where, in upholding New York's child pornography law, we expressly recognized that there was no "question here of censoring a particular literary theme. . . ." See also id., at 775, 102 S.Ct., at 3364 (O'CONNOR, J., concurring) ("As drafted, New York's statute does not attempt to suppress the communication of particular ideas").

Our cases surely do not establish the proposition that the First Amendment imposes no obstacle whatsoever to regulation of particular instances of such proscribable expression, so that the government "may regulate [them] freely," post, at 2552 (WHITE, J., concurring in judgment). That would mean that a city council could enact an ordinance prohibiting only those legally obscene works that contain criticism of the city government or, indeed, that do not include endorsement of the city government. Such a simplistic, all or nothing at all approach to First Amendment protection is at odds with common sense and with our jurisprudence as well. [4] It is not true that "fighting words" have at most a "de minimis" expressive content, ibid., or that their content is in all respects "worthless and undeserving of constitutional protection," post, at 2553; sometimes they are quite expressive indeed. We have not said that they constitute "no part of the expression of ideas," but only that they constitute "no essential part of any exposition of ideas." Chaplinsky, 315 U.S., at 572, 62 S.Ct., at 769 (emphasis added).

The proposition that a particular instance of speech can be proscribable on the basis of one feature (e.g., obscenity) but not on the basis of another (e.g., opposition to the city government) is commonplace, and has found application in many contexts. We have long held, for example, that nonverbal expressive activity can be banned because of the action it entails, but not because of the ideas it expresses so that burning a flag in violation of an ordinance against outdoor fires could be punishable, whereas burning a flag in violation of an ordinance against dishonoring the flag is not. See Johnson, 491 U.S., at 406-407, 109 S.Ct., at 2540-2541. See also Barnes v. Glen Theatre, Inc. . . .111 S.Ct. 2456, 2460-2461, 115 L.Ed.2d 504 (1991) (plurality); id. . . .111 S.Ct., at 2465 2466 (SCALIA, J., concurring in judgment); id. . . .111 S.Ct., at 2468-2469 (SOUTER, J., concurring in judgment); United States v. O'Brien, 391 U.S. 367, 376-377, 88 S.Ct. 1673, 1678-1679, 20 L.Ed.2d 672 (1968). Similarly, we have upheld reasonable "time, place, or manner" restrictions, but only if they are "justified without reference to the content of the regulated speech." Ward v. Rock Against Racism, 491 U.S. 781, 791, 109 S.Ct. 2746, 2753-2754, 105 L.Ed.2d 661

(1989) (internal quotation marks omitted); see also Clark v. Community for Creative Non Violence, 468 U.S. 288, 298, 104 S.Ct. 3065, 3071, 82 L.Ed.2d 221 (1984) (noting that the O'Brien test differs little from the standard applied to time, place, or manner restrictions). And just as the power to proscribe particular speech on the basis of a noncontent element (e.g., noise) does not entail the power to proscribe the same speech on the basis of a content element; so also, the power to proscribe it on the basis of one content element (e.g., obscenity) does not entail the power to proscribe it on the basis of other content elements.

In other words, the exclusion of "fighting words" from the scope of the First Amendment simply means that, for purposes of that Amendment, the unprotected features of the words are, despite their verbal character, essentially a "nonspeech" element of communication. Fighting words are thus analogous to a noisy sound truck: Each is, as Justice Frankfurter recognized, a "mode of speech," Niemotko v. Maryland, 340 U.S. 268, 282, 71 S.Ct. 325, 333, 95 L.Ed. 267 (1951) (Frankfurter, J., concurring in result); both can be used to convey an idea; but neither has, in and of itself, a claim upon the First Amendment. As with the sound truck, however, so also with fighting words: The government may not regulate use based on hostility—or favoritism—towards the underlying message expressed. Compare Frisby v. Schultz, 487 U.S. 474, 108 S.Ct. 2495, 101 L.Ed.2d 420 (1988) (upholding, against facial challenge, a content neutral ban on targeted residential picketing) with Carey v. Brown, 447 U.S. 455, 100 S.Ct. 2286, 65 L.Ed.2d 263 (1980) (invalidating a ban on residential picketing that exempted labor picketing). [5]

The concurrences describe us as setting forth a new First Amendment principle that prohibition of constitutionally proscribable speech cannot be "underinclusiv[e]," post, at 2553 (WHITE, J., concurring in judgment) a First Amendment "absolutism" whereby "within a particular 'proscribable' category of expression,. . .a government must either proscribe all speech or no speech at all," post, at 2562 (STEVENS, J., concurring in judgment). That easy target is of the concurrences' own invention. In our view, the First Amendment imposes not an "underinclusiveness" limitation but a "content discrimination" limitation upon a State's prohibition of proscribable speech. There is no problem whatever, for example, with a State's prohibiting obscenity (and other forms of proscribable expression) only in certain media or markets, for although that prohibition would be "underinclusive," it would not discriminate on the basis of content. See, e.g., Sable Communications, 492 U.S., at 124 126, 109 S.Ct., at 2835-2836 (upholding 47 U.S.C. § 223(b)(1) (1988), which prohibits obscene telephone communications).

Even the prohibition against content discrimination that we assert the First Amendment requires is not absolute. It applies differently in the context of proscribable speech than in the area of fully protected speech. The rationale of the general prohibition, after all, is that content discrimination "rais[es] the specter that the Government may effectively drive certain ideas or viewpoints from the marketplace," Simon & Schuster. . .112 S.Ct., at 508; Leathers v. Medlock, 499 U.S. . . .111 S.Ct. 1438, 1444, 113 L.Ed.2d 494 (1991); FCC v. League of Women Voters of California, 468 U.S. 364, 383-384, 104 S.Ct. 3106, 3119-3120, 82 L.Ed.2d 278 (1984); Consolidated Edison Co., 447 U.S., at 536, 100 S.Ct., at 2333; Police Dept. of Chicago v. Mosley, 408 U.S., at 95-98, 92 S.Ct., at 2289-2292. But content discrimination among various instances of a class of proscribable speech often does not pose this threat.

When the basis for the content discrimination consists entirely of the very reason the entire class of speech at issue is proscribable, no significant danger of idea or viewpoint discrimination exists. Such a reason, having been adjudged neutral enough to support exclusion of the entire class of speech from First Amendment protection, is also neutral enough to form the basis of distinction within the class. To illustrate: A State might choose to prohibit only that obscenity which is the most patently offensive in its prurience i.e., that which involves the most lascivious displays of sexual activity. But it may not prohibit, for example, only that obscenity which includes offensive political messages. See Kucharek v. Hanaway, 902 F.2d 513, 517 (CA7 1990), cert. denied. . .111 S.Ct. 713, 112 L.Ed.2d 702 (1991). And the Federal Government can criminalize only those threats of violence that are directed against the President, see 18 U.S.C. § 871—since the reasons why threats of violence are outside the First Amendment (protecting individuals from the fear of violence, from the disruption that fear engenders, and from the possibility that the threatened violence will occur) have special force when applied to the person of the President. See Watts v. United States, 394 U.S. 705, 707, 89 S.Ct. 1399, 1401, 22 L.Ed.2d 664 (1969) (upholding the facial validity of s 871 because of the "overwhelmin[g] interest in protecting the safety of [the] Chief Executive and in allowing him to perform his duties without interference from threats of physical violence"). But the Federal Government may not criminalize only those threats against the President that mention his policy on aid to inner cities. And to take a final example (one mentioned by Justice STEVENS, post, at 2563-2564), a State may choose to regulate price advertising in one industry but not in others, because the risk of fraud (one of the characteristics of commercial speech that justifies depriving it of full First Amendment protection, see Virginia Pharmacy Bd. v. Virginia Citizens Consumer Council, Inc., 425 U.S. 748, 771-772, 96 S.Ct. 1817, 1830-1831, 48 L.Ed.2d 346 (1976)) is in its view greater there. Cf. Morales v. Trans World Airlines, Inc. . . .112 S.Ct. 2031, 119 L.Ed.2d 157 (1992) (state regulation of airline advertising); Ohralik v. Ohio State Bar Assn., 436 U.S. 447, 98 S.Ct. 1912, 56 L.Ed.2d 444 (1978) (state regulation of lawyer advertising). But a State may not prohibit only that commercial advertising that depicts men in a demeaning fashion, see, e.g., L.A. Times, Aug. 8, 1989, section 4, p. 6, col. 1.

Another valid basis for according differential treatment to even a content defined subclass of proscribable speech is that the subclass happens to be associated with particular "secondary effects" of the speech, so that the regulation is "justified without reference to the content of the. . . speech," Renton v. Playtime Theatres, Inc., 475 U.S. 41, 48, 106 S.Ct. 925, 929, 89 L.Ed.2d 29 (1986) (quoting, with emphasis, Virginia Pharmacy Bd., supra, 425 U.S., at 771, 96 S.Ct., at 1830); see also Young v. American Mini Theatres, Inc., 427 U.S. 50, 71, n. 34, 96 S.Ct. 2440, 2453, n. 34, 49 L.Ed.2d 310 (1976) (plurality); id., at 80-82, 96 S.Ct., at 2457-2458 (Powell, J., concurring); Barnes. . .111 S.Ct., at 2469-2471 (SOUTER, J., concurring in judgment). A State could, for example, permit all obscene live performances except those involving minors. Moreover, since words can in some circumstances violate laws directed not against speech but against conduct (a law against treason, for example, is violated by telling the enemy the nation's defense secrets), a particular content based subcategory of a proscribable class of speech can be swept up incidentally within the reach of a statute directed at conduct rather than speech. See. . .111 S.Ct., at 2460 (plurality); id. . .111 S.Ct., at 2465-2466 (SCALIA, J., concurring in judgment); id. . .111 S.Ct., at 2468-2469 (SOUTER, J., concurring in judgment); FTC v. Superior Court Trial Lawyers Assn., 493 U.S. 411, 425-432, 110 S.Ct. 768, 776-780, 107 L.Ed.2d 851 (1990); O'Brien, 391 U.S., at 376-377, 88 S.Ct., at 1678-1679. Thus, for example, sexually derogatory "fighting words," among other words, may produce a violation of Title VII's general prohibition against sexual discrimination in employment practices, 42 U.S.C. § 2000e-2; 29 CFR § 1604.11 (1991). See also 18 U.S.C. § 242; 42 U.S.C. §§ 1981, 1982. Where the government does not target conduct on the basis of its expressive content, acts are not shielded from regulation merely because they express a discriminatory idea or philosophy.

These bases for distinction refute the proposition that

the selectivity of the restriction is "even arguably 'conditioned upon the sovereign's agreement with what a speaker may intend to say.'" Metromedia, Inc. v. San Diego, 453 U.S. 490, 555, 101 S.Ct. 2882, 2917, 69 L.Ed.2d 800 (1981) (STEVENS, J., dissenting in part) (citation omitted). There may be other such bases as well. Indeed, to validate such selectivity (where totally proscribable speech is at issue) it may not even be necessary to identify any particular "neutral" basis, so long as the nature of the content discrimination is such that there is no realistic possibility that official suppression of ideas is afoot. (We cannot think of any First Amendment interest that would stand in the way of a State's prohibiting only those obscene motion pictures with blue eyed actresses.) Save for that limitation, the regulation of "fighting words," like the regulation of noisy speech, may address some offensive instances and leave other, equally offensive, instancces alone. See Posadas de Puerto Rico, 478 U.S., at 342-343, 106 S.Ct., at 2977-2978.[6]

II

Applying these principles to the St. Paul ordinance, we conclude that, even as narrowly construed by the Minnesota Supreme Court, the ordinance is facially unconstitutional. Although the phrase in the ordinance, "arouses anger, alarm or resentment in others," has been limited by the Minnesota Supreme Court's construction to reach only those symbols or displays that amount to "fighting words," the remaining, unmodified terms make clear that the ordinance applies only to "fighting words" that insult, or provoke violence, "on the basis of race, color, creed, religion or gender." Displays containing abusive invective, no matter how vicious or severe, are permissible unless they are addressed to one of the specified disfavored topics. Those who wish to use "fighting words" in connection with other ideas—to express hostility, for example, on the basis of political affiliation, union membership, or homosexuality—are not covered. The First Amendment does not permit St. Paul to impose special prohibitions on those speakers who express views on disfavored subjects. See Simon & Schuster. . .Arkansas Writers' Project, Inc. v. Ragland, 481 U.S. 221, 229-230, 107 S.Ct. 1722, 1727-1728, 95 L.Ed.2d 209 (1987).

In its practical operation, moreover, the ordinance goes even beyond mere content discrimination, to actual viewpoint discrimination. Displays containing some words odious racial epithets, for example—would be prohibited to proponents of all views. But "fighting words" that do not themselves invoke race, color, creed, religion, or gender—aspersions upon a person's mother, for example—would seemingly be usable ad libitum in the placards of those arguing in favor of racial, color, etc. tolerance and equality, but could not be used by that speaker's opponents. One could hold up a sign saying, for example, that all "anti-Catholic bigots" are misbegotten; but not that all "papists" are, for that would insult and provoke violence "on the basis of religion." St. Paul has no such authority to license one side of a debate to fight freestyle, while requiring the other to follow Marquis of Queensbury Rules.

What we have here, it must be emphasized, is not a prohibition of fighting words that are directed at certain persons or groups (which would be facially valid if it met the requirements of the Equal Protection Clause); but rather, a prohibition of fighting words that contain (as the Minnesota Supreme Court repeatedly emphasized) messages of "bias motivated" hatred and in particular, as applied to this case, messages "based on virulent notions of racial supremacy." 464 N.W.2d, at 508, 511. One must wholeheartedly agree with the Minnesota Supreme Court that "[i]t is the responsibility, even the obligation, of diverse communities to confront such notions in whatever form they appear," ibid., but the manner of that confrontation cannot consist of selective limitations upon speech. St. Paul's brief asserts that a general "fighting words" law would not meet the city's needs because only a content specific measure can communicate to minority groups that the "group hatred" aspect of such speech "is not condoned by the majority." Brief for Respondent 25. The point of the First Amendment is that majority preferences must be expressed in some fashion other than silencing speech on the basis of its content.

Despite the fact that the Minnesota Supreme Court and St. Paul acknowledge that the ordinance is directed at expression of group hatred, Justice STEVENS suggests that this "fundamentally misreads" the ordinance. Post, at 2570. It is directed, he claims, not to speech of a particular content, but to particular "injur[ies]" that are "qualitatively different" from other injuries. Post, at 2565. This is word play. What makes the anger, fear, sense of dishonor, etc. produced by violation of this ordinance distinct from the anger, fear, sense of dishonor, etc. produced by other fighting words is nothing other than the fact that it is caused by a distinctive idea, conveyed by a distinctive message. The First Amendment cannot bc cvaded that easily. It is obvious that the symbols which will arouse "anger, alarm or resentment in others on the basis of race, color, creed, religion or gender" are those symbols that communicate a message of hostility based on one of these characteristics. St. Paul concedes in its brief that the ordinance applies only to "racial, religious, or gender specific symbols" such as "a burning cross, Nazi swastika or other instrumentality of like import." Brief for Respondent 8. Indeed, St. Paul argued in the Juvenile Court that "[t]he burning of a cross does express a message and it is, in fact, the content of that message which the St. Paul Ordinance attempts to legislate." Memorandum from the Ramsey County Attorney to the Honorable Charles A. Flinn, Jr., dated July 13, 1990, in In re Welfare of R.A.V., No. 89-D-1231 (Ramsey Cty. Juvenile Ct.), p. 1, reprinted in App. to Brief for Petitioner C-1.

The content based discrimination reflected in the St. Paul ordinance comes within neither any of the specific exceptions to the First Amendment prohibition we discussed earlier, nor within a more general exception for content discrimination that does not threaten censorship of ideas. It assuredly does not fall within the exception for content discrimination based on the very reasons why the particular class of speech at issue (here, fighting words) is proscribable. As explained earlier, see supra, at 2545, the reason why fighting words are categorically excluded from the protection of the First Amendment is not that their content communicates any particular idea, but that their content embodies a particularly intolerable (and socially unnecessary) mode of expressing whatever idea the speaker wishes to convey. St. Paul has not singled out an especially offensive mode of expression—it has not, for example, selected for prohibition only those fighting words that communicate ideas in a threatening (as opposed to a merely obnoxious) manner. Rather, it has proscribed fighting words of whatever manner that communicate messages of racial, gender, or religious intolerance. Selectivity of this sort creates the possibility that the city is seeking to handicap the expression of particular ideas. That possibility would alone be enough to render the ordinance presumptively invalid, but St. Paul's comments and concessions in this case elevate the possibility to a certainty.

St. Paul argues that the ordinance comes within another of the specific exceptions we mentioned, the one that allows content discrimination aimed only at the "secondary effects" of the speech, see Renton v. Playtime Theatres, Inc., 475 U.S. 41, 106 S.Ct. 925, 89 L.Ed.2d 29 (1986). According to St. Paul, the ordinance is intended, "not to impact on [sic] the right of free expression of the accused," but rather to "protect against the victimization of a person or persons who are particularly vulnerable because of their membership in a group that historically has been discriminated against." Brief for Respondent 28. Even assuming that an ordinance that completely proscribes, rather than merely regulates, a specified category of speech can ever be considered to be directed only to the secondary effects of such speech, it is clear that the St. Paul ordinance is not directed to secondary effects within the meaning of Renton. As we said in Boos v. Barry, 485 U.S. 312, 108 S.Ct.

1157, 99 L.Ed.2d 333 (1988), "[l]isteners' reactions to speech are not the type of 'secondary effects' we referred to in Renton." Id., at 321, 108 S.Ct., at 1163-1164. "The emotive impact of speech on its audience is not a 'secondary effect.'" Ibid. See also id., at 334, 108 S.Ct., at 1170-1171. (opinion of Brennan, J.). [7]

It hardly needs discussion that the ordinance does not fall within some more general exception permitting all selectivity that for any reason is beyond the suspicion of official suppression of ideas. The statements of St. Paul in this very case afford ample basis for, if not full confirmation of, that suspicion.

Finally, St. Paul and its amici defend the conclusion of the Minnesota Supreme Court that, even if the ordinance regulates expression based on hostility towards its protected ideological content, this discrimination is nonetheless justified because it is narrowly tailored to serve compelling state interests. Specifically, they assert that the ordinance helps to ensure the basic human rights of members of groups that have historically been subjected to discrimination, including the right of such group members to live in peace where they wish. We do not doubt that these interests are compelling, and that the ordinance can be said to promote them. But the "danger of censorship" presented by a facially content based statute, Leathers v. Medlock. . .111 S.Ct. 1438, 1444, 113 L.Ed.2d 494 (1991), requires that that weapon be employed only where it is "necessary to serve the asserted [compelling] interest," Burson v. Freeman. . .112 S.Ct. 1846, 1852, 119 L.Ed.2d 5 (1992) (plurality) (emphasis added); Perry Education Assn. v. Perry Local Educators' Assn., 460 U.S. 37, 45, 103 S.Ct. 948, 954-955, 74 L.Ed.2d 794 (1983). The existence of adequate content neutral alternatives thus "undercut[s] significantly" any defense of such a statute, Boos v. Barry, supra, 485 U.S., at 329, 108 S.Ct., at 1168, casting considerable doubt on the government's protestations that "the asserted justification is in fact an accurate description of the purpose and effect of the law," Burson, supra. . .112 S.Ct., at 1859 (KENNEDY, J., concurring). See Boos, supra, 485 U.S., at 324-329, 108 S.Ct., at 1165 1168; cf. Minneapolis Star & Tribune Co. v. Minnesota Comm'r of Revenue, 460 U.S. 575, 586-587, 103 S.Ct. 1365, 1372-1373, 75 L.Ed.2d 295 (1983). The dispositive question in this case, therefore, is whether content discrimination is reasonably necessary to achieve St. Paul's compelling interests; it plainly is not. An ordinance not limited to the favored topics, for example, would have precisely the same beneficial effect. In fact the only interest distinctively served by the content limitation is that of displaying the city council's special hostility towards the particular biases thus singled out.[8] That is precisely what the First Amendment forbids. The politicians of St. Paul are entitled to express that hostility—but not through the means of imposing unique limitations upon speakers who (however benightedly) disagree.

Let there be no mistake about our belief that burning a cross in someone's front yard is reprehensible. But St. Paul has sufficient means at its disposal to prevent such behavior without adding the First Amendment to the fire.

The judgment of the Minnesota Supreme Court is reversed, and the case is remanded for proceedings not inconsistent with this opinion.

It is so ordered.**

* * *

**Opinions by Justices White, Blackmun, and Stevens, concurring in various aspects of the Court's judgment, are omitted.

Endnotes

1. The conduct might have violated Minnesota statutes carrying significant penalties. See, e.g., Minn.Stat. § 609.713(1) (1987) (providing for up to five years in prison for terroristic threats); § 609.563 (arson) (providing for up to five years and a $10,000 fine, depending on the value of the property intended to be damaged); § 609.595 (Supp.1992) (criminal damage to property) (providing for up to one year and a $3,000 fine, depending upon the extent of the damage to the property).

2. Petitioner has also been charged, in Count I of the delinquency petition, with a violation of Minn.Stat. § 609.2231(4) (Supp.1990) (racially motivated assaults). Petitioner did not challenge this count.

3. Contrary to Justice WHITE's suggestion, post, at 2550-2551, petitioner's claim is "fairly included" within the questions presented in the petition for certiorari, see this

Court's Rule 14.1(a). It was clear from the petition and from petitioner's other filings in this Court (and in the courts below) that his assertion that the St. Paul ordinance "violat [es] overbreadth. . .principles of the First Amendment," Pet. for Cert. i, was not just a technical "overbreadth" claim—i.e., a claim that the ordinance violated the rights of too many third parties—but included the contention that the ordinance was "overbroad" in the sense of restricting more speech than the Constitution permits, even in its application to him, because it is content based. An important component of petitioner's argument is, and has been all along, that narrowly construing the ordinance to cover only "fighting words" cannot cure this fundamental defect. Id., at 12, 14, 15-16. In his briefs in this Court, petitioner argued that a narrowing construction was ineffective because (1) its boundaries were vague, Brief for Petitioner 26, and because (2) denominating particular expression a "fighting word" because of the impact of its ideological content upon the audience is inconsistent with the First Amendment, Reply Brief for Petitioner 5; id., at 13 ("[The ordinance] is overbroad, viewpoint discriminatory and vague as 'narrowly construed' ") (emphasis added). At oral argument, counsel for Petitioner reiterated this second point: "It is. . .one of my positions, that in [punishing only some fighting words and not others], even though it is a subcategory, technically, of unprotected conduct, [the ordinance] still is picking out an opinion, a disfavored message, and making that clear through the State." Tr. of Oral Arg. 8. In resting our judgment upon this contention, we have not departed from our criteria of what is "fairly included" within the petition. See Arkansas Electric Cooperative Corp. v. Arkansas Pub. Serv. Comm'n, 461 U.S. 375, 382, n. 6, 103 S.Ct. 1905, 1911-1912, n. 6, 76 L.Ed.2d 1 (1983); Brown v. Socialist Workers '74 Campaign Comm., 459 U.S. 87, 94, n. 9, 103 S.Ct. 416, 421, n. 9, 74 L.Ed.2d 250 (1982); Eddings v. Oklahoma, 455 U.S. 104, 113, n. 9, 102 S.Ct. 869, 876, n. 9, 71 L.Ed.2d 1 (1982); see generally R. Stern, E. Gressman, & S. Shapiro, Supreme Court Practice 361 (6th ed. 1986).

4. Justice WHITE concedes that a city council cannot prohibit only those legally obscene works that contain criticism of the city government, post, at 2555, but asserts that to be the consequence, not of the First Amendment, but of the Equal Protection Clause. Such content based discrimination would not, he asserts, "be rationally related to a legitimate government interest," ibid. But of course the only reason that government interest is not a "legitimate" one is that it violates the First Amendment. This Court itself has occasionally fused the First Amendment into the Equal Protection Clause in this fashion, but at least with the acknowledgment (which Justice WHITE cannot afford to make) that the First Amendment underlies its analysis. See Police Dept. of Chicago v. Mosley, 408 U.S. 92, 95, 92 S.Ct. 2286, 2289-2290, 33 L.Ed.2d 212 (1972) (ordinance prohibiting only nonlabor picketing violated the Equal Protection Clause because there was no "appropriate governmental interest" supporting the distinction inasmuch as "the First Amendment means that government has no power to restrict expression because of its message, its ideas, its subject matter, or its content"); Carey v. Brown, 447 U.S. 455, 100 S.Ct. 2286, 65 L.Ed.2d 263 (1980). See generally Simon & Schuster, Inc. v. Members of N.Y. State Crime Victims Bd. . . .112 S.Ct. 501, 514, 116 L.Ed.2d 476 (1991) (KENNEDY, J., concurring in judgment). Justice STEVENS seeks to avoid the point by dismissing the notion of obscene anti-government speech as "fantastical," post, at 2562, apparently believing that any reference to politics prevents a finding of obscenity. Unfortunately for the purveyors of obscenity, that is obviously false. A shockingly hard core pornographic movie that contains a model sporting a political tattoo can be found, "taken as a whole [to] lac[k] serious literary, artistic, political, or scientific value," Miller v. California, 413 U.S. 15, 24, 93 S.Ct. 2607, 2614-2615, 37 L.Ed.2d 419 (1973) (emphasis added). Anyway, it is easy enough to come up with other illustrations of a content based restriction upon "unprotected speech" that is obviously invalid: the anti government libel illustration mentioned earlier, for one. See supra, at 2543. And of course the concept of racist fighting

words is, unfortunately, anything but a "highly speculative hypothetica[l]," post, at 2562.

5. Although Justice WHITE asserts that our analysis disregards "established principles of First Amendment law," post, at 2560, he cites not a single case (and we are aware of none) that even involved, much less considered and resolved, the issue of content discrimination through regulation of "unprotected" speech—though we plainly recognized that as an issue in Ferber. It is of course contrary to all traditions of our jurisprudence to consider the law on this point conclusively resolved by broad language in cases where the issue was not presented or even envisioned.

6. Justice STEVENS cites a string of opinions as supporting his assertion that "selective regulation of speech based on content" is not presumptively valid. Post, at 2563-2564. Analysis reveals, however, that they do not support it. To begin with, three of them did not command a majority of the Court, Young v. American Mini Theatres, Inc., 427 U.S. 50, 63-73, 96 S.Ct. 2440, 2448-2454, 49 L.Ed.2d 310 (1976) (plurality); FCC v. Pacifica Foundation, 438 U.S. 726, 744-748, 98 S.Ct. 3026, 3037-3040, 57 L.Ed.2d 1073 (1978) (plurality); Lehman v. City of Shaker Heights, 418 U.S. 298, 94 S.Ct. 2714, 41 L.Ed.2d 770 (1974) (plurality), and two others did not even discuss the First Amendment, Morales v. Trans World Airlines, Inc. . . .112 S.Ct. 2031, 119 L.Ed.2d 157 (1992); Jacob Siegel Co. v. FTC, 327 U.S. 608, 66 S.Ct. 758, 90 L.Ed. 888 (1946). In any event, all that their contents establish is what we readily concede: that presumptive invalidity does not mean invariable invalidity, leaving room for such exceptions as reasonable and viewpoint-neutral content-based discrimination in nonpublic forums, see Lehman, supra, 418 U.S., at 301-304, 94 S.Ct., at 2716-2718; see also Cornelius v. NAACP Legal Defense & Educational Fund, Inc., 473 U.S. 788, 806, 105 S.Ct. 3439, 3451, 87 L.Ed.2d 567 (1985), or with respect to certain speech by government employees, see Broadrick v. Oklahoma, 413 U.S. 601, 93 S.Ct. 2908, 37 L.Ed.2d 830 (1973); see also CSC v. Letter Carriers, 413 U.S. 548, 564-567, 93 S.Ct. 2880, 2889-2891, 37 L.Ed.2d 796 (1973).

7. St. Paul has not argued in this case that the ordinance merely regulates that subclass of fighting words which is most likely to provoke a violent response. But even if one assumes (as appears unlikely) that the categories selected may be so described, that would not justify selective regulation under "secondary effects" theory. The only reason why such expressive conduct would be especially correlated with violence is that it conveys a particularly odious message; because the "chain of causation" thus necessarily "run[s] through the persuasive effect of the expressive component" of the conduct, Barnes v. Glen Theatre. . .111 S.Ct. 2456, 2470-2471, 115 L.Ed2d 504 (1991) (SOUTER, J. concurring in judgment), it is clear that the St. Paul ordinance regulates on the basis of the "primary" effect of the speech—i.e., its persuasive (or repellant) force.

8. A plurality of the Court reached a different conclusion with regard to the Tennessee anti-electioneering statute considered earlier this Term in Burson v. Freeman . . .112 S.Ct. 1846, 119 L.Ed.2d 5 (1992). In light of the "logical connection" between electioneering and the State's compelling interest in preventing voter intimidation and election-fraud—an inherent connection borne out by a "long history" and a "widespread and time-tested consensus". . .112 S.Ct., at 1855-1858—the plurality concluded that it was faced with one of those "rare case[s]" in which the use of a facially content-based restriction was justified by interests unrelated to the suppression of ideas, id. . . .112 S.Ct., at 1857-1858;. . .112 S.Ct., at 1859 (KENNEDY, J., concurring). Justice WHITE and Justice STEVENS are therefore quite mistaken when they seek to convert the Burson plurality's passing comment that "[t]he First Amendment does not require States to regulate for problems that do not exist". . .112 S.Ct., at 1856, into endorsement of the revolutionary proposition that the suppression of particular ideas can be justified when only those ideas have been a source of trouble in the past. Post, at 2555 (WHITE, J.); post, at 2570 (STEVENS, J.).

CHAPTER 7

THE THEORY OF TRULY FREE SPEECH

"Free Speech Theory and Hateful Words"*

*Nicholas Wolfson***

INTRODUCTION

A considerable body of persuasive legal literature is supporting the thesis that racist or sexist hate speech should receive reduced or even no protection under the First Amendment.[1] The arguments are coherent and powerful. The empirical premises for the new First Amendment theory are first, the scientific falsity of explicit or implicit racial or sexual stereotyping, and second, the harm such speech does to the victim. The person who is called "kike," "nigger," or "fag," suffers emotional humiliation and personal loss of dignity.[2] The victim feels threatened, humiliated, and diminished. He or she may suffer temporary or permanent psychological harm. Further, such expression tears the weave of the community in which the speech is made, breaks down civil discourse and incites weak-minded onlookers to similar thoughts and words. Finally, the ideational content of the utterance is minimal.

The traditional civil-libertarian response is predictable.[3] The First Amendment is designed to protect disgusting speech from the censorship of government. The offensiveness of the speech in question is never a reason for removing it from pro-

---

* This article appears at 60 *University of Cincinnati Law Review* 1 (1991). Footnotes have been changed to endnotes and are numbered as in the original. Reprinted with permission.

** Ellen Ash Peters Professor of Law, University of Connecticut.

tection of the First Amendment. There are the usual exceptions—e.g., fighting words,[4] obscenity,[5] defamation,[6] speech too closely "brigaded" with forbidden conduct[7]—but otherwise the government must be view-point neutral.

At this point, critics of the traditional discourse ask the cogent question, why should racist speech, which all enlightened men and women will admit is based upon false premises, be permitted? The factual assumptions underlying hate speech are to the effect that blacks or Jews or women are inferior, stupid, greedy, or inherently violent. Both critics and traditionalists in the civil liberties community agree that the assumptions are false. The bigotry expressed in such racist remarks is based on the kind of "facts" that are on a par with the assumption that the world is flat. Moreover, traditionalists and critics, I submit, agree that the hatred expressed by such speech serves no socially redeeming value.

Traditional defenders of the First Amendment make recourse to the amendment's purposes. A popular argument is that free exercise is essential to the felicitous pursuit of truth. Out of the clash of opposing ideas and opinions (some false) the truth will emerge.[8] Moreover, true ideas will be appreciated more fully only as a result of truth's clash with falsehood.[9] In addition, truth is difficult to identify, and perhaps the worst umpires or referees of truth are the oppressive arms of government which will always attempt to impose an orthodoxy consonant with the frequently corrupt interests of the bureaucracy.[10]

PRAGMATISM

Free speech principles depend upon a pragmatic belief in the nature of truth. As Posner puts it, "truth is what free inquiry—unforced, undistorted, and uninterrupted—would eventually discover about the objects of inquiry. Since the process of inquiry never ends, this implies that truth always lies beyond our horizon: it is there but we aren't."[11] The test of time is important; in a sense, truth is that consensus which develops over time. But even a widely held consensus may not hold indefinitely. New ideas and new developments can break it, as Einstein's discovery of relativity theory replaced the old Newtonian consensus. Ideas should be subjected to a Darwinian survival test mediated by vigorous free speech and inquiry which moves toward a consensus or a changed consensus, and also makes the consensus reached more acceptable.[12] In the same manner, a competitive free market economy produces over time better goods and services than a command economy.[13] Nevertheless, consensus is not always the test. Consider the fact that a majority of Americans believe in magic and astrology.[14]

The pragmatic approach is skeptical, but not completely so. That we now believe the earth is round, and one thousand years ago believed it was flat, does not mean the earth was then flat. Yet, the pragmatic because of its reference to the role of consensus in defining truth does tend to blur the distinction between fact and opinion.[15] As Posner stated, "truth" is a "process of belief formations that unfolds over time."[16]

The skepticism does not mean cynicism about the role of ideas and the clash of debate. The skepticism and pragmatism underlying the argument for free speech somewhat ironically also involves a deep faith in the worth and value of discussion, disagreement, and criticism. It is not a skepticism that entails a kind of nihilism about the impact of ideas. Although truth is always out there somewhere, beyond our ken, and absolutism is suspect, there is still an eighteenth century enlightenment belief in the wonder and majesty of argument and disputation and the quest for truth. We can do well to quote Richard Posner:

> Pragmatist skepticism about "truth" might, for example, be thought to undermine the nation's commitment to free speech. If there is no truth "out there," how can free speech be defended by reference to its efficacy in bringing us nearer to truth? Actually this is not such a difficult question. If there is no truth out there, this should make us particularly wary of people who claim to have found the truth and who argue that fur-

> ther inquiry would be futile. . . .There is knowledge if not ultimate truth, and a fallibilist theory of knowledge emphasizes, as preconditions to the growth of. . .knowledge, the continual testing and retesting of accepted "truths". . . .[17]

The pragmatic view is not limited to purely rational, logical debate. As developed below, it recognizes that the search for elusive truth utilizes rhetoric, metaphor and imagery. The human mentality influences and is influenced by poetry, emotion, symbols, action, and passion. Hence, the pragmatic view implies that protected speech includes more than the syllogism, abstract reason, and the kinds of language found in, for example, law review articles.[18]

The new critics likely will respond in the following manner: Although truth is notoriously difficult to define or find, we all agree on some things. The earth is round. The earth revolves around the sun. Genocide is evil. Not even the most ardent civil libertarian is an absolute skeptic about the search for truth. She or he will agree that hateful speech about blacks, women, Jews, and hispanics is despicable. Those old friends of the First Amendment will no doubt fear that hateful speech may destroy the sense of community that binds our society together. They will concur that the factual assumptions underlying hateful epithets—Jews plan to control the world, blacks are inferior, women are subordinate to men—are false. I expect that civil-libertarians will not concede the remotest possibility that they are in error here.

Therefore, since the truth is clear in this regard, and the false words may do great damage, why protect false hateful speech?[19] We do not permit a school curriculum devoted to the flat earth science of one thousand years ago. It follows that racist and sexist speech should be lawfully prohibited despite the First Amendment.

It is at this point that civil libertarians introduce slippery slope arguments.[20] The arguments are of a familiar type. The danger is that a policy that permits censorship based on content cannot be limited to the particular category chilled. The temptation of court and executive branch will be to broaden the breach in the doctrine of content neutrality. Censorship of racist speech may some day lead to the chilling of socialists or libertarians or Marxists or critical legal studies scholars.

The response is usually that the courts and legislatures can easily distinguish between the unique category of sexist or racist speech and all other kinds of speech. Distinguished commentators have also argued that sexist and racist speech is uniquely condemnable. They make a communitarian argument. The purpose of the government is to preserve a coherent and acceptable set of values designed to bind citizens together in a condition of dignity and civil respect. This purpose is not some kind of external, superficial operation of government. Rather government should reinforce the deep seated commonalities based on human worth that are natural to the American society. Racist speech, unlike all other categories of speech, is foreign and alien to the inherent purposes of the American society. Hence, loathsome speech should not be protected by the First Amendment.[21]

The new theorists are engaged in an intellectual pursuit that entails more than a slippery slope risk. Here, slippery slope is defined, for my purposes, as the danger that courts will take one breach in content neutrality, and in the interests of uniformity and coherence, develop other breaches. As an example of slippery slope reasoning, a court may argue that just as racist speech is emotionally inflammatory and is based on false premises about human nature, and therefore should be lawfully censored, so too should the government censor comic books that are emotionally inflammatory and promote violence in the reader.

This slippery slope is a serious risk. It is one that should cause us concern with the new theorists positions. But there is something even more ominous in their thinking, albeit related to the slippery slope argument. They have accepted as a fundamental proposition that there are certain orthodoxies that a society and a government must accept and enforce in order to maintain their worth and dignity. It is a proposition that was fundamental to western society before the successful growth of First Amendment principles. Indeed, it is the order of mind that free speech advocacy was designed to overthrow. One hundred years ago and earlier, it was commonplace to assume that society must preserve certain beliefs in order to maintain the worthy community.[22] For example, atheism should be chilled (in earlier centuries by execution) since belief in God was a basis for the good society. Atheism was regarded as fundamentally alien to the societal consensus and as a movement that would rend the fabric of society. There are many people today in our society who, while they may not recommend execution of atheists, nevertheless regard atheism as irrefutably evil and metaphysically contrary to the good society. The First Amendment restrains their ardor for censorship. The free speech principle inculcates in them a belief that expressions of ultimate falsehood and depravity must not be censored.

As this example suggests, there is nothing (except a strong version of the First Amendment) to contain the philosophy that x and only x category of speech is false and dangerous, hence must be censored. No so-called neutral truth-seeking principle will voluntarily, without government compulsion, convince every faction, group, and party not to advance their deeply held convictions that y and z categories are loathsome, and must be suppressed, once political factions succeed in imposing their views on x category of speech.

The new theorists have adopted in modern dress the old societal theories that the free speech movements of the past centuries were designed to defeat. As Leonard Levy wrote: "Neither freedom of speech nor freedom of press could become a civil liberty until people believed that the truth of their opinions, especially their religious opinions, was relative rather than absolute. . . ."[23] It is clear, then, why the new theorists reject the relativist skepticism of the traditional civil libertarians.

The move toward acceptance of absolutes signals the eventual end of First Amendment liberalism. There can be no limit of absolutes to the category of racist or sexist speech. Once we admit to a breach of content or viewpoint neutrality, because racist speech is false and dangerous, we have to fight that battle on every other front. In every dispute, we can expect the argument that the speech under threat of censorship is false, will lead to harm, and hence should be banned.

Indeed, it was just this kind of argument that was used in the fifties to attempt to ban communist speech.[24] The supporters of censorship asserted that communism was a deeply flawed doctrine that would lead to totalitarian evil. Now, even old apologists for communism admit that the censors were on target in their assessment of the falsity and danger of communist doctrine.

Civil libertarians of the day argued that suppression would lead by various slippery slope passages to censorship of good or noble ideas. Years earlier, Holmes had argued that, "Only the emergency that makes it immediately dangerous to leave the correction of evil counsels to time warrants making any exception to the sweeping command [of the First Amendment]."[25]

If we ban racist speech, how then do we not move inexorably to the suppression of other unpopular thought such as communist speech. The potential evil of communist propaganda is enormous. We have witnessed seventy years of failure, mass killings and attempted genocide by communist regimes, and the collapse of the communist regimes in the Soviet Union and Eastern Europe. Surely, the perversity and evil of totalitarian communist thought is apparent to all of us, as is the evil of racist speech. There is no principled method of separating out the two for First Amendment purposes, once we accept the premise that demonstrated falsity is the test for diminished First Amendment protection.

The new critics of the First Amendment condemn the relativism and skepticism of traditional liberalism. They are on target in this attack, because they have correctly identified the heart of First Amendment theory. They strike a receptive chord among many, because today in America, as was true when John Stuart Mill lived, we live in an age "destitute of faith, but terrified at skepticism. . . ."[26]

Absolutism in any form is fundamentally contrary to First Amendment doctrine. If certain truths are correct beyond peradventure, then what is the point of free debate, and the marketplace of ideas, in a marketplace where truth and value has been correctly determined. Mill identified the position of the new critics when he observed over one hundred years ago:

> Strange that they should imagine that they are not assuming infallibility, when they acknowledge that there should be free discussion on all subjects which can possibly be *doubtful*, but think that some particular principle or doctrine should be forbidden to be questioned because it is *so certain*, that is, because *they are certain* that it is certain."[27]

The new critics are generally men and women on the left wing of the political spectrum. But their assault on First Amendment skepticism is shared by conservatives. Willmore Kendall is a good example of the latter thinking. He has argued that a strong version of the First Amendment assumes that "society is. . .a *debating* club. . . ."[28] Kendall disagrees, asserting that "[s]ocieties. . .cherish a whole series of goods—among others. . .the *living* of the truth they believe themselves to embody already. . . ."[29] He also claims that a First Amendment driven society will "descend. . .into progressive breakdown of those common premises upon which alone a society can conduct its affairs by discussion. . . ."[30]

A far greater figure than either Kendall or the new critics argued long ago for the need to exercise censorship in order to achieve a good and just society. Plato, in *The Republic*, had no difficulty in reaching a firm belief in what was objectively good and just and true.[31] Hence he emphasized the values of censorship in the areas of nurture and education, in order to assure such goals. As he put it: "Then the first thing will be to establish a censorship of the writers of fiction, and. . .reject the bad. . . ."[32] One of the standards will be the elimination of any tales that create a fear of death, because inculcation of the virtues of bravery in battle is important for the guardians of the just society.[33] Further, literature that praises laughter must be eliminated because the guardians must be sober and solemn.[34] Third, lying will be prohibited, except by the rulers who shall have that privilege.[35] Also, literature will be monitored to assure that the youth will be temperate, obedient to commanders, and controlled in "sensual pleasures."[36] In addition, no tale that ascribes evil or vicious acts by the gods will be permitted.[37]

In a famous passage, Plato recommends the expulsion of playwrights from the ideal state, since, as he curiously puts it, actors frequently play the role of evil or weak men and women, and this is somehow a debasing practice.[38] Next he addresses music, and demands that all but a kind of stirring and martial melody line be expunged from the permitted kinds of melody.[39] All of this and more will create a just, virtuous, and courageous citizenry and ruling class, who will be in harmony with justice. One of the felicitous results, Plato observed, will be an indisposition to frequent the law courts or to become lawyers.[40]

Even where absolutes are accepted, there is a First Amendment fall back position. Mill argued that the truth cannot be understood unless debated.[41] The Jewish Talmud is an example (far older than Mill) of this position. The great scholar Rabbi Adin Steinsaltz has noted that the Talmud is "the only sacred book in all of world culture that permits and even encourages the student to question it."[42] As Edward Alexander has said, "The talmudic practice of preserving. . .rejected arguments. . .might in fact be the only stable foundation for a just reliance on the *victorious* doctrine. . . ."[43]

But in the hurly burly world of politics and power, the fall back position is weak once the society accepts the view that, for First Amendment purposes, certain thoughts and ideas are politically correct or incorrect. The burden, then, is on proponents of incorrect views to prove that they can continue to speak falsely. At best they will be relegated to a doctrine along the lines of First Amendment commercial speech doctrine. That body of jurisprudence holds that, although commercial speech gets some First Amendment protection, it is diluted. Since commercial speech is considered easily verifiable by the government, the Court permits the government to ban false speech or to monitor and correct misleading commercial speech.[44]

I have emphasized the skeptical underpinnings of First Amendment theory in the context of a free market for ideas and opinions.[45] That is, we are fundamentally skeptical about the ability of courts to separate out areas where truth is absolute, from areas where there is a fundamental inability to reach truth in some absolute sense. There are other reasons, apart from the rationale of debate as the surety of an open and free market in ideas, commonly advanced for the First Amendment. One purpose or goal is advancement of human autonomy or self-realization, whether of speaker or listener.[46] Free speech, liberally interpreted, permits the flowering of the human personality. Certainly there is substantial evidence that this is one of the commonly advanced purposes of a strong interpretation of the First Amendment. But it has its limits. I doubt that many would argue that racist and sexist speech advances human autonomy or worthy self-expression. I take it as given and true that such speech is degrading and false, and advances the most bestial elements of the human personality. Here again, the argument that can create a First Amendment wall around such loathsome speech, is the kind of skepticism discussed above.[47] That is, once we concede that certain kinds of self expression, and forms of human autonomy, are based on false and grotesque assumptions, and hence should be censored, there is no principle that can contain the search for self-expression that is worthy, and self-expression that is not. For example, the Roman Catholic Church views homosexuality as loathsome and sinful. It does not view the issue as debatable, and subject to reasonable difference. It is a matter of "God's law". Do we then ban speech advocating that life style? Once we admit that there are true orthodoxies on which courts can reach closure, such as, racist speech is false and harmful, and hence must be banned, the court will consider all other issues on which certain groups consider speech to be abominable. Executives will nominate judges, and legislatures will confirm, based on the nominees' notions of what is acceptable speech and what is not. Inevitably, the courts will begin to censor human self- expression and self-realization that is within a sphere of doubt and debate as to its truthfulness and worthiness, even though advocates deny that the sphere is doubtful.

Another reason for a strong version of the First Amendment is the contention that free speech is essential to the democratic process.[48] This expresses the fairly obvious concept that men and women, political parties, and interest groups must communicate and debate in order for the democratic process to proceed and flourish. But the cogent proposition may always be made that certain ideas and philosophies are repugnant to a worthy democratic polity. Racism and sexism, and the domination of minorities and women by others, may be mentioned as movements that, if successful, will create or maintain a society that is hateful and racist rather than democratic and free. But here again, we censor such speech at our peril because of the fallibility of the human intellect. There is, to repeat the argument made above, no principled method, once we accept the philosophy that the Court may censor speech which it regards as harmful to the democratic process, to contain the inevitable future attempts to censor all ideas and opinions which it fears will destroy the democratic process as it sees it at the given moment.

As indicated above, free speech has been justified as: first, a method to facilitate truth seeking; second, a means for assuring human autonomy and dignity; and third, a facilitator of the democratic process.[49] On analysis, human fallibility and the elusive nature of truth, underlie all three principles and their corollaries. Because we cannot be certain as to what opinions help or harm democracy, we should not censor that which we consider offensive to the democratic ideal. Because we cannot be certain as to what concepts advance or demean human autonomy, we permit vigorous debate. Needless to say, the same skepticism supports a free market in order to forward the pursuit of truth out there somewhere.

In summary, the new critics allege that, once society reaches a consensus, as in the area of racist or sexist speech, it is the duty of government to sustain true belief, and wipe out false opinion. This is a principle that is impossible to contain. In the first place, it is impossible to achieve infallibility in the judgment that a consensus has been reached. Since dissent is at issue, there will always be those dissenters who insist that truth has not been ascertained. Second, even if all mankind but one agrees on an issue, to use the famous Mill example, that does not mean that the truth has been infallibly ascertained.[50] Third, and most important, once we grant that society can infallibly pick certain opinions as "noxious,"[51] censorship will quickly extend to all areas that majorities, or powerful minority interest groups, consider dangerous. The free speech principle must permit grotesque and nasty speech, because society in the domain of speech, cannot be half skeptical and half infallible. We cannot infallibly choose the subjects that are legitimately debatable, and those that are not. Once the boundary line between the acceptable and the non-acceptable is open for judicial scrutiny and legislative action, fallible and self-interested groups will forever battle it out for the prize of legitimating censorship in one area after the next.

The strong First Amendment position I advocate is admittedly a difficult one for society to maintain. My best comparison is to the unicyclist on the high wire. It is a difficult balancing act. We maintain a strong version of the First Amendment not because the truth or usefulness of an idea or mode of self-expression cannot in many areas be ascertained to some degree of certainty. That is, we are not total skeptics. But we maintain it because we lack the capacity to distinguish areas of certainty, more or less, from areas where truth as we now see it is elusive and changeable in the future. That skepticism extends to areas of science, economics and all subjects broadly defined as political. It also extends to the role of speech as a method for facilitating the self realization of speaker or listener. And it extends to the role of speech in facilitating the political process. Once we accept that debate and inquiry must end in certain areas, we cannot limit that principle. Litigators and the courts will forever seek out subjects about which debate should end. The search will be ceaseless, and the areas of censorship will forever expand.

EDUCATION

Of course, American society, in part, does work on the basis that certain opinions and ideas have been validated. Absent that, there could be no coherent secondary school curriculum. In the hard sciences, this is a fairly facile proposition. We permit advocacy of the 'flat earth' science outside the classroom but not in it. We make a pragmatic judgment that accepted bodies of knowledge should be taught in the schools. Free speech principles apply to protect soap box, magazine, or newspapers advocacy of contrary views, such as creationism, *outside* the classroom. This is a safety valve for dissent. Obviously, creationists disagree with this limitation.

However, if we are not careful, the school system can indoctrinate students with the prevailing orthodoxy.[52] I agree that without some professional control over the curriculum, school would degenerate into chaos and propaganda, rather than education.[53] I refer in particular to the secondary classroom where young children are students. The issues get trickier at the college level where young adults are students, and diversity in teaching, no matter how 'heretical,' should be permitted. Yet even there, I admit the need for standards; the physics professor who teaches the Ptolemaic system as correct should be fired. Again, the issues get trickier with teaching varieties of political and aesthetic theory. In the latter fields, it is much more difficult to reach a consensus, no matter how defined.

The danger is that school authorities may use the curriculum process to impose on students orthodoxies that are political rather than neutral scientific principles. (Even in science, there is ample room for debate, contention, and ambiguity.) Lately, politically correct thinking has been enforced on many campuses—not merely hard scientific correctness—only one species of which is the attempted banning of racist and sexist epithets in or outside the classroom.[54] Faculty on many campuses have attempted to eliminate the "grand prejudice"[55] that western culture and civilization should occupy the center of education. Where the university is a state institution, the impact of the First Amendment on this kind of indoctrination, which involves the censorship of dissenting professors, becomes a legal as well as a moral and cultural issue.

The reference to the "grand prejudice" illustrates the point made earlier about the impossibility of cabining areas of alleged certainty from areas of uncertainty. I believe there is a fairly wide consensus that sexual and racist epithets are false and grotesque modes of speech. But it is impossible to contain censorship directed at the epithet once we grant the validity of such censorship. The university community appears to be moving toward wide agreement that racial and sexist epithets are merely shallow forms of a deeper prejudice, notably the "illusion" that western civilization and certain "dead white males" such as John Locke are valuable or worthy. The argument is that the pillars of western thought, such as Jefferson, Aristotle, and Shakespeare, who allegedly glorified royalty and imperialism, are the causes of alleged western racism and sexism. Hence they must be dismissed from the academy, or at least minimalized. In short, the university community seems to be arguing that western civilization is the intellectual cause of western racism and sexism. Molefi Asante, chair of the African-American studies at Temple, has argued for a Afrocentric curriculum, premised on the works of ancient African scholars.[56] "There are only two positions," he says, "either you support multiculturalism in American education, or you support the maintenance of white supremacy."[57]

The advocates of multiculturalism and politically correct thinking on campus argue that all knowledge is suspect since it flows from power and white domination. In order to avoid the charge that their position is equally suspect they make an exception for their lessons on race and ethnicity. Truth does reside, they assert in *their* propositions about the debilitating role of white power. Power in the hands of certified minorities is correct. Thus, since Shakespeare for example, was, as they see it, racist and imperialist, his work is of no importance except, perhaps, to prove the elements of white power in the so called academic liberal arts canon. This is a position espoused by self described left-wingers. But Marxists do not necessarily espouse such extremism. As Irving Howe, himself a prominent leftist, wrote recently, "George Lukacs, the most influential Marxist critic of the twentieth century," wrote that, "Those who do not know Marxism may be surprised at the respect for the *classical heritage of mankind* which one finds in the really great representatives of that doctrine."[58] Howe also quotes Leon Trotsky to the effect that:

> If I say that the importance of The Divine Comedy lies in the fact that it gives me an understanding of the state of mind of certain classes in a certain epoch, this means that I transform it into a mere historical document. . . .How is it thinkable that there should be not a historical but a *directly aesthetic relationship* between us and a medieval Italian book? This is explained by the fact that in a class society, in spite of its changeability, there are certain common features. Works of art developed in a medieval Italian city can effect us too. What does this require? . . . .That these feeling and moods

> shall have received such broad, intense, powerful expressions as to have raised them above the limitations of the life of those days.[59]

Some conservative followers of the law and economics movement including interest group theory make much the same charge as the multiculturalists. For example, Professor McChesney has argued that political pressure and interest group politics explain the scope of First Amendment doctrine.[60] He denies that ideas have power, at least relative to the power of economic interest. Hence, in the area of the commercial speech doctrine, he attempts to demonstrate that the Constitution, the courts, and the lawyers all mold First Amendment doctrine in response to the economic power of corporate elites.[61]

Needless to say, if legislators and judges begin to agree that white power underlies the alleged majesty of the First Amendment as well as the liberal arts canon, they will be tempted to uphold censorship in state run campuses to eliminate the influence of Plato, Aristotle, Locke and the other "dead white males." At the least, they will begin to accept the validity of arguments that the First Amendment does not necessarily bar censorship of the "grand prejudice" if "proof" can be adduced that western civilization embraces false values. Such evidence will become an accepted matter of proof in litigation upon this subject.

IDEATIONAL CONTENT OF RACIST SPEECH

The new critics argue that racial and sexist epithets are not only based upon false assumptions of fact about race and sexuality, but are also (1) devoid of ideational content, and (2) emotionally harmful to the victim. Let us take up the assertion that the insult is relatively free of ideational content, hence, should not protected by the First Amendment. The pejorative, "get lost nigger, kike, queer etc.," is arguably a mere profane grunt rather than an idea or opinion. It is also designed to intimidate rather than rationally communicate. Since the grunt is based upon factually false premises about the minority group, and is an expression of anger or fear, not a rational idea, why not ban it without fear of compromising the First Amendment?

This is an old and venerable position. Spinoza argued for free speech, so long as it was based on reason not "fraud, anger or hatred."[62] This doctrine is not endorsed by the Supreme Court. In *Cohen v. California*, the Court held that a jacket bearing the words "Fuck the Draft" was protected by the First Amendment.[63] The Court stated that "one man's vulgarity is another's lyric."[64]

Assume that the reference to "kike" was replaced by something like, "you are a Jew." From my reading of the New Testament, I have concluded that Jews were responsible for the death of Christ.[65] From my perusal of that great classic, *The Merchant of Venice*, I have concluded that Jews are greedy.[66] From my study of Marx's work on the Jews, I have decided that Jews are inherently purveyors of the worst excesses of the capitalist system.[67] From my reading of the U.N. General Assembly Resolution passed on November 10, 1975 declaring Zionism "to be a form of racism," I have ascertained that Zionism is racism.[68] From my reading of Richard Wagner,[69] and the writer Ludwig Feuerbach,[70] I have determined that Jews are depraved elements in the body politic. Hence, please leave this school or better yet leave the country.

The last paragraph is calm, deliberative and nasty. It is intellectual (in the sense of references to the learned sources) and false in its assertions. It threatens Jews and expresses anger and fear. Do we permit this kind of anti-semitic statement because it is expressed and clothed in the garments of rational thought, but ban the "Jew is kike" epithet? If we do, it appears that we are expressing a kind of elitist theory of permissible racist speech. Street vernacular won't cut it, but racism of the academy will.

The "Jew is kike" statement is popular speech based upon a two thousand year history of 'learned' and elitist anti-semitism, taught by church fathers, great literary titans, profound musical composers, famous revolutionaries, and learned scholars. It is not "low value" speech (that is, speech that conveys no political message) to use the terminology popularized by Professor Cass Sunstein and others.[71] It expresses a point of view on a public issue, the status of Jews. It is not equivalent to the proposition of a rapist. It is a disgusting opinion. As a Jew, my gut reaction is to ban the popular version as well as the more "learned." But that can not be done without fatally compromising the First Amendment.

The example of so-called rational or intellectual argumentation set forth above illustrates another point. So-called rational discourse in the realms of politics, religion, and law, let alone art or cinema, is often in reality a mixture of metaphor, rhetoric, authority, "common sense," and imagery.[72] It is not a rational logical exposition in the form mathematicians or scientists use.[73] In a secular era, it is especially difficult to reach consensus on ethical and moral issues. The abortion debate is an example. There is no mathematical or scientific route to an answer. There is no rational or logical method to determine when human life begins. The opposing camps argue by way of imagery and metaphor. One camp will appeal to the concept of murdering the unborn, the other camp will appeal to the woman's right to control her body. Political discussion usually does not proceed in a linear fashion to some truth. The death penalty presents another example. One side will publish the pictures of execution and otherwise argue the barbarity of capital punishment. The opposing camp will appeal to retribution. Another example is the debate about whether the war in Iraq was a just war. Professor Arthur Leff has gone so far (too far I believe) as to assert on a similar issue that there is no way to "prove" justness or the lack of it except by using a "louder and louder voice," "or by defining it as so."[74] The same is true for the debate between bishops of the Roman Catholic church and members of the gay community about the church's moral disapprobation of homosexuality. (Do we ban gay epithets on campus but permit the cardinals to continue teaching that homosexuality is sinful?) The debates and discussions continue sometimes indefinitely, with conclusions sometimes decided by changes in technological and economic structure. For example, it is questionable that rational discussion had a greater impact on womens' attitudes toward sexuality than the impact of the pill.

EMOTIONAL CONTENT OF HATE SPEECH

Criticism of hate speech because of its emotional content and the harm it will cause is a weak argument. Much of so called intellectual debate is frequently vitriolic and derisive. Any cursory reading of book reviews or commentaries upon other thinkers will establish the biting, often vicious cut and parry of the members of the academy. Intellectuals cringe when reading their book reviews, and, no doubt, realize that the victims of their own biting reviews, will suffer emotional harm. Mark Twain's review of the works of Fennimore Cooper is a fine example, albeit more "restrained" than some. When he was done with Cooper, the literary body lay prostrate and bleeding.[75] In a recent issue of *The New Republic*, Mickey Kaus reviewed William F. Buckley's new book, *Gratitude*.[76] The cover page read, "Mickey Kaus skewers Wm. F. Buckley Jr." In the review, Kaus called the book "lazily researched and sloppily argued."[77] Kaus suggested that a reader, knowing Buckley was the leading conservative in the United States, "might conclude that American Conservatism was in a fairly advanced state of decrepitude."[78] *The New Yorker*, in a brief review of the movie, *The Miser*, called it "tiresome, simpleminded, infantile. . . ."[79] In the *National Review*'s December 31, 1990 issue, movie reviewer John Simon called the movie, *Reversal of Fortune*, "thoroughly offensive" and found parts of it "ineffably tasteless, almost sacrilegious."[80] Simon, in the same issue, called the Broadway musical, *Shogun*, an "unqualified disaster—a bloated nightmare of stylistic miscegenation."[81] This is emotional warfare, likely to inflict serious emotional harm to the authors and performers. Do we ban it?

One of the principal conceptual bases for prohibiting racial epithets stems from the tort of intentional infliction of severe emotional distress. The Restatement (Second) of Torts defined the tort as follows: "(1) One who by extreme and outrageous conduct intentionally or recklessly causes severe emotional distress to another."[82] One commentator has observed that the "extreme and outrageous conduct" component is, in reality, the entirety of the tort.[83] The Restatement defined "outrageous," in part, as a case "in which the recitation of the facts to an average member of the community would arouse his resentment against the actor, and lead him to exclaim, 'Outrageous!'"[84] An "I-know-it-when-I-see-it" test.

The Supreme Court, in *Hustler Magazine v. Falwell*, had this to say about the word:

> "Outrageousness" in the area of political and social discourse has an inherent subjectivity about it which would allow a jury to impose liability on the basis of the jurors' tastes or views, or perhaps on the basis of their dislike of a particular expression. An "outrageousness" standard thus runs afoul of our longstanding refusal to allow damages to be awarded because the speech in question may have an adverse emotional impact on the audience.[85]

In a somewhat similar vein, John Stuart Mill stated:

> Much might be said on the impossibility of fixing where these supposed bounds are to be placed; for if the test be offense to those whose opinions are attacked, I think experience testifies that this offense is given whenever the attack is telling and powerful, and that every opponent who pushes them hard, and whom they find it difficult to answer, appears to them, if he show any strong feeling on the subject, an intemperate opponent.[86]

Outrageous, nevertheless, is a fair description of some of the battles in scholarly and political journals. Outrageous does not exhaust, but is frequently the mark of avant garde, original work in the arts and literature, as well as mediocre works straining unsuccessfully to be original. The point of the First Amendment is to protect speech that is outrageous. Speech that is sedate, that is non-controversial, that is somewhere within the confines of traditional convention and morality, seldom needs protection.

C.S. Lewis was a brilliant and talented Oxford Don, author of serious works on literature, as well as world famous novels of fantasy for children and the young at heart. He was a passionate believing Christian. He engaged in a debate with another scholar on the existence of God, on which he had written a serious work. The woman who debated him, Elizabeth Anscombe, literally destroyed his written work on the existence of God. She left him in emotional despair. He was forced to reconsider his life, his meaning and his work. Fortunately he recovered, although he did not write philosophical works proving the existence of God again. He turned instead to his novels for children. He did not change his convictions on the existence of God, despite her rhetorical and intellectual blitzkrieg.[87] As Swift once said, "You cannot reason a person out of something he has not been reasoned into."[88] Obviously no one would charge Anscombe with the tort of emotional harm, although she devastated Lewis with intent and with deliberation. Again, emotional warfare in the academy is permissible, but street language is suspect.[89]

In the end, pure reason, whatever that is, is seldom the method by which minds are changed. The use of rhetoric, metaphor, and imagery are powerful instruments for change.[90] For example, Richard Posner has correctly observed that Holmes' Lochner dissent, one of the most influential judicial pieces in American jurisprudence, was a model of rhetoric and imagery, as opposed to reason and the calm marshalling of facts.[91] If the First Amendment is going to turn on relative use of emotion, insult, injury to sensibilities of listener, the nature of speech will change in the direction of the bland and the mediocre. Judges will be thrust into content and style discrimination, required to weigh the proportion of emotion and derision to the percentage of pure reason.

A fine example of the use of action, emotion and derision is the cinematic treatment of American fundamentalists. It is no secret that screen writers and directors have not been overly kind to this minority group. They are forever depicted as ignorant, hypocritical boobs. On the silver screen, they are pictured as religious frauds who mouth the words of piety while lusting for money and sex. The pictures wound the fundamentalist; it is clear the directors intend the injury, and the intellectual content (as in many movies) may be thin. The movies are the pictorial equivalent of the epithet, "fundamentalists are lying hypocritical boobs." I surmise the new critics of the First Amendment are not proposing the censorship of the cinema. They would argue, I suspect, that racism is without question evil, but anti-fundamentalism is widely supported in the elite culture. It is therefore, not emotion, diatribe, or hatred that disqualifies speech, but rather truthfulness. We are back to the arguments considered at the beginning of this piece. Speech is to be treated as commercial speech is now treated by the Court. The government is to have the power to ban false speech, or correct misleading speech.

I have no doubt that racist and sexist insults and epithets harm the listener, and harm society. But in the final analysis, if harm to the listener is the measure by which we regulate speech, there will be nothing left of the First Amendment. When societies choose to censor, they do so because of perceived potential for harm as defined by the interests in positions of power. Speech that government considers harmless will not be censored, and there is obviously no need for a First Amendment for that kind of speech. If we deed to government the power to define what is harmful, and to censor speech that, in its opinion, will cause harm, we open the way to government thought control. As Judge Easterbrook put it, "[a]ny other answer leaves the government in control of all of the institutions of culture, the great censor and director of which thoughts are good for us."[92]

I should examine at this juncture another issue. Above,

I discussed the tort of intentional infliction of emotional distress.[93] That doctrine can serve as a basis for statutes forbidding racist and sexist speech. I discussed some objections to such a use. But should we distinguish the infliction of emotional harm on private figures from the infliction of such harm on public figures, or from racist remarks not directed at any individual. The same general issue appears in the world of libel actions.

The *Hustler Magazine v. Falwell* Court considered a parody in which Falwell was depicted as having a drunken incestuous encounter with his mother. The story was labeled a parody. The Court held that

> *public figures and public officials* may not recover for the tort of intentional infliction of emotional distress by reason of publications such as the one here at issue without showing in addition that the publication contains a false statement of fact which was made with "actual malice," i.e., with knowledge that the statement was false or with reckless disregard as to whether or not it was true." This is not merely a "blind application" of the New York Times standard. . .it reflects our considered judgment that such a standard is necessary to give adequate "breathing space" to the freedoms protected by the First Amendment.[94]

Here there was no false statement of fact since the story was an obvious satire, not a statement of fact.[95]

A possible implication of the Court's reasoning is that the core meaning of the First Amendment is to protect public political debate. When private figures are involved, the balance shifts to protection of reputation, in the case of libel, and emotional health, in the case of racist or sexist speech. This position would permit a racial epithet directed at a public figure, where a false statement of fact was involved, as long as the statement was made without actual malice. A more lenient test would be permitted for private figures. This position would also imply the protection of racial epithets directed at no one in particular, as distinguished from one directed at a particular private party. The former case would involve no infliction of emotional distress against a particular individual.

I have the following problems with such distinctions in the area of allegedly racist or sexist speech. First, it is an opening wedge in permitting increased state regulation of private speech. That is a potentially momentous intrusion. If the state can regulate the civility of discourse in matters of race or sex, there is no rational reason for preventing the state from requiring defined civility across the entire range of private conversation and speech. My examples of literary and scholarly savagery toward opponents is an example of the kind of discourse that could be regulated under cover of diminishing emotional harm and softening the edge of argument.[96] A hallmark of totalitarian societies has been the state's often successful efforts to censor and chill private speech.

Second, private speech is essential to the democratic process. Citizens form and reform their attitudes to economic, social, and financial issues by the stuff and substance of their private gossip and discourse. It is artificial to separate the two and permit censorship of the private speech. It is dangerous if we do it under the guise of chilling the infliction of emotional harm in an outrageous form. It would directly reach content that offends, but regulation of offensive speech threatens to reduce speech to syrupy irrelevance and blandness.

Third, as developed more fully below, it is impossible to limit the ban to statements only of the nature of "X, you are a kike." People differ radically in their definitions of what is racist or sexist. Indeed the terms are used sometimes with careless abandon. To some, the advocacy, for example, of anti-quota policies is racist, and in the context of a private argument, allegedly a racist epithet. In the domain of private speech, the courts would enter a thicket of the usual interpretation and development, that would inevitably act as a chill and deterrent to face to face private speech.

Fourth, private speech has been transformed in recent years. The use of four letter words has exploded. Also, the distinction between women and men in the use of profanity has largely vanished. The differences between the sexes on this score are a thing of the past. The cinema, which reflects the popular culture, every day shows the use by men and women of words like "fuck" that were unmentionable in polite society a few decades ago. In a sense, the effort by some to censor epithets is an effort to restore in modern fashion an old morality.

Perhaps most important is another point, however. The argument that racist speech directed at a private individual is more deserving of censorship than racist speech directed at the world in general is based on a curious premise. It supposes that the private epithet creates more harm than a published racist philosophical tract. This proposition is empirically dubious. Television broadcasts or books aimed at creating general racist sentiments against a group or a class are more dangerous to society than the personal insult. The latter hurts an individual, the former can influence vast groups, mold public opinion, and create a racist environment. Of course, ideas have consequences, which is why, absent the First Amendment, society always attempts to censor what it considers dangerous speech. The dangers of that approach are examined in most of the other sections of this paper.

This distinction between speech aimed at the individual and speech aimed at society at large has an interesting parallel in the area of licensing of professionals, such as attorneys.[97] Under current doctrine the unlicensed attorney or investment advisor who gives advice to an individual, face to face, violates the law and the First Amendment offers no protection. If that same individual writes a book on the law of securities, the First Amendment protects publication of the book. The argument is that the personal advice violates a personal trust, can gull the recipient, and is more action than speech. Nevertheless, the book can do immense damage if erroneous, even if widely criticized. If we accept the view that the distinction is based upon a false premise, then the First Amendment would dismantle the licensing structures in all the states.[98] Of course, one could move in the opposite direction and ban the book as emanating from a state disapproved source. This action would involve the dangers of censorship that this article addresses.

DEFAMATION

We can profit from a discussion of defamation, a category of speech that, when factually false, may not be legally protected. Many experts believe that defamation actions intimidate the press. The *New York Times v. Sullivan*[99] standard for public figures, requiring proof of actual malice, falsity, and harm to reputation was intended to preserve a vigorous and feisty press. In recent years, plaintiffs with deep pockets or attorneys on contingent fee bases have, it has been argued, succeeded in intimidating the press.[100] Even the possibility of suit, sometimes causes publishers and novelists to alter their copy. Professor Tribe has observed that since the unanimous *Sullivan* decision:

> [T]he Court has become deeply fragmented about almost every respect of libel, and the doctrine has become a frustrating tangle for all concerned—a mysterious labyrinth for those seeking to clear their names and a costly and unpredictable burden for the speakers the first amendment is designed to protect.[101]

There is a similarity between the defamation action and racist and sexist speech. Defamation is directed at a specific person.[102] The same is true for much but certainly not all racist speech. The defamatory speech must assert a false fact and harm the reputation of an individual. It differs from racist speech in that racist speech is true in the sense that when someone says "I hate you, kike," the emotion is genuine and the victim is indeed a Jew. In addition, the harm is not to reputation, but is an emotional blow of fear and intimidation. However, there is arguably an element of falseness, in that the ethnic slur is sometimes based upon a flawed and false view (albeit frequently an opinion) of the racial or gender group.

Libel of a group is probably not a valid cause of action anymore.[103] In a sense, sexist and racist speech is an offshoot of group libel. The epithet, "X is a kike," flows from the general proposition that Jews are all kikes, hence X, a Jew, is a kike. The new critics would like to reintroduce the group defamation concept.

Discourse on public or private figures is the stuff of political speech. Some speech is general, such as debate over the value of private property and the plusses of redistribution of wealth. But in the case of politics, most debate necessarily involves the criticism of individual political actors. Nixon is or is not a liar. The Keating five are or are not beholden to savings and loan largess.[104] Senator Tower was or was not an alcoholic.[105] If there were doubts, the Ariel Sharon and General Westmoreland trials demonstrated the inextricable linkage between biting critique of individual public figures and the stuff of political debate.[106] The Westmoreland trial involved the country's fundamental differences over the wisdom and conduct of the Vietnam war. The Sharon trial involved the deep divisions over Israel's conduct of the Lebanese invasion. Defamation doctrine, in effect, subjects much of political speech to the test of truthfulness (plus, of course, the *New York Times v. Sullivan* chastening requirement of actual malice). Justices Black, Goldberg and Douglas concurred in that case, arguing that the First Amendment required absolute immunity for criticisms of public officials, not the actual malice standard.[107] Actual malice "is knowledge that [the statement published] was false or [made] with reckless disregard of whether it was false or not."[108] The Westmoreland and Sharon trials reinforced the strength of Justices Black, Douglas and Goldberg's arguments. Both Westmoreland and Sharon were powerful public figures who had clear access to the press to argue their cause and to cleanse their names.[109] They did not need the libel process.

When the object of alleged defamation is a private party and the matter is not of public concern, there is no First Amendment requirement of actual malice.[110] The lack of a public figure and a public issue, tips the scales in the direction of preserving private reputation.[111] However, the First

Amendment still requires the plaintiff to show some fault on the part of the defendant.[112] The Court's distinctions between private and public figures and between private and public concerns have been widely criticized as a confusing labyrinth. For example, Professor Tribe stated that the "latest accommodation between the First Amendment and the individual's reputational interests lacks coherence. . . ."[113] He also pointed out that individuals have been suing authors of novels and films with increasing frequency for allegedly depicting them in a false and harmful way. This trend has chilled the creative expression of authors and publishers.[114]

In the case of private social talk, much speech is gossip about the foibles of our friends and neighbors. Next door neighbor Paul is or is not an alcoholic. If we are to be held at risk in such speech, as indeed we are, it is only the relative litigation adverseness of potential plaintiffs that saves us. Who could pass the day safely, if speech were actually held to the litmus test of truth to which it is held in theory? We could not utter a word without verification and audit. Imagine the following scene at a party: "What do you think of Harry?" "I cannot talk about Harry unless and until I research the truthfulness of the gossip in which I was about to engage." Defamation is, on reflection, a less than perfect doctrine, although an old and venerable one, that is workable to date only because of the relative lack of litigation. In that sense, the doctrine is much like anti-adultery laws, endurable only so long as not extensively enforced. Further, although public figures have access to the national press, local figures have access to the local press to rebut local accusations.

The end result is that much political speech, which is often about individual politicians, is subject to a truth test, subject to the actual malice criteria. The truth test also applies to private speech, except that the standard is probably negligence. Therefore, a truth test is deep in the heart even of speech that lies at the core of protected speech. With that wedge, the new critics can argue more effectively for establishing a similar test for racist and sexist speech aimed at a specific person. The contention may be met by the objection that the defamation doctrine is widely criticized and, in the opinions of many learned commentators, the *Sullivan* test, even with the malice standard, is not working well. Nevertheless, once one accepts truth as a valid First Amendment criteria, as it is accepted in defamation, the breach is apparent and difficult to contain doctrinally—that is, as a matter of the usual arguments in the law by way of analogy from one case and body of law to the next case. That difficulty is what I pointed out in the first section of this paper on truth-seeking, slippery slopes, and the First Amendment.[115]

A fact versus opinion issue lurks here. Defamation turns on the truthfulness of asserted fact, not opinion. Opinions are protected, though a recent Court opinion has perhaps fuzzed the distinction between fact and opinion by stating that opinions that are in reality implied assertions of false facts will be treated as statements of erroneous fact.[116] The judicial distinction between fact and opinion still holds in general. Some opponents of the new critics will effectively argue that sexist and racist talk is, in reality, protected opinion, albeit nasty, not assertion of fact. Indeed it is opinion which has proven remarkably resistant to the introduction of facts about the religious or racial group. The very ability and success of certain groups may lead to the less successful group hating and despising them. That is, positive facts about a given group may form the basis for prejudice. For example, Jews and Asians may be at the top of the economic or academic ladder. The hatred may be the product of fear, anger, or envy disconnected from reason and fact. "You are different, and therefore I hate you." All of these differences may be true in fact.

The distinction between fact and opinion is tricky because of the ambiguity and uncertainty of so called 'facts' and the value and clarity of many so-called 'opinions.' History is replete with the canonization of facts which on further research, debate in the free market of discourse, and study turn out to be fiction. Newton's laws, once considered the infallible key to the universe, turned out, after relativity doctrine, to be of limited application. Most would agree that the advantage of democracy over totalitarianism is an opinion, not a fact, but it is an opinion so firmly held that most would agree that the violation of it will lead to societal disaster. A healthy First Amendment should protect the publication or utterance of alleged false fact as well as alleged false opinion.

SUBJUGATED GROUPS

We cannot ignore another powerful argument of the new critics of classic First Amendment liberalism. They have maintained that the victims of racist and sexist speech are weak and oppressed groups. Blacks, gays, lesbians, and women do not have positions of power, with a few exceptions, in the media and the political structure. They cannot effectively fight back in the media or in politics in the manner of Generals Sharon and Westmoreland. Free speech for these subjugated groups is a formality devoid of substance. The words that wound them not only cannot be effectively rebutted, but also create stereotypes in society that reinforce the oppression and may create in the minds of the victims, sometimes, an acceptance of the racist stereotyping. Therefore, the alleged free market of ideas does not function for them.[117] Perhaps worse, their autonomy and dignity, values advanced by free speech, are diminished by the false speech. Democratic values are cheapened by this process, since the oppression by hateful speech lessens their ability to participate on an equal basis in the democratic process. Hence, the role of free speech in advancing the processes of democracy, another value of free speech, is perverted by the words that wound.

The new critics argue that free speech in the classic liberal mode is obsolete. It was appropriate for an age and a society in which certain articulate, powerful white males were oppressed by more powerful groups of other white males. It was an age in which great media giants had not yet arisen, and individuals could more readily than today publish pamphlets and newspapers. Now that communication is in the hands of such giants, free speech is in reality speech for the owners and editors (mostly white males) of NBC or *The New York Times* or Time-Warner or CBS. Individuals are submerged in such a society, divided from one another by self-interest. If individuals do have power, they are mostly of the Michael Milken variety,[118] wealthy and white, and, in the opinions of many, consumed by greed rather than by societal communitarian impulses. The need, then, is to use government to protect not individuals so much as subjugated minorities.

This is a powerful argument, perhaps the most persuasive of the new critics' arguments. Let us examine it closely. They recommend using the judiciary and the legislature to channel free speech. Speech, such as racist or sexist talk, will be banned by statutory law, or common law use of the tort of intentional emotional harm. Speech critical of non-subjugated groups will not be censored. Those groups do not need the protection of censorship, hence there is no reason to dilute First Amendment protection for weaker groups to criticize them. "Harry is a honky" passes, "Bill is a nigger" is banned. However, allegedly racist and sexist speech extends well beyond the simple epithet. Limiting it to that category would permit a vast quantity of more subtle, more effective racist and sexist speech, at least as defined by many feminists and minority groups. Therefore, courts will be tempted to extend the prohibited categories well beyond the simple three or four letter epithet. Novels that disparage whites may be sold. Novels that disparage blacks—in the opinion of some, *Huckleberry Finn* is such an example—will be blocked. Novels or cinema scoffing at homosexuality will be banned; artistic work or non-fiction critical of the heterosexual nuclear family get the green light. Roman Catholic teaching about the evils of homosexuality will be banned. Their teaching against birth control is suspect because, arguably, it impacts worse on poor minority families and woman, who must bear the costs of large families. Speech recommending immigration laws that favor Europeans will be banned. Speech recommending immigration laws that favor Africans or Asians will be permitted. (Some minorities may argue that Asians succeed so well in America that they are no longer a subjugated group. That will have to be litigated.) Speech criticizing quotas is presently at the border. The courts will have to determine whether such speech is inherently racist or sexist. Mainstream black groups consider quotas essential as one of the fundamental methods to end discrimination in our society. They may not consider it a border issue. Speech criticizing busing is suspect. The courts will have to determine whether such speech subjugates the minority population. Speech attacking affirmative action programs even where not involving quotas will be suspect. Again the courts will have to determine whether the speech is protected by the First Amendment, or alternatively, so injurious to minorities, as to justify its censorship. Creative jurisprudence will be necessary for speech advocating the death penalty. Such speech may, on judicial analysis, create a criminal justice structure that always executes blacks more frequently than whites. So-called classic paintings depicting rape will be questionable, another issue to be considered by the courts. Likewise, great poems, such as *Leda and the Swan*, depicting a rape by Zeus, are questionable.[119] Speeches, books, and articles advocating the role of women in the home may be censored. Beyond that, most literature more than fifty years old may be suspect because of the degradation of women and minorities reflected in it. Speech advocating non- combat roles for women are at the margin; perhaps the courts will censor them. Perhaps they are not even at the margin since they argue sexual distinctions in the work force, and hence are sexist. Scientific research that examines white deficiencies will be permitted. Research that examines minority failings will be prohibited. A requirement of political correctness would be applied in the area of speech, not just to conduct.

It is clear from this partial list, that control of racist and sexist speech involves monumental thought control. It is not surprising, since it is the consequence that classic First

Amendment liberalism has always predicted flows from breach of First Amendment content neutrality. Unless we limit censorship to the simple epithet, such as, "you are a kike", and budge not a whit from that simple category, the reach and scope of censorship will be enormous. But no meaningful doctrine that accepts the need to limit First Amendment protection in the interest of chilling sexist and racist speech can be successfully limited. Simple sexist and racial epithets, horrible as they are, are but the tip of racial and sexist stereotyping, as the new critics see it. An epithet is nothing but the crystallized street expression of racial and sexist bigotry.[120] The reason for exempting it from First Amendment protection is the falsity and perversity of the thought. The judicial doctrine will surely and inexorably reach out to accomplish its purposes, and courts will soon be considering the kinds of speech illustrated in the preceding paragraph. Since modern courts, as all attorneys and legal scholars know, move out creatively in constitutional law in search of what they deem a proper mix of intent, policy and morality, the boundaries of permissible speech will be governed by the justices' vision of the evils of sexist and racist speech. Conservative justices will reach one result, probably one not desired by the new critics, and liberal, radical, or feminist justices will reach another.

The movement toward a state imposed vision of the good society, if it materializes, would be the result of the abandonment of the traditional liberal version of the First Amendment. That philosophy was based upon an exaltation of the individual and a healthy skepticism of the wisdom of the state. Free speech facilitates the search for truth and permits the self realization of the individual. Tragically, that realization does not always result in an admirable human being. But it is a price we have to pay to avoid state authoritarianism, and thought control by bureaucrats.

A distinguishing feature of humanity is the ability and capacity to entertain thought and opinion. Animals may have some language, but humans are unique in the complexity and subtlety of our thinking. But it is impossible to separate freedom of speech from freedom of inner thought. As Albert Levi has said, "in a certain sense freedom of speech is as much a concern of the inner life as is freedom of thought."[121] If we limit it, as many post-liberal philosophers suggest, we move inexorably toward a collectivist vision of society, in which the state is used to mold the ideal society as commanded by the then dominant forces in the culture. This is why, for example, fundamentalists and radical feminists have sometimes, albeit uneasily, joined forces to attempt to censor pornographic literature.[122] Both groups, although wildly disparate, have strong notions of the right kind of society, and the disposition to use the state to advance them.

Note that I mentioned "dominant forces" above. The irony is that so called subjugated groups can gain control over the direction of speech only by their domination of the judiciary and the legislature. Their success marks the end of their subjugated status, unless we ascribe altruism to white dominant forces that grant them appropriate censorship.

One of the barriers to the use of the state to create the ideal society, as seen by the politicians in command, is the First Amendment. Speech is a vital tool for molding attitudes. The state cannot put its hand effectively on that implement, if individuals and private associations are free to speak out in opposition to state policy, and if the state is limited in its use of speech to coerce policy. The First Amendment operates as an obstacle to those goals.

The new critics emphasize the need for equality. They argue that the Fourteenth Amendment's equal protection clause emphasizes the value of equality in society.[123] Subjugated groups, arguably, lack the power necessary for competition in the market for ideas. Hence racist speech no matter how broadly construed must be censored. Other nasty speech, such as flag burning, must be protected since the victims include the powerful, those able to defend themselves in the speech arena.

Note that the argument from equality is designed to censor speech that dissents from the prevailing majoritarian political vision of the just society. This is a position that endorses a particular political orthodoxy as a systematic limit on free speech. As such it runs counter to the philosophical core of free speech and the First Amendment.[124] As the Court stated in *United States v. Eichman*, the case which voided the Flag Protection Act of 1989,

> We are aware that desecration of the flag is deeply offensive to many. But the same might be said, for example, of virulent ethnic and religious epithets, vulgar repudiations of the draft, and scurrilous caricatures. If there is a bedrock principle underlying the First Amendment, it is that the Government may not prohibit the expression of an idea simply because society finds the idea itself offensive or disagreeable.[125]

More particularly, banning speech offensive to the powerless would chill speech that disagrees with the prevailing majority view of who or what is a subjugated class deprived of free speech. Are Gays a subjugated group requiring speech priority? Those who disagree, such as the leadership of the Roman Catholic Church, will find that their free speech will be chilled because of a majoritarian determination of values regarding subjugation.

Solution of the inequality, by way of chilling speech, creates tremendous problems. We have already pointed to the massive thought control that controlled speech will create. Another problem is selection of the groups requiring protection. The selection process involves choices of values, opinions and vision of the world. Government officials or judges, if given that power, have the ability to turn society in any direction that pleases them. This is a power the First Amendment was designed to prevent. For example, evangelical fundamentalists are despised by the educated elites in the American population.[126] As Richard Neuhaus puts it: "For most Americans blessed or blighted by higher education, everything associated with fundamentalism has been indelibly poisoned. . . .Fundamentalism. . .represents all the bigotry, know-nothingness, and legalistic repression that has ever afflicted humankind."[127] Fundamentalists were, until recent years, excluded from the "public square," that is, the political life of the country.[128] In recent years, they have made a foray into that area by influencing the Republican party.[129] Certainly, in their opinion, and in the opinion of others, they are a frustrated and oppressed minority. Do we then structure government control of speech to compensate them for their lack of equality in the world of ideas and opinion formation? They might suggest the following measures: quota hiring of fundamentalists in elite universities; quota offerings on fundamentalism in universities; quota publication of fundamentalist ideas in elite journals; quota hiring of fundamentalist reporters for elite newspapers; quota hiring of creationist scientists in elite universities; production of one pro-fundamentalist movie for every three anti-fundamentalist movies; or right of reply in the editorial page for every anti-fundamentalist editorial. Naturally epithets, such as "X is an Elmer Gantry," will be banned. To the extent that speech molds behavior, such measures will, indeed, create a different America.

In short, the very choice of the disadvantaged groups is a matter of vigorously debated opinion and fact. Who deserves more speech protection: Hispanics, Blacks, and Asians? Mexicans or Puerto Ricans more than other Hispanics? Koreans more or less than other Asians? The example of fundamentalists illustrates that introducing speech control in the interest of disadvantaged groups will amount to massive government control over which groups dominate speech, which groups must get more free speech, and, in general, sovereignty over the spiritual, moral, religious, ethnic, and political direction of society. It will constitute a move in the direction of an authoritarian state, or even of a totalitarian state. It is a move toward rigid quotas in the arena of speech. The losers in the free market will always argue that they are subjugated. They will always, if we permit breach of the First Amendment, seek out government thought control to redress the balance, and shift it in their direction.

In this regard, there is some wisdom to be gained from

a recent incident in Hawaii that illustrates the complexities we invite when we begin to pit group against group, and attempt to determine which is privileged in free speech because of subjugation. A white student at the University of Hawaii complained in a student newspaper about "Caucasia." A faculty member wrote a letter to the newspaper attacking white prejudice against ethnic Hawaiians and asking him to leave the state. She maintained that the student "did not understand racism at all." He did fly home, but intended to return the following semester. Some critics called the faculty member a racist. The faculty of the philosophy department, in which the student had been enrolled, criticized the faculty member who wrote the letter. Her supporters argued for her rights to free speech. The University Center for Hawaiian Studies characterized the philosophy department as involved in "plantation tactics of threat." The argument involved use of the word "haole," a Hawaiian word which once meant foreigner but now means a Caucasian. The student had claimed that native Hawaiians use the word in a derogatory sense. Caucasians constitute 24% of Hawaii's population. Japanese-Americans constitute 23%. Ethnic and part Hawaiians make up 20%. Filipinos constitute 11%, but are the most rapidly increasing group. Caucasians and Asian-Americans are the economically most successful groups.[130]

A recent article by Mari J. Matsuda also illustrates the dangers and difficulties of affording more speech protection to "disadvantaged" groups and less to more powerful groups. She makes the specific suggestion that hateful speech by disadvantaged groups should be protected by the First Amendment.[131] Hence anti-white vicious epithets by minorities should be protected. The same kind of speech by whites directed against blacks, let us say, would be subjected to criminal prosecution. She then examines, as she puts it, "stories at the edge."[132] These are "problem"[133] cases under her definition of actionable racist speech. A problem for her is Zionism and Zionist speech.[134] Is it racist speech? And if it is, are Jews a disadvantaged group? I must admit, that as a Jew, and a supporter of Israel, her decision that this is a tough case needing analysis, and the implication that Zionism is or may be racism, is troubling to me. It should be troubling to all civil libertarians. She reassures us by asserting, "I reject the sweeping charge that Zionism is racism and argue instead for a highly contextualized consideration of Zionist speech."[135] Zionists, she believes, are off the hook, but not always; it depends on the context.[136] I trust the reader gets the message. Once we enter the domain of emasculating the First Amendment in order to censor all varieties of allegedly racist speech, we get into highly political arguments such as: is Zionism racism? I happen to believe that one who denounces the national liberation movement of the Jews as racism is an anti-semite. Hence, I will, if moved by the new critics, argue for censorship of such speech, and perhaps expulsion of the United Nations from New York, which once passed the obnoxious resolution that Zionism is a form of racism.[137]

Professor Matsuda then asserts that "[t]o the extent any racial hostility expressed within a Zionist context is a reaction to historical prosecution, it is protected under the doctrinal scheme suggested [of protecting racist speech of prosecuted groups] in this article."[138] This means that courts will examine whether Zionists critique Arab tactics and policies, and whether the level of critique reaches what the court determines to be "racist." Then courts will decide whether Jews are technically a disadvantaged group. No doubt one side will call Arab experts and the other side will call Jewish experts on the latter issue. Professor Matsuda then argues that if the Zionist asserts "generic white supremacy,"[139] this constitutes Jewish alliance with the dominant group, and the Jewish speaker loses his or her privilege to harshly criticize Arabs. (Perhaps if the Jewish speaker is a woman, she will be able to trump the litigation against her on the grounds that she is part of a subjugated sex.) Since Arabs are Caucasian, I do not quite understand the argument, but the political context of the litigation and the arguments is apparent.

Matsuda's next difficult issue is whether blacks and other minorities may engage in anti-semitic speech.[140] This question presents a knotty issue for her, since one subordinated group is dumping on another subordinated group. She analyzes the problem in one sentence. "I am inclined to prohibit such speech."[141] However, she would sometimes rely on the culture of the recipient group. She argues that "the custom in a particular subordinated community may tolerate racial insults as a form of word play."[142] She would judge it by the recipient's "community standard."[143]

There is no doubt that under her scheme the state or the private plaintiff will be free to attempt to prove that Jews are not subordinated. This attempt may involve such issues of proof as wealth of Jews, what industries they allegedly dominate, their SAT scores, and the size of their average home. The weakness in her argument is inherent in the approach that turns freedom of speech on the relative dominance or subordination of a group. It is a subject that calls for political, social, and emotional arguments of the most extreme subjectivity and personal bias. There will always be real and alleged power imbalances. In the United States, White Anglo-Saxon Protestants, Japanese, Chinese, and Jews enjoy higher economic status than Mexicans, Blacks, American Indians, and Puerto Ricans.[144] But certain groups are more successful politically and not so successful economically. The Japanese were "relatively late participants in politics on the mainland."[145] For many years, the Irish enjoyed more political than economic power.[146] Powerful families own the *New York Times* and the *Washington Post.* Males dominate the hierarchy of the Roman Catholic Church. The speech equality philosophy of the new critics cannot be contained. It requires a powerful state organ to command speech equality, as they define it, across society. The kind of society that can expropriate control of the *Times* and *Post* from inherited wealth, censor anti-feminist propaganda of the Catholic hierarchy, chill the speech of more successful ethnic groups, is the kind of society that was predominant in Eastern Europe until a few years ago, when it collapsed. It is a totalitarian society which requires a governing elite that must appropriate all power, including power over speech, for itself and the groups it decides to favor.

CONCLUSION

In the end, the arguments of the new critics turn on power. Elite white groups possess power. Subjugated minority groups and women lack power. Economic power determines everything. Speech is merely the epiphenomenon of power, to use the language of the older Marxist left. Free speech is merely a cunning device by which the dominant hierarchies cultivate and husband their dominance. Culture, books, plays, cinema, history, philosophy are products of the ruling elites. They possess no truth or value outside of their instrumental value to the elites. It is a grim world. The new critics are usually identified as men and women of the left. But the interest group theories of James Buchanan and some of his followers in the "law and economics" movement, at least when pursued in an extreme fashion, agree in essence, with the foregoing statement of the case. They have argued that law, (and, McChesney has argued, First Amendment doctrine), are merely the product of power group lobbying and influence.[147] The very scope of First Amendment doctrine turns and twists with the influence of interest group politicking. Ideas of truth, democracy, beauty, autonomy, or legal reasoning are largely irrelevant, or more accurately, radically subjective, at least until the right group, namely the new critics, reach power. Thus the entire commercial speech doctrine, giving commercial speech some protection under the First Amendment, is viewed as merely the product of lobbying and maneuvering of groups whose economic interest will be satisfied by the new doctrine.[148] The more powerful the group, the more certainly it will get the proper constitutional doctrine. Right and left agree, then, that speech, argument, reason, or emotion have no influence independent of the power of elite groups at the top of the power structure.

This is a despairing vision of society. It is nihilistic and cynical to its core. It fundamentally eschews word and book and idea as elements of society. In the final analysis, it is more deeply skeptical than the methodological skepticism that, as I discussed above, underlies traditional First Amendment doctrine.[149] It is a movement that is systematically cynical about the value of discourse. It is a philosophy, or rather a movement—we cannot believe in philosophy if all is raw power—that denies the value of everything. In order to rescue itself from total nihilism it rather arbitrarily asserts that there is no truth anywhere, except in the assertions of certain minority and feminist groups who receive the seal of approval from the ruling elites of the new movement. Those groups, ironically, do possess objective truth. Since the sole basis for denial of the present culture is the assertion that it is based on power, the new ordering, which will be based on a new power structure, is also devoid of truth. But the new critics, as a matter of fiat, deny that *their* power is subject to criticism. Shakespeare, Locke, Jefferson, and western civilization itself will be dethroned, to be replaced by a new power structure that will miraculously be valid and worthwhile, despite the corrosive skepticism and cynicism which underlies the new critics' approach to the values of our culture.

The new thinking, if successful, will decisively end the free exchange of ideas that underlies all of western culture and civilization, or indeed all cultures. Race, ethnicity, and gender will be the sole determinants of the university and the media. Because ideas are useless, because they are in reality the disguised weapons of power, with no independent validity, all discourse turns into warfare. Because legal briefs on a First Amendment case are irrelevant, the only thing for the so-called scholar to do is to measure the pocketbook and power of the litigant. This approach makes dreamy-eyed idealists out of the old legal realists. The judicial process is otherwise irrelevant. Likewise, all art and literature is to be evaluated on the basis of the race and wealth of the author or his or her patrons. Such a recipe, now embraced by so many in the academy, is a recipe for the end of discourse and the world of ideas and culture.

The free speech principle is closely linked, it is clear, to the kind of society we desire. The First Amendment envisages a culture in which competition in speech significantly affects the shape of society. More effective writers, more rhetorically-adept pamphleteers, more effective newspaper owners and editors will win the day. The results will not be to the liking of the losers in this competition. I, for one, deplore the success of Patrick Buchanan as a syndicated columnist and television commentator. At one point, his verbal assault on the Jews and Israel led A. Rosenthal of the New York Times to accuse him of anti-semitism.[150] Although I might, in a weak moment, desire a structure that censored Buchanan, I believe that the only safe system for liberty and freedom is the one we have, in which answers to Buchanan must come from other writers, not the state.

I do not wish to give the impression from the past few paragraphs that speech alone is the determinant of success or failure of disparate groups in society. We can overemphasize the influence of speech. We saw a dramatic example of this in Eastern Europe, where forty years of communist control of speech, and communist propaganda against religion and nationalism and ethnicity, broke down almost overnight to reveal that ethnic differences, ethnic rivalries, religious beliefs, and nationalism had not been dissolved by forty years of speech control. Complex patterns of culture, not yet successfully analyzed by science, explain differences among groups. Moreover, the First Amendment does not bar regulation of discriminatory conduct, such as job hiring bias, and acts of intimidation in the work place.

The First Amendment has often been justified as a method or means for facilitating the democratic process. On one level, this is a fairly tautological proposition. Democracy entails the competition of rival groups and individuals, and the settlement of disputes by periodic popular vote. Since speech is the medium by which differences are aired and debated, freedom of speech is a kind of synonym for the democratic system. It is difficult to imagine a vote in Congress, or an election in the total absence of free speech unless we wish to mimic the elections in Nazi Germany or Stalin's Russia. Speech has also been justified as a safety valve for discontent that permits a democratic society to evolve without violence.

On a deeper level, the free speech principle, in conjunction with the democratic process, helps create a certain kind of society. It entails a society in constant flux and dynamic change. Nothing is fixed, nothing is taken for granted. The marketplace of ideas is akin to the free market in goods and services. Change is the only constant. Just as consumers test out rival goods and services in the free market for products, so do consumers test out ideas in the free market of speech. Capitalism is distinct from other societies—feudal, socialist, or religious fundamentalist—in the force and rapidity of change and movement. [151] Capitalism is constantly destroying the old and creating the new. Technology and free enterprise produce the cinema and the world changes. Entrepreneurs develop the internal combustion engine and the face of the earth changes. The same occurs in the world of ideas, speech, art, and newspaper. Some thirty years ago, explicit sex was taboo in the cinema, Victorian sexual mores were not yet in tatters, and women at college lived in separate dorms and observed fixed evening hours of residence. All that has changed, due largely to the influence of free speech in the form of cinema, magazine, book, and speech, along with the influence of the pill, the automobile, and a host of other causes. Such a society has its costs. There are winners and losers. There is constant motion, stress and conflict. But there is freedom and autonomy, prosperity and initiative.

It is no accident that capitalism and free speech are so frequently present together. The free flow of information, ideas and technology is essential in the modern age. We live in an age of information. The computer, the micro chip, the fax, television, and cinema have created a universe in which the barriers to information and new ideas fail everywhere. Efforts to restrain free speech limit not only intellectual freedom, but result in a stultified and failed economic system. It is no accident that communism collapsed as this age came to fruition. Communist systems were unable to compete in the new technology and the new economies based upon the computer. The explosive mix of free speech, fax machines, and computers has created a universal knowledge and appreciation of the achievements of democracy and capitalism. Students in China, before the regime murdered them, marched with statues of liberty and slogans based upon the Jeffersonian ideals of the American revolution.

The new critics stress the value of equality above all other values. Only an authoritarian or totalitarian state can impose that goal. Only the state can place all individuals and all groups in a position of equality with all other groups. More successful groups or individuals must be restrained in speech as well as conduct. Interest group politics are suspect, and would be ended. Only the authoritarian or totalitarian state can accomplish those results. A strong libertarian version of the First Amendment is a thrcat to that goal. The new critics view free speech as a wild card that creates uncertain, unpredictable, unequal results. Hence, they desire to dampen spontaneous change and create a fixed and static society. Their efforts would fail, given the difficulties in the modern age of fax machines and the computer, to restrain the speech they detest. Disfavored speech would be driven underground but it would subsist. The result, as Thomas Emerson indicated in an earlier time, would be to magnify the possibilities of resentment and violence.[152] Indeed, the state censorship of hateful language, and more important, the subtle variations thereof, would have a contrary effect. The forbidden would gain a sort of attractiveness.

The traditional liberal vision of the First Amendment does not entail a purely individualistic society. Communitarian values are included in the First Amendment freedom of association.[153] The Supreme Court has applied the First Amendment to protect the internal governance structure of associations, not merely their speech.[154] That is, the Court has begun to bar government interference with the democratic processes of private groups. The

Court has used this approach to safeguard minority group organizations from the excesses of an intolerant government. This is a liberal, free speech method to advance the opportunity of minorities to move forward, on their own initiatives, in the American culture. De Toqueville recognized long ago that it is, in the words of Justice Kennedy, "a distinctive part of the American character for individuals to join associations to enrich the public dialogue."[155] Justice Kennedy quoted de Toqueville as follows: "Americans of all ages, all conditions, and all dispositions constantly form associations. . . .If it is proposed to inculcate some truth, or to foster some feeling by the encouragement of a great example, they form a society."[156]

Hence, the First Amendment facilitates the ability of minority groups and feminists to organize, to establish their own organizational rules and standards for membership, to agitate, to march, to demonstrate, in order to change society.[157] The same freedom permits religious fundamentalists to organize and to seek power. The new critics do not fully trust the market place in speech and ideas to accomplish the proper result. Indeed, they are concerned that speech they dislike may succeed. It was a similar fear that led government to ban free speech for millennia.[158]

ENDNOTES

1. See, e.g., Richard Delgado, *Campus Antiracism Rules: Constitutional Narratives in Collision*, 85 NW.U. L. REV. 343 (1991) [hereinafter, Delgado, *Campus Antiracism*]; Richard Delgado, *Words that Wound: A Tort Action for Racial Insults, Epithets, and Name-Calling*, 17 HARV. C.R.-C.L. L. REV. 133 (1982); Marjorie Heins, *Banning Words: A Comment on "Words That Wound"*, 18 HARV. C.R.- C.L. L. REV. 585 (1983); Richard Delgado, *Professor Delgado Replies*, 18 HARV. C.R.-C.L. L. REV. 592 (1983); Steve France, *Hate Goes to College*, 76 A.B.A. J., July 1990, at 44; Kent Greenawalt, *Insults and Epithets: Are They Protected Speech?*, 42 RUTGERS L. REV. 287 (1990); David Kretzmer, *Freedom of Speech and Racism*, 8 CARDOZO L. REV. 445 (1987); Charles R. Lawrence, *If He Hollers Let Him Go: Regulating Racist Speech On Campus*, 1990 DUKE L.J. 431; Mari J. Matsuda, *Public Response to Racist Speech: Considering the Victim's Story*, 87 MICH. L. REV. 2320 (1989); Rodney A. Smolla, Symposium, *Free Speech and Religious, Racial and Sexual Harassment*, 32 WM. & MARY L. REV. 207 (1991); Symposium, *Language as Violence v. Freedom of Expression: Canadian and American Perspectives on Group Defamation*, 37 BUFF. L. REV. 337 (1989); Symposium, *Offensive and Libelous Speech*, 47 WASH. & LEE L. REV. 1 (1990);

Some state courts have held that the objects of racial epithets may bring tort actions for intentional infliction of emotional distress. *See* David Givelber, *The Right to Minimum Social Decency and the Limits of Evenhandedness: Intentional Infliction of Emotional*

Distress by Outrageous Conduct, 82 COLUM. L. REV. 42, 66 (1982). The Supreme Court has not directly ruled on the issue. *But cf.* Collins v. Smith, 578 F.2d 1197 (7th Cir.), *cert. denied*, 439 U.S. 916 (1978) (voiding Village of Skokie ordinance criminalizing dissemination of material inciting racial or religious animus).

2. Numerous colleges and universities have enacted student conduct codes or modified old ones to chill such speech or similar speech. State universities are subject to First Amendment scrutiny. A federal district court has held unconstitutional the University of Michigan student code on discriminatory harassment. Doe v. University of Michigan, 720 F.Supp. 852 (E.D.Mich. 1989).

3. *See, e.g.*, Heins, *supra* note 1.

4. Chaplinsky v. New Hampshire, 315 U.S. 568, 572 (1942). Chaplinsky called a city marshall "a God damned racketeer" and "a damned Fascist." *Id.* at 569. The statute upheld in the case forbade "offensive" words. *Id.* Since that case, the Supreme Court weakened the fighting words doctrine when it overturned the conviction of a man who wore a jacket asserting "Fuck the Draft." Cohen v. California, 403 U.S. 15 (1971). The Court has also emphasized in later cases the need to prove imminent violence. *See, e.g.*, Texas v. Johnson, 491 U.S. 397, 408 (1989); Lewis v. City of New Orleans, 415 U.S. 130 (1974); Gooding v. Wilson, 405 U.S. 518 (1972).

5. Roth v. United States, 354 U.S. 476, 485 (1957).

6. New York Times v. Sullivan, 376 U.S. 254, 268 (1964).

7. *See* NICHOLAS WOLFSON, CORPORATE FIRST AMENDMENT RIGHTS AND THE SEC 63-66 (1990).

8. JOHN STUART MILL, ON LIBERTY Ch. II (D. Spitz ed. 1975).

9. *Id. See also* Whitney v. California, 274 U.S. 357, 375-77 (1927) (Brandeis, J., concurring).

10. Vincent Blasi, *The Checking Value in First Amendment Theory*, 1977 AM. B. FOUND. RES. J. 521.

11. RICHARD POSNER, THE PROBLEMS OF JURISPRUDENCE 114 (1990).

12. *Id.*

13. *Id.*

14. *Id.* at 115.

15. *Id.* at 114.

16. *Id.* at 114.

17. *Id.* at 466.

18. Richard Posner, *What Has Pragmatism To Offer Law?*, 63 S. CAL. L. REV. 1653, 1662 (1990).

19. *See* Ruth Wedgwood, *Freedom of Expression and Racist Speech*, 8 TEL AVIV U. STUD. L. 325 (1988).

20. JOHN NOWAK ET AL., CONSTITUTIONAL LAW 836 (3d ed. 1986).

21. Matsuda, *supra* note 1.

22. LEONARD LEVY, EMERGENCE OF A FREE PRESS 5 (1985).

23. *Id.*

24. *See, e.g.*, Dennis v. United States, 341 U.S. 494 (1951); Yates v. United States, 353 U.S. 298 (1957).

25. Abrams v. United States, 250 U.S. 616, 630-31 (1919) (Holmes, J., dissenting).

26. Mill, *supra* note 8, at 22 (quoting CARLYLE, MEMOIRS OF THE LIFE OF SCOTT).

27. *Id.*

28. *Id.* at 162.

29. *Id.*

30. *Id.* at 164-65.

31. PLATO, THE REPUBLIC *in* THE PORTABLE PLATO 353 (Scott Buchanan ed. 1977).

32. *Id.*

33. *Id.* at 364.

34. *Id.* at 368.

35. *Id.* at 369.

36. *Id.* at 370.

37. *Id.* at 373.

38. *Id.* at 383.

39. *Id.* at 384-86.

40. *Id.* at 402.

41. MILL, *supra* note 8, at 34-35.

42. Edward Alexander, *A Talmud for Americans*, 90 COMMENTARY, July 1990, at 27, 30.

43. *Id.*

44. *See* WOLFSON, *supra* note 7, at Ch. 1.

45. *See* Abrams v. United States, 250 U.S. 616, 630 (1919) (Holmes, J., dissenting).

46. *See, e.g.*, MARTIN H. REDISH, FREEDOM OF EXPRESSION: A CRITICAL ANALYSIS 11-29 (1984); Ralph K. Winter, *A First Amendment Over-View*, 55 BROOK. L. REV. 71 (1989).

47. *See supra* text accompanying notes 8-17.

48. Alexander Meiklejohn, FREE SPEECH AND ITS RELATION TO SELF-GOVERNMENT (1948); Robert Bork, *Neutral Principles and Some First Amendment Problems*, 47 IND. L.J. 1 (1971).

49. In a recent book, Professor Steven Shiffrin advanced dissent as the key value of free speech. STEVEN SHIFFRIN, THE FIRST AMENDMENT, DEMOCRACY AND ROMANCE (1990). However, he failed to articulate the criteria by which we judge certain dissent protected and other dissent not protected. *See* Book Note, *Romancing the First Amendment*, 104 HARV. L. REV. 955, 958-960 (1991). In a brief footnote, he asserted that pornography is a form of dominion over women, and hence is a form of dissent against a puritanical society that he would probably not protect. But this requires more argument than a brief footnote. He also "avoids such difficult first amendment issues as hate speech." *Id.* at 959. Hence, it seems that his notion of dissent is based on unarticulated premises, and is narrower than required to meet current issues. In addition, Shiffrin espouses an "eclectic" free speech philosophy. But eclecticism conflicts with the rest of his book that, in contradiction to his call for eclecticism, that is, multi-factor case by case analysis, emphasizes the unitary value of dissent.

50. MILL, *supra* note 8, at 18.

51. *Id.* at 23.

52. See *The Derisory Tower: 'Multiculturalism' and Racism on Campus*, THE NEW REPUBLIC, Feb. 18, 1991, at 5-48, 49-53 [hereinafter *Derisory Tower*].

53. In *Bethel School District No. 403 v. Fraser*, the Court upheld the disciplining of a high school student for "offensive" speech. 478 U.S. 675, 678 (1986). The Court stated: "[S]chools must teach by example the shared values of a civilized social order...." *Id.* at 683. *See also* Hazelwood School Dist. v. Kuhlmeier, 484 U.S. 260, 271-72 (1988). For a summary of the cases affirming Supreme Court protection of traditional First Amendment rights of state university students, see David Rosenberg, Note, *Racist Speech, the First Amendment, and Public Universities: Taking a Stand on Neutrality*, 76 CORNELL L. REV. 549, 564-69 (1991).

54. *See, e.g.*, France, *supra* note 1, at 44; *Derisory Tower, supra* note 52; Ed Gallucci, *A Gathering Storm Over the Politically Correct*, NEWSWEEK, Dec. 24, 1990, at 48; *Academic Groups Fighting the 'Politically Correct Left' Gains Momentum*, CHRON. OF HIGHER EDUC., Dec. 12, 1990, at A-3; Anne Matthews, *Deciphering Victorian Underwear And Other Seminars*, N.Y. TIMES, Feb. 10, 1991, (Magazine), at 42; John Searle, *The Battle Over The University*, N.Y. REV. OF BOOKS, Dec. 6, 1990, at 34; *Speech Codes and Free Speech*, BOSTON GLOBE, Feb. 26, 1991, (Editorial), at 14; *'The Storm Over The University': An Exchange*, N.Y. REV. OF BOOKS, Feb. 14, 1991, at 48.

55. Gallucci, *supra* note 54, at 48.

56. *Id.* at 54.

57. *Id.*

58. *Derisory Tower, supra* note 52, at 41.

59. *Id.* at 41.

60. Fred S. McChesney, *A Positive Regulatory Theory of the First Amendment*, 20 CONN. L. REV. 355 (1988).

61. *Id.*

62. BENEDICT SPINOZA, *Theological-Political Treatise, in* THE CHIEF WORKS OF BENEDICT SPINOZA, 258 (R.H.M. Elwes trans. 1883).

63. 403 U.S. 15 (1971).

64. *Id.* at 25. However, in *F.C.C. v. Pacifica Found.*, the Court supported the FCC's authority to ban radio programs that were indecent but not obscene. 438 U.S. 726 (1978). Although the Court was protecting unsupervised children in the audience, this case is part of the Court's move toward creating hierarchies of expression within the First Amendment. LAURENCE H. TRIBE, AMERICAN CONSTITUTIONAL LAW 938 (2d ed. 1988).

65. *See* Lucy Dawidowicz, *How They Teach The Holocaust*, 90 COMMENTARY, Dec. 1990, at 25, 27.

66. WILLIAM SHAKESPEARE, THE MERCHANT OF VENICE. For a discussion of the complexities of the play, see ALLAN BLOOM, GIANTS AND DWARFS 64-82 (1990).

67. KARL MARX, ON THE JEWISH QUESTION (1844).

68. Jeanne J. Kirkpatrick, *How The PLO Was Legitimized*, 88 COMMENTARY, July 1989, at 57.

69. JACOB KATZ, THE DARKER SIDE OF GENIUS: RICHARD WAGNER'S ANTI-SEMITISM (1986).

70. Michael A. Meyer, *Anti-Semitism and Jewish Identity*, 88 COMMENTARY, Nov. 1989, at 35, 37.

71. *See, e.g.*, Cass R. Sunstein, *Pornography and the First Amendment*, 1986 DUKE L. J. 589; Larry Alexander, *Low Value Speech*, 83 NW. U. L. REV. 547 (1989); Cass R. Sunstein, *Low Value Speech Revisited*, 83 NW. U. L. REV. 555 (1989).

72. *See* RICHARD POSNER, LAW AND LITERATURE: A MISUNDERSTOOD RELATION 281-87 (1989).

73. *See* POSNER, *supra* note 11, at 148-53.

74. Arthur Leff, *Economic Analysis of Law: Some Realism about Nominalism*, 60 VA. L. REV. 451, 454 (1974).

75. MARK TWAIN, *Fennimore Cooper's Literary Offenses*, in 22 LITERARY ESSAYS.

76. Mickey Kaus, *Mickey Kaus Skewers Wm. F. Buckley*, THE NEW REPUBLIC, Dec. 31, 1990, at 34.

77. *Id.* at 34.

78. *Id.*

79. Goings On About Town, The Theatre, THE NEW YORKER, Nov. 19, 1990, at 4.

80. John Simon, *Odd Couples*, 42 NATIONAL REVIEW, Dec. 31, 1990, at 46.

81. *Id.* at 49.

82. RESTATEMENT (SECOND) OF TORTS § 46 (1965).

83. Givelber, supra note 1, at 46.

84. RESTATEMENT (SECOND) OF TORTS § 46 cmt. d (1965).

85. Hustler Magazine v. Falwell 485 U.S. 46, 55 (1988). The Court admited limitations in the doctrine. "We recognized in *Pacifica Foundation*, that speech that is "vulgar," "offensive," and "shocking" is 'not entitled to absolute protection under all circumstances."' *Id.* at 56 (quoting FCC v. Pacifica Found., 438 U.S. 726, 747 (1978)). The Court further stated that it had long "recognized that not all speech is of equal First Amendment importance." *Id.* (quoting Dun & Bradstreet, Inc. v. Greenmoss Builders, Inc., 472 U.S. 749, 758 (1985)). *See supra*, note 53.

86. MILL, *supra* note 8, at 51.

87. A. N. WILSON, BIOGRAPHY OF C. S. LEWIS 213-15, 220 (1990). Wilson wrote that Elizabeth Anscombe, Lewis's opponent "was quite equal to the bullying and the exploitation of the audience to which Lewis resorted." *Id.* at 213.

88. POSNER, *supra* note 11, at 151.

89. *See supra* text accompanying notes 62-71.

90. POSNER, *supra* note 11, at 150.

91. *Id.* at 394-95 (citing Lochner v. New York, 198 U.S. 45 (1905)).

92. American Booksellers Ass'n, Inc. v. Hudnut, 771 F.2d 323, 330 (7th Cir.1985), *aff'd*, 106 S.Ct. 1172 (1986) (mem.).

93. *See supra* notes 83-84 and accompanying text.

94. Hustler Magazine v. Falwell, 485 U.S. 46, 56 (1987) (emphasis added).

95. *Id.* at 57.

96. *See supra* text accompanying notes 75-81.

97. *See* WOLFSON, *supra* note 7, at 146-50.

98. *Id.*

99. New York Times v. Sullivan, 376 U.S. 254 (1964).

100. *See* LOUIS G. FORER, A CHILLING EFFECT: THE MOUNTING THREAT OF LIBEL AND INVASION OF PRIVACY ACTIONS TO THE FIRST AMENDMENT (1987).

101. TRIBE, *supra* note 64, at 865.

102. *Id.* at 861-86.

103. In *Beauharnais v. Illinois*, the Court held in a closely decided opinion that defamation of groups was a valid cause of action. 343 U.S. 250 (1952). Tribe, in his authoritative treatise, stated that "[t]he continuing validity of the *Beaucharnais* holding is very much an open question." TRIBE, *supra* note 64, at 861 n.2. Judge Easterbrook, writing for the court in *American Booksellers Ass'n, Inc. v. Hudnut*, stated, "In *Collins v. Smith*. . .578 F.2d at 1205, we concluded that cases such as *New York Times v. Sullivan* had so washed away the foundations of *Beauharnais* that it could not be considered authoritative." 771 F.2d 323, 331 n.3 (7th Cir.1985) (citing Collins v. Smith, 578 F.2d 1197, 1205 (7th Cir.1978)), *aff'd*, 106 S.Ct. 1172 (1986) (mem.)). *But see* Note, *A Communitarian Defense of Group Libel Laws*, 101 HARV. L. REV. 682 (1988).

104. *See* Richard Berke, *Ethics Unit Singles Out Cranston, Chides 4 Others in S&L Inquiry*, N.Y. TIMES, Feb. 28, 1991, at 1.

105. *See* JOHN TOWER, CONSEQUENCES: A PERSONAL AND POLITICAL MEMOIR (1991).

106. *See* FORER, *supra* note 100, at 22-23. *See also* TRIBE, *supra* note 64, at 869-70 n.54.

107. New York Times v. Sullivan, 376 U.S. 254, 293 (Black, J., joined by Douglas J., concurring); *id.* at 297 (Goldberg J., joined by Douglas, J., concurring).

108. *Id.* at 280.

109. TRIBE, *supra* note 64, at 869-70 n.54.

110. *See* Dun & Bradstreet, Inc. v. Greenmoss Builders, Inc., 472 U.S. 749 (1985); Gertz v. Robert Welch, Inc., 418 U.S. 323 (1974).

111. *See* TRIBE, *supra* note 64, at 873-86.

112. *Id.* at 882.

113. *Id.* at 886.

114. *Id.* at 886 n.84.

115. *See supra* text accompanying notes 11-51.

116. Milkovich v. Lorain Journal Co., 110 S.Ct. 2695 (1990).

117. This article does not cover sexual harassment in the workplace, which involves speech so closely brigaded with conduct as to be beyond the scope of this article.

118. Milken was the 'genius' of 'junk' bonds who pleaded guilty to securities law violations in perhaps the most famous of financial fraud cases in this country.

119. For a discussion of this poem and issues of pornography, see POSNER, *supra* note 72, at 336-37.

120. *See supra* text accompanying notes 62-73.

121. Albert Levi, *in* MILL, *supra* note 8, at 196.

122. The Attorney General's (Meese) Commission on Pornography supported a sustained attack on pornography "adopting an amalgam of traditional and feminist objections to sexually explicit materials." Sunstein, *supra* note 71, at 589.

123. Lawrence, *supra* note 1, at 438-49; Matsuda, *supra* note 1, at 2377.

124. Some have argued that Brown v. Board of Education, 347 U.S. 483 (1954), justifies censorship of private racist speech. Lawrence, supra note 1, at 438-49. That case, it is said, established a principle of racial equality that encompasses speech. However, *Brown* forbade *state* racist *conduct*, not *private speech*. To conflate speech with conduct, and governmental action with private speech, is a fundamental error. Even if *Brown* implicitly forbad government racist speech, it cannot forbid private racist speech. Nadine Strossen, *Regulating Racist Speech on Campus: A Modest Proposal*, 1990 DUKE L.J. 484, 542-47.

125. United States v. Eichman, 110 S.Ct. 2404, 2409-10 (1990) (cite omitted).

126. RICHARD NEUHAUS, THE NAKED PUBLIC SQUARE: RELIGION AND DEMOCRACY IN AMERICA (1984).

127. *Id.* at 45.

128. *Id.* at Ch. 3.

129. *Id.* at 35.

130. Richard Halloran, *Hawaii Journal: Rare Storm Over Race Ruffles a Mixed Society*, N.Y. TIMES, Dec. 26, 1990, at A20.

131. Matsuda, *supra* note 1, at 2361-64. Professor Matsuda uses a story- telling methodology. She describes the terrible racist horror stories that individuals have undergone in their lives. This is a methodology that has become popular in recent writings in law reviews. It embodies a perplexing approach to the development of knowledge. Scientists have recognized for generations the difference between the so-called anecdotal and the statistically relevant. An individual's experience or perception may be totally at variance from the experiences or feelings or truths of the group, the community or the data as a whole.

132. *Id.* at 2361.

133. *Id.*

134. *Id.* at 2364.

135. *Id.*

136. *Id.*

137. See Kirkpatrick, *supra* note 68.

138. Matsuda, *supra* note 1, at 2364.

139. *Id.*

140. *Id.* at 2363-64.

141. *Id.* at 2364.

142. *Id.* (cite omitted).

143. *Id.*

144. THOMAS SOWELL, ETHNIC AMERICA 5 (1981).

145. *Id.* at 179.

146. *Id.* at 30-39.

147. *See, e.g.*, JAMES BUCHANAN & GORDON TULLOCK, THE CALCULUS OF CONSENT: LOGICAL FOUNDATIONS OF CONSTITUTIONAL DEMOCRACY (1962); GEORGE STIGLER, THE CITIZEN AND THE STATE: ESSAYS ON REGULATION (1975); McChesney, *supra* note 60.

148. McChesney, *supra* note 60.

149. See supra notes 11-18 and accompanying text.

150. Joshua Muravchik, *Patrick J. Buchanan and the Jews*, 91 COMMENTARY, Jan. 1991, at 29.

151. *See, e.g.*, MICHAEL NOVAK, THE SPIRIT OF DEMOCRATIC CAPITALISM, Ch. IX (1982); JOSEPH SCHUMPETER, CAPITALISM, SOCIALISM, AND DEMOCRACY 146 (3d ed. 1950).

152. THOMAS EMERSON, THE SYSTEM OF FREEDOM OF EXPRESSION 6-7 (1970).

153. A literature in opposition to classic liberal individualism, in addition to the "new critics" described in this piece, has advocated communitarian ideology and as a consequence limits on free speech where it transgresses norms of civility and rational discourse. *See, e.g.*, MICHAEL SANDEL, LIBERALISM AND THE LIMITS OF JUSTICE (1982); Frank I. Michelman, *The Supreme Court, 1985 Term—Foreword: Traces of Self Government*, 100 HARV. L. REV. 4 (1986).

154. *See* Roberts v. United States Jaycees, 468 U.S. 609 (1984); WOLFSON, *supra* note 7, at 123-39, 143-46.

155. Austin v. Michigan Chamber of Commerce, 111 S.Ct. 1391, 1424 (1990).

156. *Id.* (quoting 2 ALEXIS DE TOQUEVILLE, DEMOCRACY IN AMERICA 106 (P. Bradley ed. 1948)).

157. *See* Kenneth L. Karst, *Boundaries and Reasons: Freedom of Expression And The Subordination of Groups*, 1990 U. ILL. L. REV. 95.

158. Subsequent to the completion of this piece, the Supreme Court decided to hear a case that may involve determination of the scope of First Amendment protection of hate speech. On June 21, 1990, R.A.V. was charged with burning a cross on the lawn of an African American. The city charged him with violating a city ordinance forbidding bias-related conduct such as cross burning. The Minnesota District Court dismissed the misdemeanor charge on First Amendment grounds. *In re* R.A.V. 464 N.W.2d 507 (Minn. 1991). The Minnesota Supreme Court reversed. *Id.* The United States Supreme Court granted cert. in R.A.V. v. City of St. Paul, 111 S.Ct. 2795 (1991). [For a discussion of the *R.A.V.* decision see the Addendum in chapter 5, and for the *R.A.V.* majority opinion see chapter 6.]

CHAPTER 8

THE ENHANCEMENT OF CRIMINAL PENALTIES BECAUSE OF "HATEFUL" MOTIVATION

"Down the Passage Which We Should Not Take: The Folly of Hate Crime Legislation"*

*Marc Fleisher***

INTRODUCTION

In her dissenting opinion to *State v. Mitchell*,[1] Judge Shirley Abrahamson, while voting to uphold the constitutionality of the hate crime law that was before the Supreme Court of Wisconsin, acknowledged that if she were a member of the state legislature, she would not support such a law because she did not think it would "accomplish its goal."[2] After briefly reviewing the United States Supreme Court's unanimous decision upholding the constitutionality of the Wisconsin statute,[3] I will contend that such legislation[4] will not only "fail to accomplish its goal" but will actually do harm.

Criminal trials are peculiarly ill-suited forums in which to determine what will often be unknowable anyway—whether the victim of an interracial act of violence was intentionally selected *because of* his race.[5] Such inquiries

*This article appears at Brooklyn Law School's 2 *Journal of Law and Policy* 1 (1994). Footnotes have been changed to endnotes and are numbered as in the original. Reprinted with permission.

**Assistant Professor of Writing, Brooklyn Law School.

into the inner recesses of a defendant's mind, and attempts to draw a causal connection between the defendant's motives and the crime itself, are even more elusive in the criminal context than in the "mixed motives" cases that comprise the majority of Title VII employment discrimination cases.[6] It would be simplistic to reply that prosecutors can choose to include a "bias" count in the indictment when the evidence is sufficient to convict and decline to do so when it is not. Because interracial acts of violence tend to attract heightened media attention, and can be both provocative and painfully evocative to members of the victim's community, such acts create particularly intense political pressure upon prosecutors to charge a bias crime when the evidence truly does not support it. The public tends to assume precipitately that any interracial violence is also racially motivated.[7] Yet such assumptions often do not comport with the conclusions ultimately drawn by prosecutors and juries who must attempt dispassionately to apply the law as explained to them to the evidence as they find it. Regardless of the prosecutor's charging decision—not to mention the jury's ultimate verdict—bias-assault statutes provide yet another cause of racial tensions and loss of confidence in the already ailing criminal justice system. Moreover, they are used by prosecutors against the very members of historically disadvantaged groups that they are intended to protect.

In conclusion, I will argue that the state can more effectively respond to racially charged crimes by vigorously enforcing traditional criminal statutes to prosecute all acts of senseless violence, regardless of the racial or religious identity of attacker and victim. Accordingly, prosecutors will not be required to prove why a particular senseless attack was committed, thereby prolonging and complicating the trial and impeding the ultimate goal of swift and certain punishment.

Wisconsin v. Mitchell:[8] *Intent or Motive—What's in a Label? (The Conduct's the Thing)*

In 1989, Todd Mitchell, a young black man, began discussing the movie "Mississippi Burning" with a group of his black friends. The group discussed a scene in which a white man beats a black boy while he is praying. Mitchell asked the group, "Do you all feel hyped up to move on some white people?"[9] Soon after, a young white boy walked by and Mitchell said, "You all want to fuck somebody up? There goes a white boy; go get him."[10] Mitchell then counted to three and pointed at the boy, after which the group ran towards him, beat him into unconsciousness, and took his sneakers. The boy remained in a coma for four days.[11] At issue in *Mitchell* was the constitutionality of a Wisconsin statute which provides that defendants who commit certain crimes be subjected to greater punishment when their victim has been "intentionally select[ed]. . .because of the race, religion, color, disability, sexual orientation, national origin or ancestry of that person."[12] Mitchell was convicted of aggravated battery, which carries a maximum penalty of two years' imprisonment.[13] The jury then concluded, under the bias statute, that the defendant intentionally selected his victim because of the boy's race. This finding exposed Mitchell to a potential sentence of seven years.[14] Without this finding, the aggravated battery conviction would have carried a maximum sentence of two years.

The Supreme Court of Wisconsin reversed the court of appeals' affirmance of the defendant's conviction, holding that the bias-crime statute under which Mitchell was convicted violated his First Amendment right to freedom of speech. The United States Supreme Court granted certiorari on this issue, and in a unanimous and brief opinion, reversed the Wisconsin Supreme Court's decision, resulting in the reinstatement of Mitchell's conviction.[15]

Until the Supreme Court decision, the First Amendment issue essentially boiled down to two basic arguments. Those who challenged the constitutionality of such statutes characterized them as punishing bigoted beliefs, arguing that since the defendant was already being punished for the assault, the bias statute served merely to impose greater punishment for his bigoted motive.[16] On the other hand, proponents of these statutes countered that they were not directed at an individual's thoughts, but at his conduct, which they characterized as the "intentional selection of a victim because of his race." The defendant "is being punished for acting on those thoughts in a way that makes his conduct more reprehensible."[17]

Of course, under either characterization, determining whether an actor "intentionally selected" his victim because of his race requires a careful examination of the actor's mental state. It is truistic that one cannot make an "intentional selection" unless it is one's intent to do so, and such an intent is unlikely to arise from reasons other than bigotry. While the underlying statute—aggravated battery—merely requires proof that Mitchell intentionally injured the victim, the penalty enhancement statute requires proof that racial bias was the reason why he injured this particular victim.[18] Accordingly, the Wisconsin Supreme Court concluded that the state punished the defendant more severely for his racial motive in committing the battery.[19] It noted that motive—the reason why the defendant committed a particular social harm—is not ordinarily an element of a crime which must be proven. It is traditionally at sentencing that the judge considers motive in attempting to make a more finely calibrated assessment of moral blameworthiness.[20] However, the Wisconsin Supreme Court was unable to explain why this is constitutionally significant. After all, if it is permissible for a judge to take motive into account at sentencing,[21] why could not a legislature make a specific motive an element of the crime that must be established by proof beyond a reasonable doubt?[22] Indeed, the Court had held in a prior case that a defendant's racial bias could be considered at sentencing in a capital murder case, provided that the prosecution could show that the bias was connected to the actual commission of the crime.[23] Moreover, the Court reasoned that "motive plays the same role under the Wisconsin statute as it does under federal and state anti-discrimination laws."[24]

The Court also distinguished *Mitchell* from *R.A.V. v. City of St. Paul*,[25] in which it held that while the city of St. Paul could prohibit "fighting words" in general, it could not selectively proscribe those fighting words that it found particularly offensive.[26] It reasoned that while the ordinance in *R.A.V.* was directed at expression, the statute in *Mitchell* was "aimed at conduct unprotected by the First Amendment."[27] It characterized such conduct as "bias-inspired" and concluded that the state could reasonably single it out as causing a greater societal harm.[28]

Finally, the Court suggested that in order to prove that a particular crime is bias-motivated, the state will often need to introduce evidence of a defendant's prior statements or associations. The defendant had argued that this would have a chilling effect on speech because individuals would not feel free to express their bigotry knowing that it might later be used against them in a bias-assault prosecution. The Court rejected this concern as bordering on fatuous. It noted that the First Amendment does not preclude using evidence of a defendant's prior statements when they are probative of a material issue.[29]

WHERE'S THE PROOF?

A Hate Crime statute of the type enacted by the state of Wisconsin requires proof that the defendant engaged in two levels of conduct: (1) the battery and (2) the "intentional selection because of race." Accordingly, it requires proof of two levels of culpable mental states: (1) that the defendant intended to injure his victim and (2) that he intended to select the victim because of his race. This latter proof requirement, whether labeled as an issue of "motive" or "intent," requires a far more subtle inquiry into the defendant's mind than does proof of whether he intended to injure or kill the victim.[30] Proof that the defendant intended harm may be inferred from the conduct itself. Yet it may often remain a mystery *why* a particular act of violence occurred. It may be described as senseless, gratuitous or arbitrary. Indeed, up until the very day of sentencing, the defendant's motives may remain enigmatic, even to himself.[31] Yet under the law of homicide or assault, the unjustifiable infliction of injury is—regardless of the reasons behind it—a punishable social harm. Moreover, the very arbitrariness of an assault can legitimately be considered an aggravating factor at sentencing. Conversely, if the defendant was particularly distraught at the time of the attack, perhaps responding to provocation by the victim, the sentencing judge might well consider this to be a mitigating factor.[32] To be sure, the reason why a defendant decides to injure or kill a victim (e.g, for money, or because he hates Jews) has traditionally been characterized not as an issue of intent, but one of motive.[33] The nomenclature, however, is insignificant. A racial motive by any other name such as "intent" would be as difficult to prove.

When the race, religion, sexual orientation or gender of the victim and victimizers is different, that fact alone often creates the perception that the assailants[34] intentionally selected the victim because of his group identity. Since crimes in which racial animus may play a rolc arc ordinarily not conspiracies to target a specific member of a group,[35] but rather, are fast-escalating street encounters, how does one go about concluding whether an individual intentionally selected his victim "because of" his race? Can there be an answer? Since "hate crimes" have been compared to, and indeed are justified by employment anti-discrimination laws,[36] it might be useful to look briefly at the particular problems of proof that plague those cases.[37] This may shed light on the ways in which proving discrimination or intentional selection in the street-violence context presents even greater problems.

It should be noted, however, that there is a basic distinction between employment discrimination cases and "hate crimes." When an individual is assaulted or killed, such conduct is itself punishable.[38] In Title VII cases, the relevant underlying conduct, such as hiring, firing, and promoting is innocuous. It is only upon trying to resolve the thorny issue of whether the employment decision was made *because of* the plaintiff's race that the conduct becomes actionable. What makes the issue thorny, as anyone familiar with Title VII litigation is aware, is the typical "mixed motives" case in which it must be determined whether the employer's actions were taken "because of" the plaintiff's race, color, religion, gender, or national origin.[39] As one commentator put it, Title VII case law has revealed "a startling variety of approaches" to the meaning of the phrase "because of."[40] In determining what roles that discriminatory animus must play in finding intentional discrimination, courts have always required a showing of "but for" causality[41] for the employment decision. Recognizing the difficulty of proving causation, some courts have shifted the burden of proof to the defendant to establish that the adverse employment decision would have been made regardless of the defendant's discriminatory animus.[42]

In the "mixed motives" employment discrimination cases the courts are ineluctably required to distinguish between the employer's legitimate and illegitimate motives, trying to determine whether the same decision would have been made absent racial animus.[43] Professor Gudel has characterized this attempt as "hunting for unicorns."[44] To be sure, in the criminal context, racial animus need not be the sole factor behind the selection process.[45] It is, however, clear that if the jury concludes that the incident would have happened anyway,[46] it is implicitly deciding that race was not a "motivating factor"—that the victim was not "intentionally selected" because of his race.

Imagine, then, that you are a juror in a criminal case and must determine, from the following account of an incident, whether in assaulting the victim, the defendant "intentionally selected" him *because of* his race.

The defendant, Shannon Siegel, a white high-school student, attends a party at which he is intoxicated. He becomes angry and uses racial epithets when he sees the victim, who is black, speaking with his former girlfriend, who is white. He had already known that the two were seeing each other. The victim and the defendant had previously socialized together among a racially-mixed group of students. It was common for these students to use racial epithets when bantering with each other. The defendant's feelings of rage and humiliation intensify when a group of the guests forces him to leave because of his boorish conduct.[47] Later that evening, the defendant, aided by four of his friends, stalks and brutally attacks the victim with a baseball bat.

This account is based on a case stemming from an incident that occurred in Atlantic Beach, New York that ultimately went to trial. Although New York did not (and as of this writing does not) have a bias-assault statute, the defendant *was* prosecuted under a misdemeanor aggravated harassment[48] statute which requires that the person be harassed "because of" his race.[49]

Accordingly, the jury had to determine, under the harassment charge, whether the defendant attacked the victim *because of* his race or whether his rage was attributable more to racially transcendent factors—feelings of jealousy about a former girlfriend and feelings of humiliation at being ejected from the party. A certain callow and intoxicated youth might resort to violence and might do so regardless of his victim's race. Indeed, where is the evidence that race played any part in the incident? It cannot be in the mere fact that the victim and the defendant were of different races. The two were not strangers to each other. And given the portrait of a drunk, jealous, rejected, and humiliated adolescent, how could the jury conclude beyond a reasonable doubt that the defendant was selected because of his race? By his use of racial epithets earlier at the party?[50] If he simply used the word in anger as a crude, vulgar and offensive attempt to wound his victim verbally as well as physically,[51] that might make him a racist, but it would not establish that he intentionally selected his victim "because of" his race.[52] And how does the defendant try to convince the jury that he did not intentionally select the victim because of his race? In this particular case, the defendant's father took the stand and testified that his son had many black friends: "I'd say three-quarters of his friends are black. They have slept over at the house and call him on the phone."[53] The father also asserted that his son "idolized" one of his black friends who was away at college.[54]

It is not surprising that the defense wanted to adduce that "some of his best friends are black,"[55] although it is impossible to know what effect it had on the jury. As it so happens, the jury convicted Siegel of first-degree assault, and acquitted him of the aggravated harassment and civil rights charges.[56] As one juror stated, "We asked ourselves: 'Would this have happened if Jermaine Ewell was white?' Our consensus was it would have. There was [sic] a great number of reasons that motivated the attack. . .embarrassment, ego being bruised and jealousy."[57]

In an employment discrimination case, where the defendant acted with mixed motives, a plaintiff has a difficult enough time proving her case. In such cases, however, there may be evidence of other circumstances in which the defendant denied employment to qualified minority applicants or evidence that the person who was ultimately hired was not as qualified as the plaintiff. One thing has remained a constant throughout these cases: there must be evidence of an intent to discriminate, and as in *Price Waterhouse v. Hopkins*,[58] that discriminatory animus must be a motivating factor in the employer's decision.[59] A number of commentators believe that this requirement unreasonably ignores the existence of unconscious racism; after all, a plaintiff is no less injured by an adverse employment decision merely because the defendant himself is oblivious to his own bigotry. In the *Price Waterhouse* case, the defendants professed that they denied the plaintiff partnership status because she lacked interpersonal skills when it was more likely they were engaging in impermissible gender stereotyping. It is certainly true that many who inappropriately allow gender or race to affect their decision-making do not admit this, even to themselves.[60]

The argument that plaintiffs in employment discrimination cases should not have to prove that the defendant engaged in purposeful discrimination is surely untenable in the criminal law context.[61] Indeed, it would be unimaginable for a criminal court to conclude that the "because of" requirement of a bias-crime statute could be satisfied by a jury finding of a causal connection between a defendant's *unconscious* racial motive and the race of his chosen victim.[62]

As discussed above, for the plaintiff to prevail in the civil context, it has always been necessary to establish that the defendant had a conscious intent to discriminate.[63] The rationale for requiring a showing of such intent is even stronger in the criminal context because the consequences to the defendant are greater punishment and greater moral condemnation.[64]

Moreover, insofar as the discriminatory selection is considered an essential element of the proscribed conduct,[65] a defendant who is not conscious that he is intentionally selecting the victim because of his race would be committing an involuntary act with respect to the bias aspect of the assault.[66]

Finally, the notion, incongruous to criminal law, that an unconscious intention could provide the requisite mental state for a criminal statute is to be distinguished from the strict liability doctrine, which makes irrelevant what the defendant may or may not have been conscious of or even should have been conscious of with respect to a specific element of the proscribed conduct. A finding of unconscious intention makes manifestly relevant the existence of a particular mental event in the defendant's mind[67] and a causal connection between that event and the ultimate selection of the victim.

Two student commentators have proposed a solution to the perception that it "is difficult, if not impossible, for any tribunal to accurately identify an accused's motives at the time of the alleged offense."[68] They suggest creating a "mandatory presumption of racist motivation in all violent interracial crimes,"[69] thus shifting to the defendant the burden of proving as an affirmative defense that he did *not* act out of racial animus or intend to select his victim because of his race.[70] This proposal contemplates prosecuting only those acts of violence committed "by whites against minorities."[71] No bias statute to date, whether state or federal, has prohibited prosecution when either a non-minority is a victim or a minority is a potential defendant.[72]

Even assuming this "one-way street" approach to interracial violence did not violate the equal protection clause,[73] it would certainly be politically unpalatable.[74] These statutes are already criticized as valuing the safety of certain groups over others.[75] They have been successfully defended against such charges by the very fact that they apply to all racially-motivated assaults; theoretically, no group is to be given favored treatment.[76]

However, the aspect of the proposal which would require the defendant to prove the absence of racial motivation as an affirmative defense requires more extensive comment. Part of the rationale offered for shifting the burden to the defendant is the perceived need to curtail prosecutorial discretion in such cases.[77] Accordingly, the argument goes, District Attorneys would no longer be able to indulge their own prejudices by declining to prosecute such offenses under the guise that it is difficult to prove racial motivation.[78]

A basic problem with this approach is that if a prosecutor believes that an interracial crime was not racially motivated, it would be unethical for her *not* to exercise her discretion and simply proceed with a charge of interracial assault. A decision to charge the defendant would expose the defendant to an enhanced penalty by requiring him to prove, at his peril, the absence of racial motivation.[79] Furthermore, such "overcharging" would only serve to increase the prosecutor's plea bargaining leverage.[80] It is even legally questionable whether a conviction for "interracial assault" would withstand an appeal under those circumstances.[81]

Moreover, shifting the burden to the defendant to prove he did *not* select the victim because of his race would, even in the absence of proof of racial motivation, make it even more likely that the defendant would feel constrained to adduce the type of evidence presented by, for example, Shannon Siegel, whose father testified about all the black friends his son has.[82] In attempting to establish that he is not the type of person who would be motivated by racial animus, the defendant would probably present evidence that includes not only his past associations, but his previous statements, and even books he may have read: the very type of evidence about which proponents of bias-crime legislation themselves expressed First Amendment concerns.[83]

The difficulty of proving that the defendant intentionally selected the victim because of his race is only compounded when bias crimes involve more than one attacker, as they typically do.[84] As in the case of the principal, to be guilty as an accomplice one must "act [ ] with the mental culpability required for the commission [of the crime]."[85] Proving accomplice liability can be problematic even in simple assault cases. For example, mere presence on the scene, regardless of the person's mental state, is not enough to convict the defendant. On the other hand, if one can establish that the actor did *something* to assist another in the attack, his intent to injure is naturally inferable from his participation in the violent conduct. However, to convict any one defendant in an ostensible *bias* assault committed by a group, one would also have to prove that each defendant chose to participate in the attack because of the victim's race.[86]

PROSECUTORIAL DISCRETION, RACIAL POLITICS, AND THE MEDIA

> It seems that almost every day someone discovers—or claims to discover—racism in others and publicly denounces it, sometimes out of anguish, sometimes out of anger, sometimes out of habit, and sometimes out of political calculation.[87]

A prosecutor's decision to charge or *not* to charge a particular defendant with a bias crime will often cause resentment and increased racial tensions among members of the victim's or defendant's community.[88] Even well-meaning prosecutors, being political animals and human beings, are not immune from the pressures that members of a racial or religious constituency will bring to bear on them to charge a bias crime even when the evidence of bias motivation is ambiguous. While New York to date has no bias assault statute, such tensions and political pressures have already taken their toll. Public officials are pressured to *label* (or decline to label) a crime as bias motivated.[89] Having such a statute would additionally require prosecutors, grand juries, and petit juries to make very controversial decisions about whether the evidence is sufficient to charge or convict the defendant of a bias crime.

The climate of racial tension and sensitivity being what it is these days, the already natural tendency of people to make quick judgments and to assume the worst is particularly acute in cases of interracial crimes of violence. Indeed, some protesters even seize upon interracial violence as an emblem of "black innocence and white guilt."[90] Political activists can be particularly adept at staging street demonstrations which attract news producers because they make for "good television."[91] Television, to be sure, has always been better at depicting confrontation than at exploring ambiguity and complexity.[92] The perceived truth, as received through the media, gets fixed early in the public's mind,[93] and almost invariably turns out—once the case gets to trial—to be far more complex and elusive than originally portrayed. And this early, pre-trial truth tends to be reinforced by the "pack" instincts of journalists.[94] It is also reinforced by the reluctance, not just of the media but of public officials, to question whether a particular victim was indeed intentionally selected because of his race for fear that they themselves will be accused of racism.[95]

The Atlantic Beach incident is instructive in illustrating how the perceived pre-trial truth often develops. The incident received a great deal of media coverage.[96] One columnist, appearing on a local television broadcast, invoked the holocaust in describing the incident.[97] A protest march, although sparsely attended, was "heavily covered by the media."[98] Editorials were written by two major New York newspapers citing the incident as exemplifying the need for bias-crime legislation[99] and Anthony Lewis wrote an "op-ed" piece characterizing it as emblematic of the persistence of racism in our society.[100] Racially motivated or not, the brutal gang assault of Jermaine Ewell with a baseball bat and sticks was incontrovertibly vicious and cowardly. And it certainly *appeared* to be racist, redolent of past lynchings of black men in the south for having the temerity to look at or speak to a white woman. Siegel was appropriately charged with attempted murder, among other felonies. Yet despite there being no tactical advantage to doing so, the prosecutor also charged Siegel with the misdemeanor of aggravated harassment and with a civil rights violation.[101]

The prosecutor may well have felt constrained to do so by the widespread perception of the incident as a racial attack. But by doing so, he took on the added burden of proving that not only did the defendant try to kill another human being by smashing his head repeatedly with a baseball bat, but that the defendant would not have done so had the victim been white. While much of the public might have assumed that this was a latter-day lynching, they would never know as much about the horrific assault on Jermaine Ewell as the twelve jurors who took an oath to decide the case based on the extensive evidence presented in court. The jury was to learn that it was not just *some* "white girl" the victim was with at the party, but the defendant's former girlfriend. The jury would also find out that the victim wasn't just any black man randomly selected for a racial attack, but one of many young black people with whom the defendant had socialized[102] and that the defendant, who was drunk, and his friends had just been unceremoniously (and, it would appear, deservedly) kicked out of a party by their peers. Upon this evidence the jury concluded that Siegel did not attack Ewell because of his race, but because he was jealous, his ego was bruised, and he felt humiliated.[103]

The jury first had to consider whether it was Siegel who attacked Ewell with the bat, and if so, whether he intended to kill Ewell (attempted murder) or to cause him serious physical injury by using a dangerous instrument

(Assault in the First Degree).[104]

As to the "racial motivation" counts, what significance did the jury accord the father's testimony about all the black friends that the defendant had? Was there an extensive debate about the meaning of this defendant asking his ex-girlfriend, "What are you doing with this nigger money?" One can imagine three possible views: 1) that the evidence tended to prove the defendant selected Ewell to victimize because he was black; 2) that it merely showed his crude way of expressing his anger and jealousy; or, 3) that he used the word routinely in a variety of contexts.[105]

If New York had enacted a "Wisconsin-type" penalty enhancement statute, then Siegel's acquittal on those charges would have been significant, and not just to him. In politically or racially charged cases, a jury acquittal on a major count can carry a powerful symbolic message for many, at times reaffirming the perception that the system is racist.[106] And so, while the prosecutor might have initially appeased a pressure group by charging bias motivation, he ultimately burdened himself with having to prove this elusive element at trial. A failure to meet that burden will constitute yet another cause for racial tension. In reality, the verdict may simply reflect a conscientious jury's attempt—in the face of a difficult issue—to do justice in the specific case before it.

Even the notorious Bensonhurst case turned out to be more complex than the initial, and for many, lasting impression of it: "[t]he initial assessment evoked vivid images of a crazed urban lynch mob,[107] armed with the most primal of weapons, chasing four young blacks down a city street that they had every right to walk on, reserving the modern weaponry for the coup de grace, a bullet to the chest."[108] Despite the more complex reality,[109] this simplistic assessment persisted—and for many still persists—long after the juries hearing the cases rejected it.[110] The shooter, Joseph Fama,[111] himself was ultimately convicted of this senseless, brutal, and cowardly murder and sentenced, without benefit of a bias-crime statute, to a term of 32 years and eight months to life.[112]

It is also understandable that given the outcry that this shocking and historically evocative incident aroused, the prosecutor chose to, in effect, brand others present at the scene as murderers by presenting the jury with an accomplice liability theory that although legally plausible,[113] was rejected by a jury as tenuous if not counterintuitive. As defense lawyer Jack Eszeroff argued at summation, "Nobody has ever been shot with a baseball bat."[114]

The jury also rejected the prosecutor's contention that each defendant intentionally chose the victim because of his race.[115] Joseph Fama may have shot Hawkins because he was black. But what about the others? Were they simply responding to the challenge—the gauntlet thrown by Gina Feliciano—that outsiders described as her "black and Puerto Rican friends" were coming to the neighborhood to beat them up?[116] Had they been told that certain non-minority outsiders were coming in for the same purpose would they have shrugged it off and stayed out of harm's way?[117] With respect to trying to answer either of those questions, how does one differentiate between the tag-along,[118] indifferent to the race of the victim, who may be motivated by an adolescent desire to "score points" with his peers and the racially-motivated participant? When Russell Gibbons, the black youth who supplied some of the bats which were ultimately wielded by members of the group, asserted that race had nothing to do with it and that he was merely backing up his buddies in an anticipated rumble, was he more credible on this point because he himself is black?[119] These are some of the issues which prosecutors must confront in bias-crime charging decisions, just as they do in any ordinary group crime: did each defendant have the mental culpability required for the commission of the crime? Ignoring for the moment whether the prosecutor could possibly fathom the respective *motives* of each member of the group, if the media, community activists, and the public in general paint them with the broad-brush rubric of "lynch mob," what is the likelihood that the prosecutor will even try to make these *mens rea* distinctions? And if she has the political courage and the ability to do so, how will she explain them to the public?

"CALLING IT BOTH WAYS"

In basketball, coaches often scream "call it both ways!" at the referee for making a call against a player when, in the coach's view, a comparable foul had previously been committed, but not called, by an opposing player. Sometimes, referees will call what is perceived as a "give back" or "make-up" foul. This means that the referee unjustly whistles the player for an infraction to compensate for a controversial call made against an opposing teammate, as part of a general attempt to even out the close calls during the course of the game.[120]

The perception that the prosecutor may not be "calling it both ways" in an interracial incident is more likely to occur if one of the calls she has to make is whether the victim was intentionally selected because of his race. For example, many whites in Bensonhurst could not understand why what they viewed in their neighborhood as a case of mistaken identity was portrayed as racial while at the same time the assault by black and latino youths on the white Central Park jogger was not.[121] In fact, the New York County District Attorney's office assiduously *avoided* approaching the brutal gang rape and attempted murder of the jogger as a racial issue.[122] Tactically, the prosecutor had nothing to gain by injecting race as an issue in the trial. Yet, as it happens, evidence existed that one of the defendants, Jermaine Robinson, later explained that he participated in the attack to avenge a beating he once suffered by a gang of white youths[123] and he asserted that others in the gang were also "going to get some whites."[124] Had New York enacted a penalty enhancing bias-crime statute, a decision not to indict on that count, in the aftermath of Howard Beach and Bensonhurst, would inevitably be viewed by many as exercising a double standard. Yet a decision *to* indict would be premised on an exceedingly shaky rationale. Would it really make sense to single Robinson out as the most culpable of the defendants because he had it in his mind that he was selecting the jogger because she was of the same race as a mob who once attacked him? Among the many who either brutally gang-raped or sexually abused her and beat her so severely that she lost 80 percent of her blood and suffered substantial brain damage, would there truly be a coherent rationale for singling Robinson out on the basis of bias?

In any event, Robinson's racial revenge statement can just as plausibly be interpreted as an after-the-fact rationalization[125] rather than an accurate report of what was truly going on in his mind at the time. But there still would be that pressure on the prosecutor to "call it both ways," to indict him for bias assault. Had a white person made an analogous custodial statement about why he chose his black victim, and asserted that his gang was "going to get some blacks," he surely would have been indicted for bias assault.

The Nassau County District Attorney's office, which had included misdemeanor racial bias charges in the prosecution of Shannon Siegel, proved that it would "call it both ways" in its recent 93-count indictment against the Long Island Railroad alleged mass murderer Colin Ferguson. By all accounts, the gunman was a tormented, deeply disturbed individual with a racial persecution complex.[126] Not content with twelve counts of murder, nineteen counts of attempted murder, thirty-four counts of assault and assorted gun possession charges, all of which taken together exposed Ferguson to 175 years in prison,[127] the prosecutor charged Ferguson with the misdemeanor of "intent to harass, annoy, threaten and alarm" his victims "because of their race, color or national origin."[128] Accordingly, if the case goes to trial, much of the focus will be on race and proving that had the train been filled with black people whom the deranged defendant would not consider to be "Uncle Toms," he would never have engaged in this carnage. Who benefits from this?[129]

The recent turmoil in the Crown Heights section of

Brooklyn, New York exemplifies how the existence of a bias assault statute elevates the pressure to "call it both ways" and creates an additional reason for members of the community to perceive the criminal justice system as favoring one group over another. Racial tensions between the Orthodox Lubavitcher Hasidim and the black community had existed for some time in Crown Heights[130] but came to a head when a Lubavitcher driver lost control of his car and tragically killed a seven-year-old black boy named Gavin Cato.[131] The district attorney's office concluded that the death was accidental and not the result of criminal negligence on the part of the driver. Therefore, no charges were brought against him. Some members of the black community reacted in anger, in part, because of a long-standing perception that the police gave preferential treatment to the Lubavitchers. In this case, there was a perception that the driver was tended to by emergency medical personnel and whisked off to the hospital before anything was done for the mortally wounded boy.[132] However, the police asserted that they merely wanted the driver taken away as quickly as possible to avoid a riot since a large and angry crowd had assembled after the accident. Some time later, the infamous Crown Heights riots occurred in which, to the chant of "kill the Jew," a young rabbinical student named Yankel Rosenbaum, visiting from his native Australia, was knifed to death.[133] A young black man, Lemrick Nelson, was indicted for murder and ultimately acquitted by a jury composed predominately of racial minorities.[134]

About a month later, Moshe Katzman, a 24-year-old rabbinical student, was arraigned in Brooklyn Criminal Court on charges that he was among a crowd that beat Mr. Nimmons, a black man, hit him with a rock and a stick, and shouted epithets such as "black nigger."[135] Leaders of the ultra-orthodox sect maintained that its members caught Mr. Nimmons in the act of burglarizing a post-graduate rabbinical school.[136] Mr. Nimmons admitted to police that a set of tools turned into the local precinct, including a screwdriver, a wrench, a box cutter, and an awl were his, but said that he was not carrying them for illegal purposes.[137] As it turned out, Mr. Nimmons had an extensive criminal record that included a conviction for possession of burglar's tools.[138] Perhaps eager to convince the black community that the Hasidim were *not* in fact given special treatment, the police commissioner and the mayor immediately categorized the assault on Nimmons as racially motivated.[139] Meanwhile, the Brooklyn District Attorney, already having been blamed by Jewish residents for his office's failure to achieve a conviction against Nelson for the Rosenbaum slaying, was at the same time accused by black activist Al Sharpton as being too close to the Hasidim. Indeed, Sharpton, not uncharacteristically, called for a special prosecutor in the Nimmons case. Lost in the cacophony of these disputatious voices was the following: (1) given Mr. Nimmons's criminal record and the tools he admittedly possessed at the time, he probably *was* attempting to commit a burglary; (2) given the sheer numbers of Hasidim who were there, and the injuries sustained by Mr. Nimmons, he may well have been criminally assaulted—instead of simply held until the police arrived—as a form of vigilante street justice;[140] and (3) given the fact that suspected robbers and burglars of all races and religions have, from time to time, been the victims of street justice when caught by angry and frustrated citizens of all races and religions, there was no basis to conclude that, because the respective races of these angry citizens were different from that of the suspected felon, racial epithets notwithstanding,[141] *this* particular case of vigilante justice was racially motivated.

Since Nimmons never appeared to testify in the grand jury, the case was dismissed. Had Nimmons testified, and had New York enacted a bias assault statute, it is fair to assume that his alleged principal assailant, Moshe Katzman, would have been charged under it, given the conclusions already drawn by the mayor, the police commissioner, and the District Attorney's representative. At trial, the prosecutor would then have had to prove beyond a reasonable doubt that despite the alleged victim's extensive criminal record for the same or similar crimes[142] and despite his possession of what could reasonably be characterized as burglar's tools,[143] he was assaulted not because he was thought to be in the process of committing a burglary, but because he was black.

Within a day of that incident, according to a white sixteen-year-old girl, a black teenager tried to steal her purse and when she resisted, he called her a "Jewish bitch."[144] Imagine the prosecutor, after charging Moshe Katzman for a bias assault against a career criminal, now trying to explain to his Jewish constituents that like as not, the teen-age robber opportunistically chose his victim not because of her religion but because she seemed good prey and, in the face of her resistance, expressed his frustration and resentment by uttering anti-semitic and gender-biased remarks.[145]

"CALLING IT AGAINST MINORITIES"

It is readily apparent that bias statutes have been and will continue to be used against the very disadvantaged groups whom these statutes are meant to protect.[146] In addition to the danger of majoritarian prosecutors enforcing these laws discriminatorily is the disturbing reality of the disproportionate number of minorities who commit the very types of crimes which will expose them to penalty enhancement.[147] Worse still, the instances in which whites have been the victims of hate crimes perpetrated by blacks is on the rise.[148] Those who make the cogent argument that "bias-inspired"[149] violence "inflicts distinct emotional harms on [its] victims"[150] unquestionably mean *minority* victims.[151]

It is somewhat ironic, then, that the bias-crime case decided by the Supreme Court concerned the victimization of a white boy, Gregory Reddick, by a young black defendant, Todd Mitchell. The question must be asked: was the harm done to Gregory Reddick, a white boy who did not grow up experiencing the pain and degradation of racism, distinctly greater than would have been any vicious, brutal and arbitrary attack upon an innocent, unoffending fourteen-year-old boy? Adding to the irony is that the attack was prompted by the defendant's angry response to a scene from "Mississippi Burning"[152] in which a white man, with impunity, beats a young black boy who is praying. Now, thirty years after the scene depicted in "Mississippi Burning," Mitchell may well hear his "bias-enhanced" sentence as society's message that he should be punished more severely because he, a black man, victimized a *white* boy, rather than a black boy. And how might the black community of Milwaukee have reacted? The vast majority may well have deplored the attack itself. They may also have viewed the use of a "penalty enhancer" in this instance with a certain sardonic irony, having experienced the ravages of black-on-black crime and perhaps felt that the police and prosecutors do not give those cases quite as much attention.[153]

CONCLUSION

If bias-assault statutes will result in difficult proof problems, exacerbate racial tensions, and be used against the very groups they were intended to protect, then why enact them at all? The ostensible answer is that such statutes send a message that society condemns such conduct and views it as particularly serious.[154] However, once the press conferences announcing the enactment of such statutes are held and the message sent, one is left with real, not symbolic, legislation which creates real, not symbolic problems. In any event, a message can effectively be sent by enforcing statutes that do not include a second tier of proof with respect to whether the defendant chose his victim because of race. For example, New York City has created a bias-crime unit within its police department. While its determinations of what is or is not a bias crime is, as discussed previously, treacherous, the very existence of the unit itself sends the message that such crimes are being treated seriously by law enforcement. And of course the very public and rigorous prosecutions of the Howard Beach, Bensonhurst and Julio Rivera "gay bashing"[155] murder cases sent a message without the need of penalty-enhancing bias-crime legislation.

Moreover, there are legislative responses to such incidents which will not bring with them the kind of self-defeating baggage that comes with bias statutes. For example, the overwhelming majority of bias crimes are committed by groups of four or more.[156] In the state of New York, one of the aggravating circumstances which raises robbery in the third degree to robbery in the second degree is the presence of at least one accomplice.[157] It is self evident that when a victim is confronted by more than one person with either the use or the threat of immediate use of force,[158] his fear of harm is likely to be greater as will be the potential for harm. This is so, despite the fact that the crime of robbery is not defined as requiring injury to the victim. Why then, is there no analogous provision in the New York assault statutes? The policy for making the participation by two or more people an aggravating circumstance is even stronger for assaults which, by definition, require that the victim suffer physical injury.[159]

Moreover, although hate crimes are ordinarily not committed by organized groups,[160] when there has been a previous agreement, as for example, when a white supremacist group sets out to terrorize a black family which has just moved into the neighborhood, both state and federal conspiracy laws can be used to sentence the defendants consecutively to the substantive crime that was ultimately committed.[161]

As for homicides, the existing statutes provide ample punishment and opportunity to send a message. After all, was the message sent by the convictions in Bensonhurst, Howard Beach and the Julio Rivera killing in Queens any less resounding because the homicide statutes under which the defendants were convicted did not require proof of *why* innocent blood was shed?

ENDNOTES

1. 485 N.W.2d 807 (Wis. 1992), *rev'd*, 113 S. Ct. 2194 (1993).
2. *Id.* at 818 (Abrahamson, J. dissenting).
3. Wisconsin v. Mitchell, 113 S. Ct. 2194 (1993). * * *
4. This article will address only assaults and homicides committed because of the affiliation of the victimized person. It will not address bias-motivated harass-

ment and vandalism. The definitions of "assault" or "battery" vary from state to state. Hereafter, "assault" or "battery" will be used to mean the intentional causing of physical injury to another.

5. For convenience, I will use "race" to include race, color, religion, national origin and sexual orientation. These are the categories enumerated in the Anti-Defamation League's Model Bill. It reads, in pertinent part: Intimidation A. A person commits the crime of intimidation if, by reason of the actual or perceived race, color, religion, national origin or sexual orientation of another individual or group of individuals, he violates Section __ of the Penal Code. CIVIL RIGHTS DIVISION, ADL LEGAL AFFAIRS DEPARTMENT, ADL LAW REPORT: HATE CRIMES STATUTES: A RESPONSE TO ANTI-SEMITISM, VANDALISM, AND VIOLENT BIGOTRY, app. A (1988 & Supp. 1990) [hereinafter *ADL MODEL BILL*].

6. *See generally* Paul J. Gudel, *Beyond Causation: The Interpretation of Action and the Mixed Motives Problem in Employment Discrimination Law*, 70 TEX. L. REV. 17 (1991).

7. For example, on November 15, 1993, two black youths approached an Israeli rabbinical student in the Crown Heights section of Brooklyn and demanded his wallet. As he began to hand the wallet to them, one of the assailants shot him in the lower back. As the pair fled without the wallet, one of them said "[expletive] Jew." Was this an afterthought, a spontaneous addition of insult to injury or proof that the victim was intentionally selected because he was Jewish? Rabbi Jacob Goldstein, chairman of Community Board 9, saw no ambiguity in it: "If they said that, it's absolutely a bias crime." The victim himself was more circumspect: "I'm confused. I'm not sure to this minute whether it was because I'm a Jew or they really did want my money." Kyle Smith, *Victim: Crown Heights Thug Called Me %&* Jew,* N.Y. POST, Nov. 16, 1993, at 2. Supporters of this legislation themselves acknowledge that the use of a racial or religious epithet does not, in and of itself, provide proof beyond a reasonable doubt that the victim was intentionally selected because of his race or religion. *See e.g.,* Brief *Amicus Curiae* of the Anti-Defamation League in Support of Petitioner [hereinafter *ADL Brief*]; *Mitchell*, 113 S. Ct. 2194. However, one cannot expect the general public to view such crimes from this dispassionate perspective, nor be attuned to the rigorous proof requirements of a criminal prosecution.

8. 113 S. Ct. 2194 (1993).

9. *Id.* at 2196.

10. *Id.* at 2196-97.

11. *Id.*

12. WIS STAT. § 939.645 (1990) ("penalty; crimes committed against certain people or property"). This statute is adopted from the Anti-Defamation League's (ADL) model hate-crime statute which uses such language as "by reason of the actual or perceived" race. ADL MODEL BILL. As of the Wisconsin Supreme Court's decision in *Mitchell*, twenty-five other states had enacted such penalty-enhancement statutes. *See Mitchell*, 485 N.W.2d at 811.

13. WIS STAT. § 939.645.

14. WIS STAT. §§ 939.05 and 940.19(1m). *Mitchell* was ultimately sentenced to four years. 485 N.W.2d at 809.

15. The Wisconsin Court of Appeals held that Mitchell waived his equal protection claim and rejected his vagueness challenge outright. State v. Mitchell, 473 N.W.2d at 2 (Wis. Ct. App. 1991). The Wisconsin Supreme Court declined to address both claims. 485 N.W.2d at 809 n.2 (Wis. 1992). Mitchell renewed his Fourteenth Amendment claims in the Supreme Court, but since they were not developed below and fell outside the issue upon which the Court granted *certiorari*, the Court did not reach these claims either. 113 S. Ct. at 2197, n.2.

16. *See* Susan Gellman, *Sticks and Stones Can Put You in Jail, But Can Words Increase Your Sentence? Constitutional and Policy Dilemmas of Ethnic Intimidation Laws*, 39 UCLA L. REV. 333, 343 (1991). In its majority opinion in *Mitchell*, the Supreme Court of Wisconsin based much of its reasoning on Professor Gellman's article. *See generally Mitchell*, 485 N.W.2d 807 (Wis. 1992).

17. James Weinstein, *First Amendment Challenges to Hate Crime Legislation: Where's the Speech?*, 11 CRIM. JUSTICE ETHICS 6, 8 (1992) (Symposium: Penalty Enhancement for Hate Crimes). For a persuasive articulation of the premise that

racially motivated violence causes an "added injury," *see id.* at 10-13.

18. The American Civil Liberties Union, among others, argued in its *amici* brief, that all the statute technically requires is intentional selection based on race for whatever reason. Brief *Amicus Curiae* of the American Civil Liberties Union in Support of Petitioner [Authored by Stephen R. Shapiro (counsel of record) and John A. Powell], *Mitchell*, 113 S. Ct. 2194 (1993) [hereinafter *ACLU Brief*]. While this may be accurate as a matter of conceptual possibility, in reality, such "intentional selections" will invariably be motivated by racial bias.

19. 485 N.W.2d 807, 811-13 (Wis. 1992); 113 S. Ct. at 2197.

20. Assuming there is no justification for injuring or killing another, the defendant has committed a social harm regardless of motive.

21. 113 S. Ct. at 2199.

22. As the ACLU noted in its *amici* brief, including motive in the definition of a crime affords greater protection to the defendant. ACLU Brief at 14, n.14.

23. *See* Barclay v. Florida, 463 U.S. 939 (1983) (plurality opinion) (holding Constitution did not prohibit sentencing court in capital murder case from taking into account elements of racial hatred in murder). *Compare* Dawson v. Delaware, 112 S. Ct. 1093 (1992) (holding evidence at sentencing phase of capital murder case of defendant's membership in Aryan Brotherhood inadmissable because not related to specific crime).

24. 113 S. Ct. at 2200. The Court specifically referred to Title VII "which makes it unlawful for an employer to discriminate against an employee 'because of such individual's race, color, religion, sex, or national origin.'" *Id. See* 42 U.S.C. § 2000e-2(a)(1) (1988).

25. R.A.V. v. City of St. Paul, 112 S. Ct. 2538 (1992).

26. 113 S. Ct. at 2200-01. Such proscriptions, reasoned the majority, are impermissibly content based. *See also R.A.V.*, 112 S. Ct. 2538, 2542.

27. 113 S. Ct. at 2200-01.

28. Citing the briefs from the state and its *amici*, the Court noted that a state legislature could rationally conclude that "bias-motivated crimes are more likely to provoke retaliatory crimes, inflict distinct emotional harms on their victims, and incite community unrest." *Id.* at 2201.

29. 113 S. Ct. at 2201. Of course, this is incontrovertible. For example, in a criminal trial, evidence that a non-Arizona resident stated, "I'm looking forward to my trip to Phoenix on Friday," would be probative of the fact that the defendant had the opportunity to commit the crime in Phoenix that Saturday. Because of the statement's relevance to the issue of identity, its use against him at trial would neither violate his First Amendment right to express his enthusiasm about a city nor chill his constitutional right to interstate travel. Unfortunately, the Court chose to illustrate the point with a uniquely infelicitous example—a forty-six-year old treason case: Haupt v. United States, 330 U.S. 631 (1947). *See Mitchell*, 113 S. Ct. at 2201-02. In *Haupt*, the Court held admissible evidence of conversations carried on "long prior to the indictment," 330 U.S. at 642, because they revealed the defendant's "sympathy with Germany and Hitler and hostility toward the United States." Accordingly, the Court reasoned, these statements were probative of the defendant's treasonous intent. *Mitchell*, 113 S. Ct. at 2202 (citing *Haupt*, 330 U.S. at 642). In effect, the Court left the door wide open to the admission of evidence of past associations and conversations that are ostensibly probative of a defendant's racist intent. *But cf.* Dawson v. Delaware, 112 S. Ct. 1093 (1992). Of course a trial judge would have to conclude that the probative value of this evidence outweighed its potential for prejudice. *See* FED. R. EVID. 403(b). The potential for prejudice would be that the jury might, in effect, use the evidence to punish the defendant for his bad thoughts. As Professor Weinstein notes, this potential First Amendment problem is not limited to hate crime prosecutions. Weinstein, *supra* note 17, at 20 n.58. For example, in a recent Florida case, a white defendant became involved in a verbal altercation about a minor traffic accident. The defendant was indicted for first degree murder for the death of the black man with whom he had argued. Florida v. Loeb. (4th Jud. Cir. Duvall County 1992) (available on VHS as *Trial Story, People v. Loeb*, Courtroom Television Network, Video Library Service, 600 Third Avenue, New York, N.Y. (212) 973-2822). The defendant contended that he acted in self defense. The

prosecution's own witnesses agreed that the deceased had threatened the defendant with a brick. The issue was whether the defendant reasonably believed that the deceased continued to pose a threat of deadly force when the defendant shot him. The defendant was a member of a white supremacist organization. The prosecution was permitted to offer evidence of previous racist writings of the defendant and show a video of a local television interview he gave in which he expressed his extreme racist views. The court, in determining that the evidence was relevant to prove motive, concluded that it did not unduly prejudice the defendant. However, one juror acknowledged that the evidence of the defendant's racist views had a profound impact on her: "It showed me what a dark heart he had. It shocked me; I've never been the same since." She also asserted that the jury made substantial use of the evidence to "help determine motive." Telephone interview with juror (Feb. 23, 1994). No doubt the judge's inclination to admit the evidence would have been even stronger had the crime charged actually required the prosecution to prove a racist motive.

30. One commentator argues, in the employment discrimination context, that intention is not necessarily a mental state that can be located in the mind. Gudel, *supra* note 6, at 82-88. *See also* A.C. MACINTYRE, THE UNCONSCIOUS: A CONCEPTUAL STUDY 53 (R.F. Holland ed. 1958). In the criminal context, this is intuitively appealing when one considers, for example, how quickly and easily a gun can be fired, without the actor necessarily hearing himself think "I intend to kill you." *See generally* Gudel, *supra* note 6. Professor Gudel argues that the defendant's conduct should be interpreted as one would interpret a painting or a text instead of trying to find the intent of the Title VII defendant, and then impose a tort model of "but for" causation between that intention and the discriminatory act. *Id.* at 86-87. However, he ultimately acknowledges that to understand the conduct as discriminatory, one will ordinarily have to inquire into the defendant's state of mind. *Id.* at 87-88.

31. Even if the defendant thinks he knows why he did it, the answer to the question "What were *the* reasons?" may well differ from the answer to the question, "What were *his* reasons?" *See generally* R.S. PETERS, THE CONCEPT OF MOTIVATION (R.F. Holland ed. 1958).

32. Indeed, murder may be reduced to manslaughter when the jury finds that the defendant acted out of a "heat of passion" resulting from adequate provocation, *see e.g.*, California v. Berry, 556 P.2d 777 (Cal. 1976), or acted under "extreme emotional disturbance" for which there was "a reasonable explanation or excuse." MODEL PENAL CODE, § 210.3 (1991).

33. *See* WAYNE R. LAFAVE & AUSTIN W. SCOTT, CRIMINAL LAW § 3.6 at 227 (2d ed. 1986). *See also* Gellman, *supra* note 16, at 364-66.

34. I use the plural because "[t]he overwhelming majority of bias crimes are committed in groups of four or more." Abraham Abramovsky, *Bias Crimes: A Call for Alternative Responses*, 19 FORD. URBAN L. J. 875, 887 (1992) (Citing Daniel Goleman, *As Bias Crime Seems to Rise, Scientists Study Roots of Racism,* N.Y. TIMES, May 29, 1990, at C1).

35. For example, a white supremacist group plots the attack on a newly-arrived black family in the neighborhood, or a gang of "gay bashers" cruises a neighborhood in search of a gay victim. Bias crimes "are usually street crimes spontaneously committed." Tanya Kateri Hernandez, Note, *Bias Crimes: Unconscious Racism in the Prosecution of Racially Motivated Violence*, 99 YALE L.J. 845 (1990). *See also,* James Jacobs, *Rethinking the War Against Hate Crimes: A New York City Perspective,* 11 CRIM. JUST. ETHICS 55 (1992) ("Hate crime appears overwhelmingly to be a phenomenon of individuals and youth gangs, not of organized racist and homophobic groups."); Brian Levin, *Bias Crimes: A Theoretical and Practical Overview,* 4 STAN. L. & POL'Y REV. 165, at 167 (1992/1993).

36. *Mitchell,* 113 S. Ct. at 2200.

37. For an intelligent and thought-provoking review of the history of Title VII litigation on the issue of proof of discriminatory treatment in the workplace, and what the author views as the underlying fallacy of the courts' approaches, *see generally* Gudel, *supra* note 6.

38. Therefore, the taking on of an additional and elusive level of proof is unnecessary to convict and punish the defendant. Later in this article I argue that taking on this burden of proof undermines, rather than promotes, the goal of swift,

certain and even-handed prosecution of all unjustified acts of violence.

39. These "mixed-motive" cases comprise the bulk of Title VII litigation. It is rare when evidence exists that an employer's sole reason for rejecting an applicant was personal animus towards the applicant's race. *See* Gudel, *supra* note 6, at 27. As Senator Case stated it in the Congressional hearings: "If anyone had an action that was motivated by a single cause, he is a different kind of animal from any I know of." 110 CONG. REC. 13837-38 (1964).

40. Gudel, *supra* note 6, at 27. Professor Gudel's article presents an excellent and thorough review of the approaches taken by the circuit courts before the Supreme Court decided *Price Waterhouse v. Hopkins*, 490 U.S. 228 (1989).

41. As Professor Gudel notes, to his chagrin, it is "universally accepted by courts and commentators, that the problem of mixed motives is a problem of causation, similar to problems of causation in tort law in which the causal link that courts must discover is one between an external event (the allegedly discriminatory act) and an internal entity or event (the discriminatory 'intent' or 'motive')." Gudel, *supra* note 6, at 19.

42. *See* Gudel, *supra note* 6, at 19. This approach was adopted in *Price Waterhouse*, 490 U.S. 228 (overruled in part and codified in part in the Civil Rights Act of 1991, 42 U.S.C. § 2000e-2(m) (Supp. III 1991) (the 1991 Act retained the "but for" causation). Accordingly, the plaintiff would lose under a "but for" analysis if she were rejected for employment because of her race or gender but another applicant was so well qualified that he would have been hired even had the employer not rejected the plaintiff for impermissible reasons. Gudel, *supra*, note 6, at 96. In the criminal context, the only ostensible analogy to this "after-the-fact" approach which takes the bigoted employer off the hook would be the situation in which a gang's racial motives are placed into doubt because, during a rampage, they ultimately attacked a member of their own race as well. *See* SULLIVAN *infra* note 121 at 114.

43. A line of cases, however, interprets the mixed motives cases as giving the defendant the right to use after-acquired evidence of a legitimate reason to justify an employer's decisions. *See* Ann C. McGinley, *Reinventing Reality: The Impermissible Intrusions of After-Acquired Evidence in Title VII Litigation*, 26 CONN. L. REV. 145 (1994) (publication pending).

44. Gudel, *supra* note 6, at 96. To convict a defendant for an act of violence, however, juries need not even imagine their existence.

45. *See, e.g.*, United States v. Bledsoe, 728 F.2d 1094, 1098 (8th Cir.), *cert. denied*, 469 U.S. 838 (1984).

46. *See* State v. Wyant, 597 N.E. 2d 450 (Wis. 1992), *vacated* 113 S. Ct. 2954 (1993) (subsequent history omitted).

47. *See* Michael Alexander, *"I never Hit Him"; Suspect in Ewell attack says black youth was friend*, NEWSDAY, Nov. 19, 1992, at 4. (Nassau & Suffolk ed.).

48. Aggravated harassment in the second degree. N.Y. PENAL LAW § 240.30 (McKinney 1991 & Supp. 1994).

49. The statute provides, in pertinent part: A person is guilty of aggravated harassment in the second degree when, with intent to harass, annoy, threaten or alarm another person, he: . . . 3. Strikes, shoves, kicks, or otherwise subjects another person to physical contact, or attempts or threatens to do the same because of the race color, religion or national origin of such person. *Id. See also*, N.Y. CIV. RIGHTS LAW §§ 40-c (Discrimination), 40-d (Penalty for Violation) (McKinney 1993) (This section of the Consolidated Laws of New York provides civil remedies for discrimination, and defines "harassment" by reference to N.Y. PENAL LAW § 240.30).

50. There was apparently some conflict at the trial about whether racial epithets were used. One witness alleged that the police coerced her to say that she heard the defendant use racial epithets and another witness was unable to recall the use of racial slurs. Michael Alexander, *Damaging Testimony in Beating Trial*, NEWSDAY, Oct. 31, 1992, at 12 (Nassau & Suffolk ed.). For the purpose of this discussion, I will assume that the defendant did use racial epithets earlier at the party.

51. The defendant's former girlfriend, Nicole Diamond, testified that he had previously asked her "[w]hat are you doing with nigger money?" At the party, Diamond told Ewell, the victim, about the remark. Michael Alexander and Eric Nagourney,

Guilty of Assault, Siegel Innocent of Attempted Murder, NEWSDAY, Nov. 22, 1992, at 3. There was no evidence that racial epithets were used during the attack.

52. Indeed, the ACLU, which submitted an amicus brief supporting the constitutionality of the Wisconsin statute, has opposed a Florida bias statute which merely requires that in committing a crime the defendant "evidence[] prejudice." *See* ACLU Brief, at 8 n.6; FLA. STAT. § 775.085(1) (1991). The Florida statute shifts the focus from the conduct of "intentional selection." On its face, it permits punishment of people who appear to be racists while committing a crime more than non-racists who commit crimes or for that matter, racists who do not evidence their racism as they are committing the crime. *See* Richards v. Florida, 608 So. 2d 917 (Fla. App. 1992) (holding statute "does not define with sufficient due process particularity what additional criminal act is required").

53. Alexander, *supra* note 47.

54. *Id.*

55. This is the very type of abstract evidence of a defendant's racial attitudes of which the admissibility is highly questionable when offered by the prosecution because it has no connection to the crime charged. *See generally, supra* note 29 and *infra* note 83. While the Supreme Court took a cavalier approach to the issue of the state offering such evidence, it did not even address the fact that the defendant himself has the right to adduce character evidence that he is not a racist, and will often feel constrained to do so. *See* FED R. EVID. 404(a)(1). However, it is not clear what constitutes evidence of not being a racist, nor at times what a "racist" is, as the use of the word is ever expanding and ever open to different opinions as to its meaning. As reported in the New Republic, a white man in Ohio also tried to prove he was not a racist by citing his relationships with black people. This prompted the following cross-examination:

> Q.And you lived next door to [Mrs. Ware, a 65-year-old black neighbor]?
> A. Yes
> Q. Never had dinner with her?
> A. No
> Q. Never invited her to a picnic at your house?
> A. No
> Q. I want you to name just one [black] person who was a really good friend

of yours. Jeffrey Rosen, *Court Watch: Bad Thoughts*, NEW REPUBLIC, July 5, 1993, at 16.

56. Siegel was sentenced to the maximum penalty for first-degree assault: five to fifteen years. *See* N.Y. PENAL LAW § 120.10 and Art. 70 (McKinney 1987).

57. Craig Gordon, *The Jermaine Ewell Case; What's Next? After Siegel's conviction, fewer witnesses against others*, NEWSDAY, Nov. 23, 1992, at 3 (Nassau and Suffolk ed.). The jury was instructed that under both the aggravated harassment and civil rights charges it would have to conclude that race was the *sole* factor which motivated the defendant to attack the victim. This is contrary to the federal courts' interpretation of its "private action" bias-crime statute, 18 U.S.C. § 245 (1983), which reads, in pertinent part: (b) Whoever, whether or not acting under color of law, by force or threat of force wilfully injures, intimidates or interferes with, or attempts to injure, intimidates or interferes with, or attempts to injure, intimidate or interfere with— (2) any person because of his race, color, religion or national origin and because he is or has been—(B) participating in or enjoying any benefit, service, privilege, program, facility or activity provided or administered by any State or subdivision thereof; *See, e.g., Bledsoe*, 728 F.2d 1094 (8th Cir. 1984) (discriminatory animus can be one of a number of motivating factors). *See also* United States v. Ebens, 800 F.2d 1422, 1429 (6th Cir. 1985). However, by concluding that the attack would have occurred even if Ewell had been white, the jury was implicitly concluding that it was not a motivating factor at all.

58. 490 U.S. 228 (1989).

59. Price Waterhouse v. Hopkins, 490 U.S. 228 (1989). Once the plaintiff establishes that it was a "motivating factor," the burden shifts to the defendant to establish that the employment decision would have been made anyway. This retains, as the dissent pointed out, the requirement of "but for" causation while tinkering with procedure. Id. at 279-94. In the criminal context, without this "but for" requirement, one is

no longer punishing conduct but instead punishing attitudes divorced from conduct. In any event, if a jury considers race a "motivating factor" in an assault, it would be paradoxical also to conclude that had the victim *not* been of that race, he would have been assaulted anyway.

60. *See* Stephen Carter, *When Victims Happen to be Black,* 97 YALE L.J. 420, 442 (1987). *See also* Charles R. Lawrence III, *The Id, the Ego, and Equal Protection: Reckoning with Unconscious Racism,* 39 STAN. L. REV. 317 (1986-87); R.S. PETERS, *supra* note 31.

61. In criminal law, an individual is only considered to have intentionally done something when it was his "conscious objective" to do so. *See, e.g.,* N.Y. PENAL LAW § 15.05(1) (McKinney 1987). Accordingly, it would be a contradiction in terms to suggest that the defendant unknowingly intended to select a victim because of race or intentionally selected his victim because of race when he was merely negligent or reckless with respect to the possibility that race inspired his selection. Imagine, for example, that the jury concluded that although Siegel *himself* sincerely disavows it, the *real* reason he attacked Jermaine Ewell was that he couldn't tolerate the notion that a black man was with his white ex- girlfriend. Suppose it further concludes that he would not have resorted to violence had Ewell been white. Should he be punished more severely for what the jury concludes was his unconscious motive? Consider the recent case of the American sailor who pleaded guilty in a military court to murder with intent to inflict great bodily harm. The fatal beating of the defendant's fellow shipmate was appallingly severe. The attack was widely perceived, by both sides of the debate over the military ban on homosexuals, as motivated by the victim's sexual orientation. Although there was no bias-crime statute under which the defendant could be prosecuted, the possibility that this was a case of gay bashing arose at the sentencing phase of the proceedings. The defendant testified that he had a temper: "I prayed that I could get rid of it, but I cannot." A psychiatrist testified that steroids, alcohol, and severe beatings suffered as a child at the hands of his stepfather may have helped trigger the defendant's violent rage. When asked whether he killed the victim because of the victim's homosexuality, the defendant responded, "No, I didn't. In all honesty I did not attack him because he was a homosexual." *See Tearful Murderer Discounts His Victim's Homosexuality,* N.Y.TIMES, May 27, 1993, at A16. How might a prosecutor prove him wrong? By calling a psychi-atrist to testify that the defendant was a homophobe who had long-simmering unconscious conflicts about his sexuality which inexplicably came to the fore in a homicidal rage? Ironically, such evidence would provide a plausible mitigating defense under MODEL PENAL CODE § 210.3(1)(b) (extreme emotional disturbance). Once it is acknowledged that the defendant is guilty of murder, should the defendant be punished more severely if the jury concludes that although the victim's race or sexual orientation was not his conscious reason for committing the act, psychiatrists and the jury know better?

62. Nevertheless, a student commentator suggests that statutes should address "spontaneous violence" caused by "unconscious racism." *See generally,* Hernandez, *supra* note 35. This issue could only arise under those statutes, such as the model statute drafted by the ADL, which omit the words found in the Wisconsin statute—"intentionally selects"—and simply refer to the victim being assaulted "because of" his race. It is certainly plausible to conclude that a person acted the way she did "because of" an unconscious motive. *See, e.g.,* MACINTYRE, *supra* note 30, at 60. Bias-crime statutes have been attacked in the past as being unconstitutionally vague on the theory that they do not specify the *mens rea* with respect to the conduct of selecting the victim. *See, e.g.* Richards v. State, 608 So. 2d 917, 921 (Fla. App., 3d Dist. 1992) (statute unconstitutionally vague because in providing for enhanced punishment when the defendant merely evidences prejudice in committing the underlying crime, "it is not clear whether a conscious prejudice is even required apart from the proscribed act itself, whatever that might be."); *see also* State v. Van Gundy, 1991 WL 60686 (Ohio App. 1991), 624 N.E.2d 722 (Ohio 1994); Gellman, *supra* note 16, at 355-57. In *Mitchell,* 113 S. Ct. 2194 (1993) the Supreme Court offered no guidelines whatsoever as to how such statutes should be drafted to pass Constitutional muster. The ACLU, in its *amici* brief had requested that the Court do so. *See* ACLU Brief. Some courts have resolved the problem by reading in a requirement that the defendant intentionally select the victim because of his race. For example, the California Court of Appeals considered an

attack against a statute prohibiting crimes "committed against [a] person. . .for the purpose of. . .intimidating or interfering" with her constitutional rights "because of the other person's race." CAL. PENAL CODE § 422.7 (1994); People v. Joshua H., 17 Cal. Rptr.2d 291 (Cal. App. 1993). The court simply inferred that the statute required proof of a specific intent as to both the deprivation of the individual's constitutional or statutory rights and as to the act being committed "on account of the person's status." *Id.* at 295. This is consistent with the federal courts' interpretation of 18 U.S.C. § 245 as requiring that the defendant "willfully injured. . .[the victim] because he was a black man." *See, e.g.*, United States v. Bledsoe, 728 F.2d 1094, 1097 (8th Cir. 1984). In *Bledsoe*, the Eighth Circuit went on to explain, as other federal courts have done, that while race need not be the sole motive, it must be a "substantial motivating factor." *Id.* As such, one would have to conclude that "'but for' the victim's protected status, the perpetrator would not have selected the victim for the crime." Wisconsin v. Mitchell, 485 N.W.2d 807, 827 (Wis. 1992) (Bablitch dissenting) (arguing that the words "because of" in the statute are not unconstitutionally vague). In *Oregon v. Plowman*, 838 P.2d 558 (Ore. 1992), the statute at issue proscribed two or more persons from causing injury to another "because of their perception of that person's race." OR. REV. STAT. § 166.165(1)(a)(A) (1989). The defendant argued that this invites prosecution whenever the race of the victim is merely different from that of the defendant. The court concluded that the "because of" language required establishing a "causal connection between the infliction of injury and the assailants' perception of the group to which the victim belongs." The court analogized this standard to certain aggravating factors in Oregon's murder statute in which a causal connection must be established between the murder and the victim's status as a witness, a juror, or some one else connected to the criminal justice system. By implication, the victim must be someone "whom the assailants have *targeted because of* their perception that the victim belongs to a particular group." *Plowman*, 838 P.2d at 563 (emphasis added). Later in this article, I will argue that the mere difference in race often causes the public to assume that the act was racially motivated, which intensifies pressure on prosecutors to indict for a bias crime even when evidence of such motive is problematic.

63. *See, e.g.*, 42 U.S.C. § 1981 (1991).

64. *See, e.g.*, Pamela S. Karlan, *Discriminatory Purpose and Mens Rea: The Tortured Argument of Invidious Intent*, 93 YALE L.J. 111 (1983). As Professor Karlan points out, in distinguishing constitutional law from criminal law cases, "[t]he central concern for equal protection law is remediation for victims; [in contrast to criminal law] any burden laid on equal protection defendants is incidental." *Id.* at 117. *See* definition of "Intention" *supra* note 61.

65. *See* State v. Mitchell, 113 S. Ct. 2194 (1993); *Plowman*, 838 P.2d 558. This is the linchpin of the argument that such statutes are constitutional because they punish conduct that the state may reasonably view as more harmful to society. To be sure, as the Supreme Court acknowledged, there is a necessary interrelationship between the conduct and the mens rea. *See Mitchell,* 113 S. Ct. at 2199. Indeed, the very word "selection" implies conscious choice.

66. National Conference of Commissioners on Uniform State Laws & American Law Institute, MODEL PENAL CODE § 2.01 (1980). The model statute provides in pertinent part:(2) The following are not voluntary acts within the meaning of this section: . . .(b) a bodily movement during unconsciousness or sleep.

67. *See generally* MACINTYRE, *supra* note 30, at 45. Psychiatric testimony about unconscious motives may of course be relevant when the defendant himself interposes the defense of insanity.

68. Helen L. Mazur-Hart, *Racial and Religious Intimidation: An Analysis of Oregon's 1981 Law*, 18 WILLAMETTE L. REV. 197, 204 (1982); *see also* Note, *Combatting Racial Violence: A Legislative Proposal,* 101 HARV. L. REV. 1270 (1988).

69. Marc L. Fleischauer, Comment, *Teeth for a Paper Tiger: A Proposal to Add Enforceability to Florida's Hate Crimes Act*, 17 FLA. ST. U.L. REV. 697, 701 (1990).

70. Such burden shifting is generally constitutional so long as the state proves beyond a reasonable doubt all the elements of the crime as it is defined by the legislature. *See* United States v. Patterson, 432 U.S. 197 (1977). Under this proposal, the state would merely have to prove (1) the underlying crime of assault, and (2) that the defendant is white and the victim is a member of a minority group. However, as one of the proponents acknowledges, the definitions of "white" and "minority" are themselves subject to ambiguity. *Combatting Racial Violence, supra* note 66, at 1272 n.9. Then, in the second phase of what would be a bifurcated trial, the defendant could attempt to prove that the victim was not intentionally selected because of his race.

71. *See Combatting Racial Violence, supra* note 68, at 1272 ("it is limited to interracial violence directed at minorities. . . .[Such] crimes would carry a heavier punishment than regular intraracial or inter-minority crimes of physical violence." *See also* Fleischauer, *supra* note 69, at 703 ("only criminal penalties involving white offenders and minority victims should be enhanced"). Fleischauer emphasizes that "it will be absolutely necessary to exempt minority offenders from the presumption of racist intent in interracial crimes." *Id.* at 703. For convenience, he uses the term "race" to include the following categories: "race, religion, ethnicity, color, ancestry and national origin." *Id.* at 703 n.38. Accordingly, under this proposal, any violence between blacks and Jews would not qualify since blacks are a racial minority and Jews are a religious minority, nor between Asians and Blacks, as Asians would be considered a minority under "national origin." And since sexual orientation does not fall within Fleischauer's categories, *any* assaults on gays, even those committed by straight White Anglo-Saxon Protestants, would not be included under his proposal.

72. Jacobs, *supra* note 35.

73. *See* Regents of the University of California v. Bakke, 438 U.S. 265 (1978); *see also* City of Richmond v. J.A. Crosson Co., 488 U.S. 469 (1989).

74. For example, during the Crown Heights disturbances, the killing of Yankel Rosenbaum, committed as a mob of blacks yelled "kill the Jew," *see* Stephen Labaton, *Reno To Take Over Inquiry In Slaying In Crown Heights*, N.Y. TIMES, Jan. 26, 1994, at A1, would not be covered by such a statute as it was committed by a member of a "disadvantaged minority."

75. *See, e,g.,* Gellman, *supra* note 16, at 389.

76. *See* Nat Hentoff, *No: Equality among Victims*, A.B.A. J., May 1993, at 45. ("Why should one victim be more precious than the other in the eyes of the law?"). Hentoff's point is not merely one of favoritism. He questions whether bias attacks are more harmful to the community than any other type of violence. To the extent that Hentoff's question may imply favoritism toward minority groups, the answer comes from, for example, the dissenting opinion of Judge Bablitch in *State v. Mitchell* ("[This statute] singles out no particular group for different treatment, and thus no suspect classification is involved"). 485 N.W.2d at 830. *See also*, Mazur-Hart, *supra* note 68, at 215 (the statute is easily defended from equal-protection attack because it "applies equally to all racial and ethnic groups"); Grannis, *supra* note 3, at 215 ("Penalty enhancement statutes do not. . .punish crimes against certain groups. Rather they can be applied to crimes against members of any group, thus avoiding the equal protection problem. . . ."). It should be noted that the equal protection argument in *Mitchell* was not that these statutes unjustifiably afford minority groups greater protection from assault. The defendant, after all, was a black youth being charged with a racial attack against a white boy. He argued instead that the statute discriminates against the poor and uneducated because they are the ones most likely to *commit* the underlying crimes eligible for penalty-enhancing bias statutes. *Mitchell*, 485 N.W.2d at 830 (dissenting opinion) The Supreme Court, while unanimously agreeing with the Wisconsin court dissenting judges' view that the statute did not violate the First Amendment, declined even to address the respondent's equal protection argument as untimely. Wisconsin v. Mitchell, 113 S. Ct. 2194, 2198 n.2 (1993).

77. *Combatting Racial Violence, supra* note 68, at 1274.

78. *Id.* at 1274. The author states: "Because the ambiguous and complex nature

of the concept of racial motivation precludes anything except subjective judgments about the presence of racial motivation, prosecutors can give effect to their own racist sentiments under the pretext of finding no racial motivation." *Id.* at 1275. Of course, the evidence will be no less "ambiguous" or "complex" to a jury. Shifting the burden of proof to the defendant merely makes it more likely that he will be convicted by jurors exercising particularly "subjective judgments." Both the ACLU and ADL, in their *amici* briefs, cited the very fact that the state of Wisconsin made "intentional selection" an element of the crime which must be proven beyond a reasonable doubt as significant in addressing First Amendment and due process concerns that defendants might be convicted on marginally relevant evidence concerning their statements and beliefs. *See* ACLU Brief at 22. *See also,* ADL Brief, at 23.

79. *See* MODEL CODE OF PROFESSIONAL RESPONSIBILITY EC 7-13 (1993); MODEL RULES OF PROFESSIONAL CONDUCT Rule 3.8, cmt. (1983) (prosecutor's obligation to seek justice).

80. In 1988, the New York City Legal Aid Union opposed the enactment of bias legislation in part because it believed prosecutors would be given a coercive plea-bargain advantage over the defendant in being able to "trade" the bias-motivated crime for the underlying crime. Richard Barbieri, *Legal Aid Union Opposing Higher Penalty in Bias Cases,* MANHATTAN LAWYER, June 14-20, 1988, at 3.

81. *See* People v. Lyde, 469 N.Y.S.2d 716 (N.Y. App. Div. 1983). In New York, a defendant is guilty of robbery in the first degree when he displays "what appears to be a pistol." N. Y. PENAL LAW § 160.15(4) (McKinney 1988). It is, however, an affirmative defense, reducing the charge to robbery in the second degree, when what is displayed is not a loaded weapon readily capable of producing death." N.Y. PENAL LAW §§ 160.15(4), 160.10(2)(b) (McKinney 1988). In *Lyde,* the defendant was convicted of robbery in the first degree because he failed to request a jury charge on this affirmative defense. The evidence established, and the People conceded on appeal, that what the defendant displayed was a toy gun. On appeal, the First Department reduced the first degree robbery conviction to second degree in the "interest of justice," declaring it error "to submit to the jury the crime of robbery in the first degree." *Lyde,* 469 N.Y.S.2d at 717-18. It is now the practice of the District Attorney's Office in New York County not to charge robbery in the first degree—which would force the defendant to raise the affirmative defense—when it knows that what was displayed was not a loaded weapon. Likewise, if the prosecutor believes that the defendant would satisfy the requirements for the affirmative defense to Felony Murder, she will not charge Felony Murder and require the defendant to interpose the affirmative defense. Interview with Kristine Hammann, Assistant District Attorney and Director of Training, New York County District Attorney's Office, Mar. 4, 1994.

82. *See supra* text accompanying notes 53-55.

83. In focusing its First Amendment concerns on the type of evidence that would be admissible to establish that a crime was motivated by bias, defenders of these statutes, such as the ACLU, were not only caught short by the Supreme Court's blithe disregard for these concerns, but seem to have ignored the pressure that will be placed on *defendants* themselves to adduce this type of evidence. *See supra* note 55. Under the rules of evidence, the defendant himself may adduce evidence about his character to prove he is *not* the type who would assault someone because of his race. FED. R. EVID. 404(a)(1); *see also* N.Y. CRIM. PROC. LAW § 60.40(2) (1992) (prosecutor can then rebut defendant's evidence of his good character). Once he does so, the door opens for an adjudication that might aptly be entitled: "Are you now, or have you ever been a racist?" The limitations placed on the *state* to adduce such evidence stem not only from the First Amendment, but from basic rules of evidence. The potential for prejudice to a defendant in revealing his racist speech or associations will probably outweigh its probative value when unconnected to the specific crime charged. *See, e.g.,* FED. R. EVID. 403; People v. Ventimiglia, 420 N.E.2d 59 (N.Y. 1981). *Cf.* Dawson v. Delaware, 112 S. Ct. 1093 (1992) (at sentencing phase of capital murder case, evidence of defendant's membership in Aryan Brotherhood inadmissible because not connected to murder of victim). *But see* Wisconsin v. Mitchell, 113 S. Ct. 2194, 2201 (1993) (*citing* Haupt v. United States, 330 U.S

631, 642 (1947)) (allowing evidence of conversations carried on "long prior to the indictment"). A related principle is that prior bad acts or crimes of a defendant are inadmissible to show he has the propensity to commit the particular crime with which he is charged or, for that matter, crimes in general. FED. R. EVID. 404(b).

84. *See* Abramovsky *supra* note 34.

85. N.Y. PENAL LAW § 20.00 (McKinney 1987).

86. Regarding the attack on Jermaine Ewell, *see supra* notes 47-57 and accompanying text, Stephen Worth, the attorney for Siegel's accomplice, James Peralta, stated, after his client pleaded guilty, "It was a matter of backing up his buddies, right or wrong." Michael Alexander, *3-to 9-year Sentence in Ewell Beating* NEWSDAY, June 8, 1993, at 27. If true, that would make Peralta an accomplice only to the assault itself. If he correctly believed that Siegel was intentionally selecting Ewell because of his race, he could be guilty of the separate and less serious crime of criminal facilitation with respect to that charge. *See* N.Y. PENAL LAW Art. 115 (McKinney 1987). Given that most participants in bias crimes are teenagers, *see, e.g.,* Abramovsky *supra* note 34, at 887, whose assaultive behavior is sudden and unplanned, *see generally, supra* note 35, determining the respective motives of each participant would be, to say the least, enormously difficult and, as another decision forced upon prosecutors, judges (who must rule on the legal sufficiency of evidence) and juries, another gratuitous cause of racial tensions. Indeed, the attempt to prove accomplice liability for the murder of Yusuf Hawkins in the Bensonhurst case—even without the additional burden of proving that each defendant intentionally selected the victim because of his race—was a dismal failure. *See* Hedges, *infra* note 108.

87. Andy Logan, *Race to the Finish*, NEW YORKER, Oct. 18, 1993, at 48.

88. In discussing the possibility of a bias-assault bill being enacted in the New York State legislature, Frank Breslor, counsel to the Senate Codes Committee, said the issues to be worked out included "whether calling attention to the racial, ethnic or political differences of the parties of a crime will really further the climate of racial harmony or make it worse." Barbieri, *supra* note 80, at 3. *See infra* McQuiston note 129.

89. Indeed, the New York City police department at one point expanded the definition of bias crimes because of pressure from advocacy groups for minorities who felt the numbers of reported incidents were misleadingly low. The definition came to include crimes in which bias was "some part of the impulse." Alison Mitchell, *Police Find Bias Crimes are often Wrapped in Ambiguity,* N.Y. TIMES, Jan. 27, 1992, at B2. However, the New York police department subsequently altered its policy to refrain initially from calling *any* incident a "bias crime" and began to limit its conclusion that the defendant was motivated by bias to the characterization "possible bias crime." It did so upon the realization that identifying crimes of violence which are motivated by bias is often elusive and that labeling crimes as such is itself a cause of racial tension. This occurred after New York City Mayor David N. Dinkins rather precipitately labeled an assault by Hasidic Jews as a bias attack against a black man they alleged was trying to commit a burglary. "It's a heavy burden on the mayor's office to make the right call each time," said government consultant Joseph Giordano, referring to the mayor having set a precedent by commenting shortly after each ostensibly bias-motivated incident. Jane Fritsch, *Police Dept. Vows a New Caution in Labeling Crimes as Bias Cases,* N.Y. TIMES, Dec. 22, 1992, at A1. It is questionable as to who benefits from a mayor's pre-indictment public conclusion about the guilt of a suspect of any crime, much less one which has a racial dimension. At the very least, the mayor need not make public pronouncements about whether a victim was intentionally selected because of race to denounce a random act of violence (or vigilantism) as a crime against humanity and as destructive to the body politic.

90. SHELBY STEELE, THE CONTENT OF OUR CHARACTER 14 (1990). Steele characterizes it as "victimization metamorphosed into power via innocence." Steele further writes: But this formula. . .binds the victim to his victimization by linking his power to his status as a victim. And this, I'm convinced, is the tragedy of black power in America today. It is primarily a victim's power. . . .So we have a hidden investment in victimization and poverty. One sees evidence of this in the near happiness with which certain black leaders recount the horror of Howard Beach, Bensonhurst and other recent instances of racial

tension. As one is saddened by these tragic events, one is also repelled at the way some black leaders—agitated to near hysteria by the scent of victim power inherent in them—leap forward to exploit them as evidence of black innocence and white guilt. *Id.* at 14-16.

91. Perhaps no one is better at creative confrontations than the Reverend Al Sharpton. As one author has put it, "His mastery of pithy phrases that worked just right on the evening news shows were a boon for producers and reporters." JOHN DESANTIS, FOR THE COLOR OF HIS SKIN: THE MURDER OF YUSUF HAWKINS AND THE TRIAL OF BENSONHURST 105 (1991). As one observer of television news in general explains it: The one ingredient most [television news] producers interviewed claimed was necessary for a good action story was visually identifiable opponents clashing violently. This, in turn, requires some form of stereotype:. . .[for example] black versus white. . . . Demonstrations or violence involving less clearly identifiable groups make less effective stories, since, as one CBS producer put it, "It would be hard to tell the good guys from the bad guys." JERRY MANDER, FOUR ARGUMENTS FOR THE ELIMINATION OF TELEVISION 274 (1978), (*quoting* EDWARD J. EPSTEIN, NEWS FROM NOWHERE: TELEVISION AND THE NEWS (1973)). It is, in part, for this reason that racially charged incidents tend to be considered "big news." JACK LEVIN & JACK MCDEVITT, HATE CRIMES: THE RISING TIDE OF BIGOTRY AND BLOODSHED 197 (1993). The authors give as an example the coverage of a Ku Klux Klan rally on August 16, 1992. It took place in Janesville, Wisconsin, which has a population of 50,000. About a hundred klansmen attended as well as approximately the same number of anti-Klan demonstrators. The rally was covered not only by the local TV stations, but by newspapers from Milwaukee and Madison. Ultimately, it became a national news story when the talk-show host Geraldo Rivera punched a klansman. *Id.* at 197-98.

92. As Robert McNeil, executive editor and co-anchor of the "McNeil-Lehrer News Hour" explains it, producers of news shows believe "that bite-sized is best, that complexity must be avoided, that nuances are dispensable, that qualifications impede the simple message, that visual stimulation is a substitute for thought, and that verbal precision is an anachronism." Robert McNeil, *"Is Television Shortening Our Attention Span?,"* 14 N.Y.U. EDUCATIONAL QUARTERLY 2 (Winter 1983).

93. It is interesting to note that in compiling statistics on bias crimes, one of the criteria the FBI uses is whether the public perceives these crimes to be motivated by bias. Joseph M. Fernandez, Comment, *Bringing Hate Crimes into Focus—The Hate Crime Statistics Act of 1990, Pub. L. No. 101-275*, 26 HARV. C.R.-C.L. L. REV. 261, 286 n.129 (1991).

94. As one journalist wrote: "Above all, we know that the greater the horror, the better the story; journalists, too, operate within a pack psychology." JIM SLEEPER, THE CLOSEST OF STRANGERS: LIBERALISM AND THE POLITICS OF RACE IN NEW YORK 201 (1990).

95. *See generally* Sam Roberts, *Race and Politics: Issues that Most Still Sidestep*, N.Y. TIMES, July 19, 1993, at B3.

96. Of the newspapers subscribed to by Nexis, there were forty stories in the first nine days after the incident. The Chicago Tribune falsely reported that the attack occurred "as [the victim] talked with a white female classmate." *Black Teen Beaten by Gang of Whites*, CHI. TRIB., June 7, 1991, at 20.

97. Similarly, the Crown Heights disturbances, in which blacks vented rage over an automobile accident in which a Hasidic driver killed a seven-year-old black boy, were hyperbolically characterized by, among others, the Republican candidate (and soon to be mayor-elect) Rudolph Giuliani, as a "pogrom." Bob Herbert, *In America; Dangerous Turf*, N.Y TIMES, Oct. 3, 1993, § 4, at 15.

98. Steve Jacobson, *Dealing with a Tragedy*, NEWSDAY, June 9, 1991, at 7.

99. Editorial, *A Better Response to Hate Crimes*, N.Y. TIMES, June 8, 1991, at 22; Editorial, *Moral Outrage Isn't Enough to Help Alfred Ewell*, NEWSDAY, June 6, 1991, at 66 (Nassau & Suffolk ed.).

100. Anthony Lewis, *The Color of His Skin*, N.Y. TIMES, June 10, 1991, at A17. There were, to be sure, articles written by one New York Times reporter in which area residents, both black and white, spoke of the incident as incongruous in an integrated

area they described as relatively free of racial tension. *See* Sarah Lyall, *Sharpton Gets Mixed Reception in Protest March at Atlantic Beach*, N.Y. Times, June 9, 1991, at 34. There was also an article in which the principal defendant, Shannon Siegel, was described by area residents as having many black friends and himself seeming to identify with black people. Sarah Lyall, *Atlantic Beach Struggles to Explain Assault on Black Youth*, N.Y. Times, June 7, 1991 at B1.

101. Siegel's defense to the crime charged was that it was not he who participated in the attack on Ewell. Since the jury could not rationally conclude that he "punched, kicked, shoved or otherwise annoyed [Ewell] because of his race," N.Y. PENAL LAW § 240.30 (aggravated harassment), without also concluding that it was Siegel, among others, who intended to kill or seriously injure Ewell with a baseball bat, the prosecutor had nothing to gain by tacking on this misdemeanor charge because it could not result in a longer sentence. *See* N.Y. PENAL LAW § 70.25 (McKinney 1987). There was, however, a tactical disadvantage—the jury might, in a compromise verdict, convict him of this misdemeanor charge and acquit on the more serious felony charge. Moreover, by including these charges, the prosecutor was ensuring that the trial would be longer and the issues for the jury more complex.

102. Siegel's father testified that about "three-quarters of his friends were black." Ewell, the victim, testified that Siegel was an acquaintance of his with whom he had gotten a ride into New York City a few times. Siegel testified that Ewell was his "friend." *See* Alexander, *supra* note 47, at 4.

103. Gordon, *supra* note 55.

104. The jury ultimately convicted Siegel of the assault charge and he was sentenced to the maximum of five to fifteen years. This means he must serve five years before being eligible for parole and would serve no more than ten years if he does his time without disciplinary problems.

105. Such language was often used in the group. One black student reportedly said that Siegel liked rap music and hung out with black students and sometimes acted as though he were "really black on the inside." Said a white student, "The way you see him walk, and the way you see him talk, as far as you know, Shannon is black." Sarah Lyall, *Atlantic Beach Struggles to Explain Assault on Black Youth*, N.Y. TIMES, June 6, 1991, at B1.

106. The converse is often true as well; when the twelve citizens in question apply the law to the facts in a manner which jibes with our perception of the case, the verdict is often said to "restore our faith in the system." As UCLA Law professor Peter Arenella put it: We have come to look at our criminal justice system as more than a mechanism to decide guilt or innocence but also as a mechanism to somehow resolve fundamental rifts in the community. People naively expect that a trial can somehow give them justice, but that is literally impossible because people in the community have different substantive expectations of what justice demands. Seth Mydans, *Looking to the Courts for Catharsis*, N.Y. TIMES, Oct. 3, 1993, at § 4, at 3.

107. Indeed, one columnist compared it to the 1955 lynching of Emmett Till. *See* Les Payne, *Don't Call Racial Harmony Justice*, NEWSDAY, May 27, 1990, at 11. Another journalist attended a forum entitled "Youth, Media, and Race Relations" at which two black students who attended school at Bensonhurst joined white students in complaining that "the media had presented a picture of Bensonhurst so grotesque that none of them, black or white, could recognize it." SLEEPER, *supra* note 94, at 305. Referring to the column in Newsday, one of the black students, Jason Garel, said, "Give me a break! Up here, African Americans are victims much more often in their own neighborhoods. You people in the media influence a lot of people. You don't realize that you have great power. I go to Bensonhurst every day to school, and my mom expresses a lot of fear now." *Id.* at 306. Both of the black students with whom Sleeper talked after the forum expressed the opinion that the "Hawkins killing was more about 'turf' and the psychology of 'Packs' than about color—precisely what the black attorney Charles Simpson told me in defending Jon Lester in Howard Beach." *Id.* at 307.

108. DESANTIS, *supra* note 91 at 81 (1991). The incident actually began when a neighborhood crack addict, Gina Feliciano, told "everyone," including one of the defendants,

Keith Mondello, that as a surprise to the neighborhood, on her birthday, her Hispanic friends were bringing a large group of their black friends to "beat the shit out of all of yez." *Id.* at 59. A large group of white neighborhood youths, perhaps as many as thirty, gathered and as was the custom in anticipation of a rumble, proceeded to "break out the bats." *Id.* at 60. As DeSantis writes: The idea among any of the participants who answered the call to arms on Sixty-eighth Street that they may have been doing something wrong probably never occurred to most of them. Rumbles between groups from different blocks was [sic] certainly acceptable, even mandatory behavior, and if anyone had second thoughts, tremendous real or imagined peer pressure might have much to do with a decision to go ahead and come. *Id.* at 62. Some of the bats were supplied by a black member of the Bensonhurst gang, Russell Gibbons, and his white friend Charles Stressler. *Id.* at 71. At one point, a neighborhood teenager, having spotted Yusuf Hawkins and his four friends, who were there merely trying to find an address in response to an ad for a used car, called to the others: "They're here! They're here! Black kids are here!" *Id.* at 75. DeSantis then describes the scene: The four black youths heard footsteps approaching. Luther turned and saw a group of white men—he would later figure twenty or thirty—coming toward them from further down the street. . . .[T]he mob surrounded the four blacks. . . .There were shouts of 'Is this them?' 'What are you niggers doing here?' somebody hollered. Yusuf, Luther, and Troy were half-herded and half-propelled around the nearest corner, at Bay Ridge Avenue. Yusuf, clutching his half-eaten Snickers bar, pressed his back against the brick wall. 'We're looking for an address,' Troy said, offering the crumbled piece of the Buy-Lines. Keith Mondello—who was to be indicted for murder—looked at Stressler and shook his head. 'I ain't gonna hit them. These are babies,' he said. 'They're kids. These aren't them.' 'I ain't gonna hit them either,' Stressler said, and turned to leave as an excited John Vento ran up and the larger crowd pressed closer. 'Is this them? Is this them?' Vento asked, and drew back his arm, preparing to hit Hawkins. A short figure dressed in all white, later identified by witnesses as Joseph Fama, stepped forward. In his right hand was a .32-caliber chrome-plated revolver. 'To hell with beating them up. I'm gonna shoot the nigger!' he reportedly said. James Patino hollered 'No!' But it was too late. Yusuf's jaw dropped as he saw the pistol pointed directly at him. He stammered and managed to get out a stifled 'Oh, shit!' Four quick pops sounded in rapid succession, and Yusuf Hawkins screamed as he reeled and staggered for about twelve feet, clutching his chest. He crumpled to the pavement, still clutching the Snickers bar. *Id.* at 76.

109. *See generally, Id.*

110. Defendants Patino, Stressler and Curreri were acquitted of all charges. Defendants Mondello, Serrano and Vento were convicted of lesser charges. Robert D. McFadden, *U.S. Decides Not to Pursue Hawkins Case*, N.Y. TIMES, Dec. 21, 1991, § 1, at 21. The Vento jury, "stunned" by what they perceived as the weakness of the prosecution's case, included four black people and one Hispanic person. According to one juror, the jury as a whole did not perceive the incident as racially motivated: The impression you got from the coverage of this case was that it was a racist incident," said one of the jurors, "We all felt that this was really more about mistaken identity and that if the four youths had gone to the same section of Bensonhurst on any night, other than that night, these people would not have been involved in a racist incident. Chris Hedges, *Man Acquitted on Major Count in Racial Killing*, N.Y. TIMES, July 4, 1990, § 1, at 1.

111. Fama, who had a 72 IQ, was described as having "depressed intelligence, memory and cognitive flexibility consistent with early brain injury." DESANTIS, *supra* note 91, at 73 (*quoting* the State University of New York Health Science Center Department of Neurology, based on examinations conducted "as late as 1987"). Fama also had a history of violence.

112. *See* William Glaberson, *Judge Gives Maximum Sentences To 2 in Bensonhurst Murder Case*, N.Y. TIMES, June 12, 1990, at A1. In New York, this means that he must serve 32 years before he is *eligible* for parole. *See generally* N.Y. PENAL LAW Art. 70.

113. Section 20.00 of the New York Penal Law provides: When one person engages in conduct which constitutes an offense, another person is criminally liable for such conduct when, acting with the mental culpability required for the commission thereof, he solicits, requests, commands, importunes, or intentionally aids such person to engage in such conduct. N.Y. PENAL LAW § 20.00. If one characterizes the "conduct which constitutes an offense" as the

actual shooting of Hawkins, then the others present at the scene of the crime were not guilty as accomplices since the evidence strongly suggests that Fama acted on his own impulse. It is however plausible to characterize the conduct as joining a volatile gang, some of whom were armed with bats, "under circumstances evincing a depraved indifference to human life" creating "a grave risk" that someone might be killed in *some fashion*. *See* N.Y. PENAL LAW § 125.25(2) (McKinney 1987).

114. DESANTIS, *supra note* 91, at 232. *See* Hedges, *supra* note 110.

115. *Id.* The prosecutor charged all the defendants with the same misdemeanor civil rights statute used against Shannon Siegel, despite the fact that it would not expose the defendants to additional jail time.

116. The juries concluded that this was a not a racial incident but a case of mistaken identity; had Hawkins been in the neighborhood on any other night, this would not have happened. *See generally, supra* note 110.

117. A rumble was not an uncommon occurrence nor frowned upon by many of the young men of Bensonhurst. Indeed, for some of them, it was "mandatory behavior." DESANTIS, *supra* note 91, at 62.

118. The tag-along who intentionally aids the principal in the assault or homicide with the *mens rea* necessary for the crime is certainly guilty as an accomplice to assault or homicide.

119. Gibbons was *not* prosecuted for the murder of Hawkins even though his conduct fit the state's theory of accomplice liability like hand to glove. If one followed the logical extension of the prosecution's theory of the case, Gibbons, in supplying the bats, intentionally aided others to engage in activity which created a grave risk of death that someone might be killed. *See* N.Y. PENAL LAW § 125.25(2). While one cannot presume to know the motives of the prosecutor in declining to indict Gibbons, it is fair to assume that a black defendant's presence as a co-defendant would have undermined, if only subliminally, the theory that the alleged accomplices were motivated by race. Defense attorney Mathew Mari believes that having Gibbons as a witness at his client's trial was a significant factor in convincing the jury that the case was about mistaken identity, not race. Telephone interview with Mathew Mari, Nov. 19, 1993 (on file with the author).

120. *See* EARL STROM WITH BLAINE JOHNSON, CALLING THE SHOTS: MY FIVE DECADES IN THE NBA 32 (1992) (Strom himself denies ever doing this).

121. DESANTIS, *supra* note 91, at 128. *See also* Lorrin Anderson, *Crime, Race, and the Fourth Estate,* 42 NATIONAL REVIEW 52 (1990). Except for the statement of one defendant, there was no evidence that the attack was racially motivated. Among the victims of the marauding gang was an elderly Latino man. TIMOTHY SULLIVAN, UNEQUAL VERDICTS: THE CENTRAL PARK JOGGER TRIALS 23 (1992). A study done by a "think tank" about media coverage of the "central-park jogger" case found that of the 406 news items examined during a particular fifteen day period, 54 cited race as a possible factor. There were only six references to it as a crime against women." *Id.* at 57. The other day this author told a white person about an incident which took place in a predominately white neighborhood. A man was walking down the street and came upon a group of black teenagers who passed him on both sides. He inadvertently brushed shoulders with one of them who then turned around and said: "Hey man, you dissed me." The teenager then pummeled the man, knocking him to the ground, and shot him, leaving him in the street where he was almost hit by oncoming traffic. His life may well have been saved by a good samaritan, a black woman, who then helped the police find and arrest two of his assailants. When my interlocutor learned that the victim was white, he immediately concluded that racial bias motivated the youths. Yet anyone who lives in a violent neighborhood, or reads newspapers, should know that such stories—in which schoolchildren kill each other over real or imagined slights—have distressingly become ever more common. Indeed, in October of 1993, Jesse Jackson noted that 362 black people under the age of 21 had been killed by other blacks in New York City alone that year. *See also* Robert D. McFadden, *Report Finds 20% of Students in New York City Carry Arms*, N.Y. TIMES, Oct. 15, 1993, at B3; Bob Herbert, *Blacks Killing Blacks*, N.Y. TIMES, Oct. 20, 1993, Op-ed, at A23. Of course, these incidents don't automatically become racially motivated simply because the victim is of a race different from that of the assailant. Yet racial tensions have reached the point where such incidents are almost

invariably viewed through a racial prism, so that if racism could ostensibly have been the motivating factor, it is assumed to be so.

122. Robert Morgenthau, the District Attorney of New York County, unequivocally asserted in a press conference that race was not at issue in the case. *See* SULLIVAN, *supra* note 121, at 167.

123. *Id.* at 166-67.

124. *Id.* at 67. Robinson also admitted in his written statement that his accomplices called some cyclists "fucking white people." *Id.* However, it is worth noting that among the victims of this marauding gang was a dark-skinned Hispanic man. Accordingly, how could it be proven that the jogger was chosen because she was white rather than because she happened to be the first woman to appear at that fateful moment?

125. Although this statement does not even ostensibly provide a mitigating defense, it is possible to imagine a situation in which a member of an historically disadvantaged group chose a white victim under circumstances that might legitimately *reduce* his actions from murder to manslaughter. *Split Second,* a play by Dennis McIntyre, tells the story of a black police officer who catches a white car thief late at night on a deserted west side street. While he has the thief handcuffed, the latter unrelentingly taunts him with ever increasing vituperativeness, ultimately spewing the vilest racist tirade imaginable. The officer, enraged, suddenly shoots and kills him. DENNIS MCINTYRE, SPLIT SECOND (Samuel French, Inc. 1984). Normally, this would provide a viable mitigating defense of "heat of passion" resulting from provocation, *see, e.g.,* CAL. PENAL CODE § 195(2) (West 1988), or "extreme emotional disturbance." MODEL PENAL CODE § 210(1)(b).

126. When caught, Ferguson had notes in his pockets expressing racial animosities towards whites, Asians, and "Uncle Tom" blacks. *See* Lena Williams, *After Train Killings, Worry About Backlash,* N.Y. TIMES, Dec. 13, 1993, at B6; *See also* Richard Perez-Pena, *Woman in '92 Subway Dispute With L.I.R.R. Suspect Says All the Signs Were There,* N.Y. TIMES, Dec. 13, 1993, at B6; Jonathan Rabinovitz, *Judge Delays Ruling in L.I.R.R. Shooting Case,* N.Y. TIMES, Jan. 5, 1994, at B6.

127. As the prosecutor put it, "it is not infinity, but it will do." *See* John T. McQuiston, *Grand Jury Indicts Suspect on 93 Counts in Attack That Killed 6 on Long Island Rail Road,* N.Y. TIMES, Jan. 19, 1994, at B5.

128. *See* N.Y. PENAL LAW § 240.30 (aggravated harassment). These misdemeanor charges will simply merge with the ultimate sentence. *See generally, supra* note 101.

129. As Jesse Jackson concluded "We should not derive from this a race motif, but a sick motif." *See* John T. McQuiston, *Mineola Woman is 6th to Die in Rail Shooting,* N.Y. TIMES, Dec. 13, 1993 at B1. One shooting victim later declared, "Race is not the issue here. For anyone to say that these shootings were racist. . .misses the point and trivializes the horror." *See* Thomas F. McDermott, *He Stared Blankly at Me, then Fired,* N.Y. TIMES, Dec. 17, 1993, at A39 (op-ed.).

130. Alison Mitchell, *Grand Jury Hears Evidence in Crown Hts. Case,* N.Y. TIMES, Dec. 8, 1992, at B1 (mentioning frequent charges by black residents that "Hasidim get preferential treatment by the police and countercharges by Orthodox Jews that the legal system provides them with no protection against crime by blacks").

131. John Kifner, *Clashes Persist in Crown Heights for 3d Night in Row,* N.Y. TIMES, Aug. 22, 1991, at B1.

132. *Id.*

133. Apparently, but for the negligence of medical personnel at the hospital who failed to notice a second knife wound on his body, Rosenbaum would probably have lived. John Kifner, *Stabbing Victim's Brother Seeks Answers,* N.Y. TIMES, Nov. 11, 1991, at B3.

134. George F. Fletcher, Convicting the Victim, N.Y. TIMES, Feb. 7, 1994, at A17.

135. Alison Mitchell, *Dinkins Faces New Criticism in Crown Heights,* N.Y. Times, Dec. 3, 1992, at A1.

136. *Id.*

137. *Id.*

138. After this incident, he was convicted and sentenced to two years for *inter alia,* two counts of criminal possession of stolen property. Patricia Hurtado, *'Beating*

Victim' Found Guilty, NEWSDAY, July 28, 1993, at 23 (City ed.).

139. Patricia Hurtado, *Hasidic Anger; 100 jam B'kln courthouse*, NEWSDAY, Dec. 3, 1992, at 5 (City ed.).

140. Black activist Al Sharpton made the point that no matter what Nimmons was doing, he did not deserve to be assaulted by his captors. Catherine S. Margold, *The Reformation of a Street Preacher*, N.Y. TIMES, Jan. 24, 1993 § 6, at 18. It would have to be established that a citizen making an arrest exceeded the force necessary to do so. *See* N.Y. PENAL LAW § 35.30 (4) (McKinney 1987).

141. As stated before, the use of racial epithets does not necessarily mean that the speaker intentionally chose the victim because of his race.

142. As the complaining witness, there would be no limitations on the defense attorney's right to cross-examine him about every conviction and bad act he may have committed. *See* FED. R. EVID. 609 (limitations on cross-examination about prior convictions apply to defendants only).

143. Nimmons, who had previously been convicted of possession of burglar's tools, had in his pocket, at the time of the incident, "a sharpened screwdriver; a sheet-metal knife; a T-bar lug wrench; a pizza cutter and a plastic instrument." Hurtado, *supra* note 139, at 5.

144. Alison Mitchell, *Dinkins Faces New Criticism in Crown Hts.*, N.Y. TIMES, Dec. 3, 1992, at A1.

145. *See* Smith, *supra* note 7.

146. Referring to hate speech statutes, one commentator has noted: "it may actually be angry members of underprivileged groups that end up being prosecuted most often" under these laws. KENT GREENAWALT, SPEECH, CRIME, AND THE USES OF LANGUAGE 301 (1989). *See also* ACLU Brief at 22-23 (citing Gellman, *supra* note 16, at 387. A black man was charged in Florida for "Evidencing Prejudice While Committing an Offense" under FLA. STAT. § 775.085 (1991) because in threatening a white police officer, he used the epithet "white cracker." The charges were ultimately dropped for insufficiency of evidence. *Hate Crime Charge Dropped Against Black Man in Florida*, N.Y. TIMES, Aug. 31, 1991, at 10. *See* Gellman, *supra* note 16, at 361 n.134.

147. Mitchell himself argued that the statute violated equal protection because a disproportionate number of the crimes eligible for penalty enhancement under the statute were committed by the "poor and uneducated." State v. Mitchell, 485 N.W.2d 807, 830 (Wis. 1992).

148. James Garafalo reported that in New York, "a surprising proportion of the racial incidents handled [in 1987 and 1988] by the BIIU [Bias Incident Investigating Unit]—209 of 585—were directed against whites. This figure does not include acts of anti-semitism which the author categorizes as "religion cases." JAMES GARAFALO, BIAS AND NON-BIAS CRIMES IN NEW YORK CITY: PRELIMINARY FINDINGS 5 (Nov. 9, 1990) (unpublished manuscript, presented to the American Society of Criminology, on file with the author) (cited in Levin, *supra* note 35). More recently, the Southern Poverty Law Center's Klanwatch, which monitors hate crimes, reported that in the last three years, 46 percent of racially motivated killings were committed by blacks. *See* Peter Applebome, *Rise Is Found in Hate Crimes Committed by Blacks*, N.Y. TIMES, Dec. 13, 1993, at A12.

149. This is the Supreme Court's characterization. State v. Mitchell, 113 S. Ct. 2194, 2200.

150. *See, e.g., ACLU Brief*, at 18.

151. These statutes are primarily intended "for groups that have been the traditional targets of bigotry" who "bear the special burden of being selected for victimization on the basis of their race or other characteristics." Grannis, *supra* note 3, at 33. Indeed, those who have been most vigorous in their support for bias statutes have been representatives of historically disadvantaged groups (for example, the ADL and the Gay and Lesbian task force).

152. MISSISSIPPI BURNING (Orion 1988) (directed by Alan Parker). The movie had a number of scenes evoking the brutality and injustices blacks were subjected to in Mississippi in the early 1960s.

153. To be sure, this perception can and does exist independent of whether a

particular jurisdiction has a bias-crime statute. However, the possibility of enhancing the penalty when the victim is white will tend to reinforce the perception that a white-dominated criminal justice system cares less about black- on-black crime. Indeed, a black person is more likely to be executed for killing a white person than for killing another black person. *See* McCleskey v. Kemp, 481 U.S. 279 (1987). Moreover, both blacks and whites will not fail to notice that because of the response from black activists and greater media coverage, prosecutors give more attention to the occasional racially charged white on black crime than to the quotidian tragedy of black on black crime. I say "occasional" because, as Brian Levin, a strong proponent of Hate Crime legislation, has noted, "a black is far more likely to be victimized by another black than by a racially motivated assault" and "[a] Jew is more likely to be killed in a motor vehicle accident than to be personally victimized in an anti-Semitic incident." *See* Brian Levin, *supra* note 35, at 172, nn. 83-84 (citing BUREAU OF JUSTICE STATISTICS, U.S. DEP'T OF JUSTICE, REPORT TO THE NATION ON CRIME AND JUSTICE 12 (2d ed. 1988).

154. Certainly it provides an easy way for politicians to demonstrate to their constituents that they are doing something about a problem without actually doing anything about it. *See, e.g.,* Weinstein, *supra* note 17, at 16 ("Enhancing punishment for racially motivated crimes seems to me to be part of a larger American syndrome of adopting harsh punishment as an expedient response that deals only with the most superficial manifestations of complex, deep-seated problems.").

Moreover, one can well imagine a legislator's fear of a negative "soft on crime" thirty-second commercial depicting a menacing looking skinhead with the following voice-over: "Opposed legislation that would have cracked down on vicious hate crimes which have torn at the fabric of our society." On the flip side, there appear to be certain legislators in New York who have balked at such legislation—which also protects those who are intentionally selected because of their sexual orientation— for fear that support for a law which would ostensibly protect, among others, gays and lesbians from violence, would actually be interpreted by their conservative constituents as support of the "gay lifestyle." Perhaps, in *their* imagination, they see a negative thirty-second commercial depicting a homophobe's worst nightmare, a flamboyantly effeminate man mugging for the cameras in a gay pride parade, as the ominous if dulcet baritone voice-over tells the world that they have supported legislation which would give "special consideration" to "deviants."

155. *See* Curtis L. Taylor & Peg Tyre, *2 Queens Men Convicted In Fatal Gay-Bias Attack*, Newsday, Nov. 21, 1991, at 5. *See also,* Joseph P. Fried, *2 Get 25 Years to Life in Gay Man's Slaying in Queens,* N.Y. TIMES, Jan. 11, 1992, at 23.

156. *See* Abramovsky, *supra* note 34, at 885.

157. N.Y. PENAL LAW § 160.10 (McKinney 1988) (Robbery in the second degree) provides in pertinent part: A person is guilty of robbery in the second degree when he forcibly steals property and when: 1. He is aided by another person actually present....

158. *See* N.Y. PENAL LAW § 160.00 ("Robbery; defined").

159. *See generally* N.Y. PENAL LAW Art. 120.00 (McKinney 1987). In New York, proposed bill § 1424 (Feb. 2, 1993), asserts that "[c]urrent New York State Law treats too leniently the crime of assault." Proponents of § 1424 would create a new crime called "gang assault" in which the defendant must be aided by "two or more persons actually present," and would accordingly be punished more severely. This proposal also calls for the sentencing judge to "consider as a factor in sentencing whether the crime was bias motivated."

160. Jacobs, *supra* note 35, at 57.

161. *See* 42 U.S.C. § 1985 (1981) (conspiracy to interfere with civil rights) (defendant need not be acting under color of state law). That the crime of conspiracy does not merge with the substantive crime is well settled in New York. *See, e.g.,* People v. Epton, 227 N.E.2d 829, 836 (N.Y. 1967) (citations omitted). One can conspire to commit a crime without ever committing it, and commit a crime without having previously conspired to do so. *See also* 42 U.S.C. § 1983 (deprivation of civil rights under color of state law); People v. McGee, 399 N.E.2d 1177 (N.Y. 1979).

CHAPTER 9

THE END OF THE ROAD

"The University in the Manner of Tiananmen Square"*

*William Van Alstyne***

The university academic council assembled in the room where it customarily met. The agenda had been distributed well in advance. Alternative formulations of a new university offensive verbal conduct rule were under consideration this afternoon. The council would finally decide the appropriate standard to submit to the Board of Trustees. These were the choices to be discussed and voted on today:

> RULE I. *No member of the faculty, student body, or staff shall engage in any verbal conduct that renders the environment on campus, or some part thereof offensive.*[1]
>
> *1ST ALTERNATIVE RULE I. No member of the faculty, student body, or staff shall engage in any verbal conduct that renders the environment on campus, or some part thereof offensive. This rule shall apply, however, only if the verbal conduct is of a sexual nature, and not otherwise.*
>
> *2ND ALTERNATIVE RULE I. No member of the faculty, student body, or staff shall engage in any verbal conduct that renders the environment on campus, or some part thereof offensive. This rule shall apply, however, only if the verbal conduct is of*

---

*This essay appears at 21 *Hastings Constitutional Law Quarterly* 1 (1993). Reprinted with permission.

**William R. and Thomas C. Perkins Professor of Law, Duke University. [With thanks to Daniel Defoe, for his useful original essay, *The Shortest Way With the Dissenters: Or Proposals for the Establishment of the Church* (London, 1703); and also to Catharine MacKinnon, Richard Delgado, Mari Matsuda, Charles Lawrence, Thomas Grey, and Cass Sunstein for their highly instructive views.]

a sexual or religious nature, and not otherwise.

3RD ALTERNATIVE RULE I. No member of the faculty, student body, or staff shall engage in any verbal conduct that renders the environment on campus, or some part thereof offensive. This rule shall apply, however, only if the verbal conduct is of a sexual, religious, or racial nature, and not otherwise.

4TH ALTERNATIVE RULE I. No member of the faculty, student body, or staff shall engage in any verbal conduct that renders the environment on campus, or some part thereof offensive. This rule shall apply, however, only if the verbal conduct is of a sexual, religious, racial, or other nature reflecting an improper and unreasonable attitude toward others according to the common standard of the university community, and not otherwise.

A Short History of How the University Came to Adopt the 4th Alternative to Rule I

i.

The rule first proposed for approval and vote was the rule simply forbidding offensive speech. This, of course, was the essential idea of RULE I. The general purpose of the rule was simply to make the campus a more pleasant environment for those participating in the university, to create a hospitable environment in which to carry on work—whether as students, faculty, administration and staff, or as regular and valued employees.

But this original, broadly-framed proposal was quickly dismissed as, at best, well-intended but nevertheless poorly conceived. The idea was too sweeping. Could complaints be brought and charges pursued before a committee empowered to put anyone at risk insofar as the committee were satisfied, after investigation and hearing, that one's "verbal conduct" did—in *some* fashion—seriously offend others (and so, as to them, render the environment, or some part thereof, offensive)? Surely, offensiveness per se could not be an appropriate test. This was vastly too broad and altogether too chilling for anyone's taste. It reached all "verbal conduct" rendering "the environment" on campus, or any part of the campus, "offensive." But what would that mean? An "offensive environment," it was asked, for example, to *whom*? To students attending a particular class? To others, not in that class, who learned what was said by a faculty member or other students? Not offensive to students (or not only to students), but offensive to other faculty, to trustees, to alumni on campus, to administrators, or to staff? "Offensive," moreover, *in what way*? Merely in one's choice of particular terms?[2] In the very nature of the information imparted?[3] Or, rather, the conclusions summarized or offered as opinion, in or out of class? Or "offensive" merely in the apparent callousness of one's values as such—values affronting the values of others on campus, or on some part of the campus where they worked?

The entire notion of proceeding in this way was hopeless. The implicit censorship of the proposal, and the standard it employed, were too much like the chilling fatwa issued worldwide on Salman Rushdie for having authored his religiously offensive (blasphemous) work of fiction, THE SATANIC VERSES—a work condemned and an author sentenced to death for his offensive (mis)portrayal of the life of the Prophet. No member of the council was willing to accept any rule cast in terms so loose as to lend themselves to levelling the campus in any of these ways. The proposal as projected in RULE I was quickly tabled. The council turned at once to the first alternative proposal, hoping it would avoid most—perhaps all—of the problems compelling the council's decision not to recommend the original version of RULE I.

ii.

Initially, *1ST ALTERNATIVE RULE* I looked considerably more promising because it was so much more specific and narrow. It had come to the council as a concrete proposal from a special task force on sexual harassment. It had particular point because of the still recent (and disturbing) Clarence Thomas-Anita Hill hearings that nearly all had seen on network broadcasts. And it was given particular point, too, by the council's own understanding that some rule roughly of this sort was expected of the university under federal law. Titles VI and VII of the Civil Rights Act of 1964, as amended, and Title IX of the Educational Amendments Act of 1972, evidently required all institutions receiving any federal assistance to forbid sexual harassment. The proposal was designed specifically to meet that requirement, and in doing so it tried not to go beyond that specific concern. In contrast with RULE I, it was thus deliberately very limited; it would reach only offensive verbal conduct "of a sexual nature," as it took exact care so to say.[4]

In the course of discussion, however, the council came to understand that *1ST ALTERNATIVE RULE* I would put the university in a most awkward position—for what the rule left out. While the rule was initially well-received (it was taken for granted that it was meant principally to protect women on campus from being subjected to humiliating remarks, denigrative jokes, etc.), as now drafted it left out of account *religiously* denigrative or humiliating verbal conduct of a like sort (e.g., "jokes" about Jews). Evidently, these would not be treated in the same fashion as abusive verbal descriptions of women (or of men). Was this really to be so? It required but little discussion for the council to concede that the failure to include verbal conduct of a religiously aspersive nature was a mistake insofar as *1ST ALTERNATIVE RULE* I treated the humiliation of others by religion as of unequal concern (indeed, by its terms, of NO concern) as humiliation by sex. So to avoid that impression the council moved to *2ND ALTERNATIVE RULE* I.[5]

iii.

But the discussion about abusive or offensive "verbal conduct of a sexual or religious nature," now subject to the proposed rule, only made the council more sharply aware that the same point made as to religion applied with at least equal force to verbal conduct of a racially-aspersive (and offensive) nature as well. And how was one to feel about that? Was it to be true that offensive utterances (i.e., denigrative utterances) would be subject to complaint only if insulting toward others based on gender or religion? Was *racial* disparagement truly to be treated as *less* inappropriate on campus, or less subject to sanction (indeed, subject to *no* sanction at all)? How was that possible? The very idea was startling. Something was clearly wrong.

Several council members suggested that this must be a red herring. Though the new rule would, by its terms, reach only verbal conduct of a "sexual nature" (now amended to include religious disparagement), and only then insofar as it rendered the campus environment (or some part thereof) "offensive", and though the new rule admittedly did not apply to "racist" verbal conduct, it was false to claim that such behavior was somehow thereby in any way meant to be condoned. Presumably—this in answer to a sharp question—it was already subject to discipline by some other rule. If not (and the speaker conceded that there seemed to be no such specific rule), then assuredly it should be added, and added quickly, as it easily could be.

Several thought this surely must be right. In response to the first point, however, there seemed to be no pre-existing, adequate rule the previous speakers could point to. Moreover, whatever might have been thought in the past, it provided no reason to leave out offensive racial verbal conduct from the proposed rule, insofar as the council itself was now about the specific business of recommending what was to be *the* proper regulation of unacceptable offensive verbal conduct at the university. Additionally, as a member of the council observed—and this point seemed especially strong—in having already extended the rule to make clear that offensive verbal conduct of a religious nature was to be covered, to fail to include the same treatment of race could rightly be regarded as a callous inversion of priorities—an act of willful discrimination by the council itself. The point hung in the air, awaiting a satisfactory response.

iv.

But before the council even moved to a vote on *3RD ALTERNATIVE RULE* I[6] (as, by now, many had already been persuaded to do), the discussion had become increasingly awkward for others in the council. Prompted by the unexpected turn the more general discussion was taking, they had begun thinking of still other issues, and other analogies. By leaving out verbal conduct denigrating to others (and making the campus environment oppressive to them) by yet *other*, indistinguishable kinds of belittling depictions, remarks, jokes, or posters—because of physical characteristics ("cripples"?), sexual orientation ("faggots"?), or national origin ("the yellow peril"?), for instance,—indeed, by cordoning off only such verbal conduct as reflected offensively on some characteristics but not others (age, sexual orientation, national origin, veteran status, obesity?), the rule was discriminatory in the bias of its restricted coverage: denying all others any standing to complain, and dismissing any complaint they might have as evidently of no equal worth—notwithstanding that this "speech" (this "verbal conduct") was belittling to them, notwithstanding that it reduced them to stereotype, and notwithstanding that it subjected them to an offensive environment on campus or some part thereof. So what was the principle the rule sought to capture, after all? What did the council think it—the council itself—was actually about? How should the council frame a suitable rule neither overinclusive nor underinclusive of what "verbal conduct" was appropriate to forbid?

More members of the council stirred uneasily in their seats. The university surely must, they had thought, work in the best way it could to assert a clear substantive stance on the right way of thinking about gender, religion, and race. In large part, that very supposition was itself built into the rule. In large part, moreover, many understood this to be part of the very function of the university (was it not?)—to educate their students, their employees, and themselves on just such questions? Moreover, as already noticed, in some measure that position was obvious from the formulation of the rule the council already had previously (albeit tentatively) approved. And, whether or not all agreed that that was so—about the proper mission of the university—at a minimum it was already virtually settled by the council as being so to the extent that it would forbid "offensive" verbal conduct respecting characteristics of gender, religion, or race, so to ban these abusive and hurtful acts from prejudicing the environment. So much had already virtually been agreed to, had it not?

But was it true that the university had no equally determinable position on the "right" way of thinking, or expressing one's views, about *other* characteristics or differences? For example, about sexual orientation, or about age, or about national origin, or about economic class? But if not, then *why* not? How did it distinguish what it was prepared to do from what it was not prepared to do? In other words, on what basis would it be a mere Pontius Pilate[7] on these other things, when it was agreed on the things already proposed for the rule? In the face of baneful remarks belittling others for their sexual orientation, whether made to them or of them,[8] for example, would the university nonetheless refuse to consider the matter as of the same complain able sort as when baneful remarks of a religiously or racially aspersive sort were the object of complaint? Why should that be? And how would one account for the university's stance? *What was its principle?*

And, again, *why was it necessary?* The council had resolved that it would not leave some "verbal conduct" to the inadequate response of a mere "free speech" campus. So much as this was already settled and clear. If the university would no longer leave some to the mercy of the "free speech campus," but would so leave others, it needed to explain its principle "up front." It necessarily followed that the proper concern of the council and the right object of the right kind of rule, was to explain its principle up front, to identify the metric of the rule and explain why certain offensive statements were forbidden and others not, to give a foundation—not a mere institutional *ipse dixit*—adequately distinguishing what offensive statements were forbidden from those statements not forbidden, regardless of their offensiveness, to distinguish mere bigotry (if that were the point of distinction) from what, though offensive, had value of some sort, on which account it would not be made the object of this rule (though it seemed to reflect other attitudes one might equally resent, equally feel offended by, equally believe to be wrong or demoralizing), as many might believe to be true of Salman Rushdie's THE SATANIC VERSES—which no university would, or ought to be, prepared to forbid. Until *that* task was done, moreover, *no* useful, *principled* rule could be adopted adequately distinguishing verbal conduct that would not be appropriate to forbid from that which the university would not tolerate or condone.

V.

The challenge laid down seemed to be worthy and fair to the council. In the course of the afternoon, it struggled at length to meet this challenge as best it could. In the end, however, the council could do no better than to adopt *4TH ALTERNATIVE RULE* I.[9] For even after elaborate further efforts to be more specific, it was agreed that nothing significantly more instructive or more specific could be done. The council's own discussion served principally to make clear what perhaps should have been obvious all along—that there was really no principle the council could state beyond "the principle" announced on the face of *4TH ALTERNATIVE RULE* I, and, in fact, it did quite accurately reflect the operative standard after all else was said and done.

Predictably, as all agreed, not *all* "denigrative" or *all* "negative" depictions were uniformly thought appropriate to forbid. Even if expressed emphatically, they might be correct or, if not perfectly correct, at least "understandable," and thus not condemnable as offensive "mere bigotry" as such. Necessarily, that is, some offensive speech (i.e., speech offensive to some persons because, in their view, denigrating of them) was not to be forbidden, consistent with the council's rejection of original RULE I. A proper rule had to allow for this understanding. And *4TH ALTERNATIVE RULE* I did so, articulating the differentiating principle as crisply as circumstances would allow. A substantial number of council members shared the view, for example, that the European discovery and subsequent displacement of Native Americans, beginning with Columbus and San Salvador, could be described as "genocide." In keeping with that view, many likewise thought it not inappropriate—quite understandable, in fact—for Native American students to express themselves very aggressively about certain subjects, i.e., to speak aggressively about whites—of the "white man," and of "the white man's rape" of the continent, and "the white man's racism" as well. Oppositely, however, a denigrative description of Native Americans (as "aborigines," or as "backward peoples" with a "primitive culture") would not pass without notice. And, moreover, at the least they were quite prepared to vote for a rule sanctioning *offensive stereotype depictions of Native Americans if concretely carried into verbal conduct so to make some part of the campus an "offensive environment" for Native American students subjected either directly or indirectly to such affronts.* They were confident their colleagues were willing to do no less.[10]

Other members disagreed with this example (they thought it somewhat ill-chosen and subject to a good deal of uncertainty that their colleagues hadn't allowed for[11]), though they admitted that their colleagues' view of its appropriate treatment was not without some measure of reason, as they felt start here about several, still different examples other council members put forth.

As one such example, a member of the council asked whether *pedophilia*—a pronounced or even exclusive erotic longing for sexual intimacy with youngsters—was a category of "sexual orientation" the council believed to be indistinguishable in entitlement to be treated with equality of protection from verbal abuse on campus according to the proposed rule? The question went largely unanswered. Several council members stiffened at the question, suspicious of why such a matter was even raised, unless as a snide suggestion aimed actually at them, as gay and lesbian persons (which they were). Was the question raised to draw them out, either to "defend" their own gay or lesbian orientation in front of the council, or otherwise to accept the unstated but implied comparison of themselves with *pedophiles*?

Unknown to these council members, however, the question was asked by a faculty member interested in testing the council's principle—an anguished faculty member who himself subscribed to pedophile magazines and who lived in terrible dread of having his own orientation discovered. Moreover, he fully believed that the sexual distinctions drawn by others were themselves merely self-serving. He had hoped the council would respond not with silence, but positively to his idea. Inwardly, he was filled with dismay that his question had been treated as some miscarried, or tasteless, out-of-place remark.

One member of the council hesitantly suggested that whether such an orientation would be protected by the verbal conduct rule would perhaps depend, at least partly—perhaps entirely—on "whether the leading national professional psychiatric and psychological organizations still regarded such a person as sexually deviant rather than normal," in which case, he supposed, descriptions of pedophiles as "deviates" "needing treatment," could not be described as expressions of "bigotry," whereas descriptions of gays and lesbians as "deviates" "needing treatment" would be subject to sanction under the rule.[12] But this altogether hapless effort to respond, so to draw some distinction according to how professional psychiatric and psychological organizations happened to classify such things, served only to make the matter that much worse.

But by now it was altogether apparent that this entire line of discussion would prove disastrous if allowed to proceed topic by topic, along any such lines as this. Other members of the council swiftly drew from this exchange the same conclusion as had already become quite obvious to others—that the council could not possibly go on in this way, now to adjudicate what was acceptable for some to say and what was not insofar as it made the environment offensive to others in some particular way. And it could not possibly make a definitive list of essentially forbidden expressions, so to distinguish them from unforbidden expressions, and adequately explain the difference—as it now was at risk of seeming to do. Neither could it possibly provide a suitable guideline list framed in any sufficient way to catch all that should be caught on the one hand (whatever that was), and yet leave untouched everything else, however offensive, appropriately protected by an ample academic freedom and an ample campus freedom of speech.

The thing to be done, therefore, was not to give up, but instead to stop with such agreement as could be reached now, so to frame the rule simply, specifically in the terms already proposed in *4th Alternative Rule* I. Beyond this, the council clearly was not the appropriate place to settle anything else. Rather, as actual incidents might arise, consistent with the standard now framed on the face of the proposed rule itself, the appropriate hearing board could sort them out: as complaints might be brought, hearings held, decisions made, and sanctions applied. In brief, the particular application of *4th Alternative Rule* I would be determined under the procedures provided in Rule II.[13]

To be sure, this regime might have its own difficulties, but so much was unavoidable, no matter what the council might do. The assumption should be the practical one that "everyone would know" (or in any event quickly learn) what the "core" of unacceptable verbal conduct was to consist of and why. Nor would it be particularly helpful, it was agreed, for the council, having already framed the rule, to get into "explanations" or provide examples (they might themselves be insulting and misunderstood, or somehow taken the wrong way by some). Obviously, some basic sense of the community would inform the hearing committee; the council was both willing and eager to assume that it would. There was, nearly all agreed, no obvious superior alternative to meet the objections that had been raised than that proposed by *4th Alternative Rule* I. Operating under this reformulation of Rule I, the proper committee, already provided for under Rule II, would decide the appropriate disposition of each actual incident, *according to the metric of the rule itself.* And so the council decided to do.

vi.

In the end, the key to the success in the final formulation and adoption of *4TH ALTERNATIVE RULE* I was the consensus on basic principle. Its basic principle was really quite clear, was it not?[14] And much unlike original RULE I (which, the council pointed out to its own satisfaction, had been squarely defeated), *4TH ALTERNATIVE RULE* I refused to make offensiveness *per se* the test. *4TH ALTERNATIVE RULE* I was both different from and far better than original RULE I because it was neither overinclusive nor underinclusive of properly sanctionable verbal conduct according to its own terms. Unless one's verbal conduct was *both* offensive *and also* of a nature reflecting an improper *and* unreasonable attitude toward others, as the rule declared, then one's verbal conduct remained outside the reach of the rule, i.e., it would not be subject to complaint and to sanction. This struck the council as being exactly as it should be.

As thus amended and perfected, the rule was no longer underinclusive because it would now treat "all like cases alike," so to apply equally, for instance, whether the object of one's denigration were some mental characteristic of others (e.g., "retards"), some physical characteristic ("cripples"), some sexual orientation characteristic ("faggots"), or some other characteristic including (but now no longer limited to) race, religion, or gender. Rather, expressions of bigoted animus calculated to diminish the sense of self worth of others on campus, and to make the environment on campus[15] a humiliating or oppressive place for them, would be reached whether of a sexual nature or some other nature. In that way, the amendment to the rule represented an obvious gain.

Yet, the rule was not overinclusive, for it was no longer driven by the same censorship standard of original RULE I. *That* standard, such as it was, and now rejected, was that the mere offensive, denigrative, belittling, or discriminatory character of one's speech (i.e., speech willfully designed to express a harsh or a negative view of others or of their practices), would, on that account, make it subject to complaint. But under the new rule, while this characteristic of one's speech was retained as a necessary condition, it would not be a sufficient condition. Specifically, that one's verbal conduct *might* express an animus toward others *and* be offensive to them, or that it belittled them, their beliefs, or their attitudes, or their values in some way, would *not* render it subject to complaint unless, in addition to being offensive in the manner or substance of its content (and whether or not it was of a sexual nature), *it also reflected an improper and unreasonable attitude according to the common standard of the university*—and all of this according to the specific terms of the rule itself.

So, to take a clear instance, applying this branch of the rule, even "hateful" denigrative expressions about a neo-Nazi student group on campus would be within the realm of protected expression, insofar as such expressions of rejection, based on a shared repugnance regarding neo-Nazis, could *not* be considered "unreasonable" or "improper" for a member of the university community to hold as a view, or to reflect straightforwardly in their speech. That they—the very persons or group(s) targeted by such speech—may feel themselves humiliated by such speech, that they may not like the way they are thus depicted, or that they may believe they are misunderstood, however, is neither here nor there, for surely one has a right to present one's opinions on neo-Nazis, whether neo-Nazis find themselves offended or not.[16] Neo-Nazis are *properly* left to the mercy of the free speech campus,[17] just as others[18] *properly* are not. The whole challenge, of course, is to know how to draw the distinction. The example was, all agreed, an excellent example in serving so well to illustrate the real value of the full terms of the rule.[19]

Those terms were crafted with care so to provide the most honest statement of what the rule—or any (i.e., *every*) rule of just this sort—actually represents in the end. The council agreed this was so, and shortly thereafter likewise agreed it was time to adjourn. First, however, the two salutary rules, *4TH ALTERNATIVE RULE* I and RULE II, were approved to the accompaniment of two cheers for a better campus environment, for academic freedom, and for the due protection of an appropriate freedom of speech. And only then did the members of the council file out from the room in which they had met. Except for a small lingering group off in one corner—who thought they caught a slight whiff of diesel fumes, and a slight sound, as of tanks clanking, as in some far away deserted Square.

Endnotes

1. *See also* Rule II ("Any member of the university community who engages in any verbal conduct contrary to Rule I shall be subject to suspension, dismissal, or other appropriate sanction as the Committee on Offensive Verbal Conduct shall decide.").

2. E.g., graphic, rather than euphemistic, usages or depictions?

3. Information, for instance, some might deem inappropriate to present (due to its offensive implications), like tabulations of SAT scores by race, or tabulations of HIV infection rate variations correlated by specific sex practices of various groups?

4. 1st Alternative Rule I: "No member of the faculty, student body, or staff shall engage in any verbal conduct that renders the environment on campus, or some part thereof, offensive. This rule shall apply, however, only if the verbal conduct is of a sexual nature, and not otherwise." (Note the comportment of this draft to the E.E.O.C. requirement, 29 C.F.R. § 1604.11 (1992), directing employers to stake all steps necessary, including developing appropriate sanctions," to eliminate "verbal conduct of a sexual nature [having] the purpose or effect of creating an. . .offensive working environment.").

5. 2nd Alternative Rule I: "No member of the faculty, student body, or staff shall engage in any verbal conduct that renders the environment on campus, or some part thereof, offensive. This rule shall apply, however, only if the verbal conduct is of a sexual or religious nature, and not otherwise." (The council was well advised to make this adjustment in the proposed rule; a footnote accompanying the E.E.O.C. directive to employers, see supra note 4, declares that the "same principle" requiring them to take action against "verbal conduct of a sexual nature [having] the purpose or effect of creating an. . .offensive working environment" applies identically in respect to such conduct of a religious nature as well (and so, too, as to race). *See* 29 C.F.R. § 1604.11, n.1(1992)).

6. 3rd Alternative Rule I: "No member of the faculty, student body, or staff shall engage in any verbal conduct that renders the environment on campus, or some part thereof, offensive. This rule shall apply, however, only if the verbal conduct is of a sexual, religious, or racial nature, and not otherwise."

7. I.e., refusing to pass judgment.

8. Under the rule as it stood, it was the "environment" that mattered. It was not crucial that sexually demeaning expressions need be personally directed to a particular individual, for example, for certainly the display of sexually demeaning posters of women "as such" were meant to be reached under the rule as it now stood—and so, too, of course, in equivalent circumstances regarding race or religion as well.

9. 4th Alternative Rule I: "No member of the faculty, student body, or staff shall engage in any verbal conduct that renders the environment of the campus, or some part thereof, offensive. This rule shall apply, however, only if the verbal conduct is of a sexual, religious, racial, or other nature reflecting an improper and unreasonable attitude toward others according to the common standard of the university community, and not otherwise."

10. They suggested, moreover, that under the federal civil rights acts (and the E.E.O.C. regulation, *supra* note 4), the university might be in violation of the federal acts were it not so to act and were it to fail to insure an environment for Native American

employees, students, faculty, or staff, free of such denigrative stereotype depictions in the very day-to-day places where they would be expected to carry on their work within the university itself.

11. For them, the example was troublesome partly because of its asymmetry—even as apparently exhibited in their colleague's own illustration: that it would privilege one offensive kind of group epithet ("white persons" as "racists"?) while not privileging another (Native American peoples as "backward" or as subject to some other denigrative characterization or some equivalently dismissive stereotype). Did their colleagues mean to suggest that the one hostile description (e.g., addressing whites as "racists") was less offensive, or somehow more legitimate (i.e., *more warranted*?) than the other? On what basis might they think; so (or did they not regard this as genuinely contestable, though not everyone would be inclined to agree)? Or was it their view, rather, that a properly considered rule will lay down one kind of verbal conduct standard for certain students, faculty, staff, and employees, but a different standard for others whose expressions of animus were simply not to be treated the same way? Possibly. And possibly for a reason. But if so, what kind of rule is this, and how would one expect it to work? May not such a rule seem itself to say that some students (minority students?) are regarded not as being more in the right than others, but merely more pardonable as to their polemical excesses because not really equal after all (on which account they are not to be held to the same expectations of verbal behavior toward others on campus as others are expected to maintain toward them)? But insofar as this were its evident message, would it actually work to support them (as their colleagues obviously intended), or might it merely further undermine them—in so treating their offensive depictions of others as something the university expects others to pass off or ignore? Or were their colleagues suggesting that even if each such description may be thought to be equally off the mark, and equally offensive in stigmatizing terms (e.g., whites as "racists"), still, given the status of some students on campus, their outbursts (such as they may be) are far more readily understandable, given the conditions they are unequally made to confront on campus, and, so, ought not be treated the same way. But how does this explanation really help at all?

Similarly, in thinking about a different (but related) example, these council members wondered whether the rule as applied, as their colleagues had it in mind, would likewise mean to exempt from complaint denigrative speech that complains of, that belittles, or that dismissively stereotypes "white male European faculty members" and thereby makes the working environment offensive to them, but not likewise exempt denigrative speech that belittled or that stereotyped women faculty or "faculty persons of color"? If it declines to act in the same way in respect to each, however, how will the university explain its policy and its failure to treat "like complaints" alike? (On the other hand, if it acts with equal vigor so to reach both kinds of belittling verbal conduct equally, whose interests may thereby seem in fact to be more substantially served?)

12. He had in mind, of course, that such organizations had altered their views regarding homosexuality some few decades earlier, no longer regarding such an orientation as abnormal (and thus not a condition one would seek to "treat" as these same organizations previously held), but they had made no similar transition for pedophilia and a number of other sexual interests of a still somewhat more exceptional kind.

13. Rule II: "Any member of the university community who engages in any verbal conduct contrary to Rule I shall be subject to suspension, dismissal, or other appropriate sanction as the Committee on Offensive Verbal Conduct shall decide."

14. Assuming one thinks so, how might one best express it? (And if one thinks it is somehow lacking in some particular, what different principle might one prefer to put in its stead?)

15. Or some part thereof.

16. Indeed, what kind of university would it be that had a rule forbidding one to point out what one thinks to be the undesirable traits or qualities of persons of *this* sort (whatever one thinks persons of "this" sort means)?

17. As also might be true, say, of those whose sexual taste may run to children (i.e., *pedophiles*) and similar deservingly disreputable groups, individuals, or beliefs, the im-

pugning of which could not be said to reflect an "improper and unreasonable attitude" according to the common standards of the university.

18. I.e., all those protected by the proposed rule.

19. That certain verbal conduct offending men on campus (e.g., reiterated descriptions depicting them as lascivious, to be watched out for as prone to sexual exploitation, to violence, to rape, and to the subordination of women) would likewise not be subject to the rule, most on the council thought likely as well (unless one were prepared to declare that such negative depictions, cautions, and warnings (about men) would be held to reflect to an "unreasonable" and "improper" attitude, which they thought unlikely—for who is prepared so to insist that they do?). That such depictions may be resented by many men, or rejected as false by at least some men, as well as stigmatizing of them, as well as offensive, is neither here nor there. For again, this rule avoids making these matters (the alleged felt falseness of the depiction, the resentment of those depicted, or its offensiveness to some person or some group) a sufficient ground, as it rightly should. But, in contrast with these cases, on the other hand, perhaps most (perhaps all) expressions of animus or belittlement of gay or lesbian persons (though not necessarily of pedophiles), or of women (though not necessarily of men), or of most racial groups (though not necessarily of whites), when carried into offensive words or graphics on campus, would be subject to complaint and to definite sanction under RULE II—reflecting (as they surely would be held so to reflect) an "improper" as well as an "unreasonable" attitude according to the metric of the rule. On all such matters, the rule is fully equal to the demands made upon it according to its own terms: the rule takes suitable care to identify the proper framework for correct judgment—not the framework of what "outsiders" think, but what "the university" thinks on each of these matters ("the common standard of the university" is the standard made to count). What could be more appropriate than this, in framing a speech code for the university, neither overinclusive nor yet underinclusive of university-sanctionable speech?

INDEX